Left Behind

Left Behind

A New Economics for Neglected Places

PAUL COLLIER

ALLEN LANE
an imprint of
PENGUIN BOOKS

ALLEN LANE

UK | USA | Canada | Ireland | Australia
India | New Zealand | South Africa

Penguin Books is part of the Penguin Random House group of companies
whose addresses can be found at global.penguinrandomhouse.com

First published in Great Britain by Allen Lane 2024

003

Copyright © Paul Collier, 2024

The moral right of the author has been asserted

Set in 12/14.75pt Dante MT Std
Typeset by Jouve (UK), Milton Keynes
Printed and bound in Great Britain by Clays Ltd, Elcograf S.p.A.

The authorized representative in the EEA is Penguin Random House Ireland,
Morrison Chambers, 32 Nassau Street, Dublin D02 YH68

A CIP catalogue record for this book is available from the British Library

ISBN: 978–0–241–27916–8

Contents

I.

On the Cusp

This book is about places that once felt prosperous but now have fallen behind. They are found all over the world, even in rich countries that have poor regions. Despite having a steel industry for centuries, South Yorkshire's core industry crashed in the 1980s and the region is now the poorest in England. The same phenomenon is common in middle-income countries: Colombia's once-prosperous Caribbean Atlantic is now much poorer than the booming region around the capital, Bogotá. Sometimes, entire countries have regressed. Zambia was once richer than its rival copper exporter, Chile; now the average income of Zambians is less than a tenth of Chileans'. Not only has Zambia become a left-behind country but within it there are regions, exemplified by its Copper Belt, that have been more extremely affected – lagging behind the more prosperous capital city, Lusaka. The Copper Belt is a left-behind region in a left-behind country. I work in all these places and hear two burning questions: Why have we fallen behind? What can we do to catch up?

As an economist rigorously trained in the dominant Anglo-American school of thought, I know there are orthodox answers to questions about the policies appropriate for places hit by a shock. Their intellectual origin is in Chicago, where Milton Friedman visualized a complex theory of why market forces could be trusted to put things right through the image of a harp with taut strings. Adverse shocks, like the collapse of a mining industry, were analogous to plucking the harp's strings: though they oscillate for a while, they soon settle back to their initial state. The shock will lower wages and property prices; that will create opportunities; and because the market is greedy for them, money will flood in, driving wages and prices back up again.

That idea was a premature certainty that has turned out to be wrong. Yet it rapidly hardened into an orthodoxy. In Oxford's Economics Department, I used to teach those theories. By the 1980s, the ideas were regarded as part of the established axioms of orthodox economics. Adherence became a touchstone of sound thinking.

Britain's Treasury implemented them far more dogmatically than any other major economy. Other finance departments in Europe or the US were influenced either by alternative schools of thought or by pragmatic responses to reality. (Although Friedman and Chicago were economically dominant during the presidency of Ronald Reagan, monetarism was never unchallenged in the US.) Furthermore, the Treasury is exceptionally powerful, while Britain's left-behind regions have been denuded of authority. Their story is emblematic of the remorseless pursuit of an economic doctrine in the context of a highly unequal relationship of political power: and that makes it globally valuable. It clarifies what has been happening in many other highly centralized poorer countries like Zambia and Colombia, in which some regions have fallen far behind.

Certainty is always dangerous: it led to the disaster of the Vietnam War. *The March of Folly*, the American historian Barbara Tuchman's devastating critique of Robert McNamara, culminates with the skewering phrase: he had 'the gift of certainty'. McNamara's vaunting self-confidence rested on a supreme belief in the power of quantification, and in his own managerial abilities. He was certain that America would win in Vietnam and intimidated presidents into accepting this.* Britain's Treasury also possesses the gift of certainty. Regardless of what happened to a shock-hit region, it never questioned its ideas.

As a teenager I read Voltaire's comic classic, *Candide*, featuring

---

* In his later life I knew McNamara: he was deeply penitent for his mistakes and passionately committed to helping places left behind, especially in Africa. But in one sense, his previous confidence remains astonishing in view of his record. At Ford, his over-confident forecasts of consumer tastes produced the marketing disaster of the Edsel, and he left Ford to become Secretary of Defense.

the buffoon Dr Pangloss, who believes that everything that happens is always for the best; we live in the best of all possible worlds. Voltaire's target was the pre-revolutionary Catholic Church and its certainties of divine benevolence. By remaining passive in situations when his actions could have been decisive, Dr Pangloss is repeatedly responsible for catastrophes, but never has any doubts that he was in the right.

The convictions of Chicago's Friedman and Britain's Treasury were worthy of Voltaire's satire: their propositions were the economics of Dr Pangloss. We are the custodians of taxpayers' money. Our duty is to resist any special pleading or attempts to impede market forces. As the experts, we know better, and so our duty is to exercise our authority: nowhere is deserving of any exceptional consideration. The market is right. Public money will be place-blind. The market knows best, so public money will follow wherever private investment leads.

This kind of logic created a canonical catastrophe.

The only high-income countries in the world where this dangerous nonsense was religiously implemented were England and Wales.* Beginning in the mid-1970s, the Treasury kept tightening its control over local government, with the predictable effect that every English and Welsh region fell behind London and its hinterland as public money chased private money into South-East England. The territories under tightening Treasury control rapidly became the most unequal in the Western world, while it acquired uniquely centralized powers.

The response to this divergence of everywhere else from South-East England has been mounting political unrest. By 2022 political pressure from the regions had reached a crescendo. In an explicit admission that the market had not delivered benefits equally, a

---

* Scotland escaped Treasury control once the Scottish Nationalists saw the potential of the discovery of North Sea Oil and came out with the winning slogan 'It's Scotland's oil'. Northern Ireland slipped out of Treasury control for the very different reason that ending IRA violence depended upon devolution to a joint Protestant–Catholic local administration. Both countries soon had their own parliaments.

laissez-faire Conservative government created a high-profile new Department of Levelling Up. Had the market worked, there would be no need to level anything up. The department had its own Cabinet Minister, who announced a detailed three-year programme in which he would coordinate new regional spending by other ministries. The minister was clever and capable, and his programme was impressive. Through his media appearances he succeeded in raising national awareness of the brutal consequences of past Treasury policies. But as a strategy for achieving change in Whitehall, the new initiative failed. The Treasury viewed the new department as another instance of local and regional interference.

The Treasury's ultimate trump card was that it controlled the budget for the new department. Despite being announced to the nation as the government's flagship programme, the budget awarded to it by the Treasury was, astonishingly, zero. The department's only source of funds was money shifted within the budget already granted by the Treasury to the Home Office Ministry, of which Levelling Up was a small part. But even this money infuriated the Treasury, so it intensified its control by scrutinizing every penny awarded to local governments. This was so effective in preventing spending that by the end of its first year only 5 per cent of the (very modest) levelling-up budget had been spent: the flagship was unable to leave port owing to lack of fuel.

Yet the mantra of being place-blind used to justify this approach to left-behind regions was not applied to decisions pertaining to London, where the Treasury is itself based. While no money could be found for the new government department, a cost-overrun for London's glitzy Elizabeth Line of £5 billion was quietly funded. This alone comfortably exceeded the unspent levelling-up money. At its worst, the Treasury's organizational culture reflected a core of double standards: overconfidence amounting to self-indulgence towards its successful heartland, and arrogant indifference towards those neglected regions left behind.

This premature orthodoxy of place is wrong. Its effects on millions of human lives have been tragic; and even on standard economic criteria it is a bad model that systematically mis-predicts. Before I started working on this book, I had questioned aspects of the model, but as I wrote I began to see just how wrong it was. Far from needing the same approach everywhere, we need policies that vary according to the local context. Far from those clever people in Chicago or the Treasury knowing what to do everywhere, agency should rest with local people who are better placed to judge what might work in their context. Often, nobody can know what will work best until patterns emerge from these local variations. Far from a style of leadership by command, we need modest leaders who win trust by sacrificing their own self-interest.

For some years I have immersed myself in pathbreaking fields of research beyond economics. Without that re-education, I could not have reached the exhilarating lightbulb moment – the reward that drives academic research. I felt a sense of freedom and exhilaration in being liberated from dogmas whose effects have been arrogant and cruel. Even economics has not stood still; subversive research in regional economics can now explain why market forces claimed as benign by Friedman are in fact perverse, accentuating collapses. But the breakthrough progress in understanding human behaviour has primarily taken place in other disciplines.

Remarkable recent advances in evolutionary social psychology confirm that humans are an unusually pro-social mammal. We have evolved to learn from each other, accumulating communal collective minds which guide our actions. We live in communities-of-place whose collective minds guide our children; we spend most of our day in communities-of-work whose collective minds guide new recruits. Within each, we come together for common purposes unattainable by individuals. But as these communities each build their future, their paths can diverge. Some places and organizations can become trapped in misleading ideas through which they fall behind, while others happen on those conducive to prosperity. In principle, left-behind communities can learn from those that are more successful, but ideas do not necessarily spread between them easily. The divergence between communities due to differences in ideas reinforces the punchline of the new insights of regional economics: left-behind places can get stuck on a slower trajectory than successful places owing to the perverse effects of market forces and the community's misinterpretation of them.

Social psychology also provides insights into how a left-behind community can catch up by forging new common purposes. Its hopeful message is reinforced by a brilliant and disruptive breach in biological orthodoxy. Just as trees in a forest link up through distributed intelligence to achieve common purposes like defence against a parasite, humans do the same: many actions of our bodies achieve common purposes on the autopilot of our distributed intelligence. Advances in both social psychology and biology show the overriding influence of our community on our actions.

This contrasts starkly with the still conventional economic notion that our actions are the result of rational calculations made by selfish individualists. Although still embedded in economic models of place, those ideas are founded on a crude 1950s view of evolution in which the survivors were presumed to have survived because of their selfishness. Other economic models are belatedly moving on from that untenable belief to another individualist psychology, termed Decision Theory, which disparages our capacity to take decisions: our brains are depicted as wonky computers prone to biases that need to be overridden by those who know better. Few economists are as yet familiar with the recent critique of those ideas on decision-taking advanced by social psychology. It demotes the supposed limitations of the individual brain in favour of the remarkable cognitive powers of humans in a networked community: for good reason, we tend to rely on our collective mind.

This points us to the importance of relationships within communities. Recent advances in moral philosophy have complemented those in social psychology by breaking free of four chill decades of Utilitarianism, in which relationships of kindness and trust within communities were ignored as morally irrelevant.[1]

Political science now illuminates far more clearly the irreducible role of the state: those functions that are not just useful but vital – the state's *sinews*. No society starts with these sinews; they have to be built. Some societies, like Haiti, have been unable to build them and so teeter on the brink of anarchy. Others, such as Russia, are states that are powerful but abusive because their power is unchecked. Political science has begun to explain these variations and connect with the moral philosophy of good leadership.

Finally, the recent field of complex decisions taken in the context of radical uncertainty is the intellectual support for the importance of rapid learning from experiments. It explains the extraordinary power of some leaders to overcome uncertainties and reset their society around a common purpose. That power can be put to good uses, as by President Zelensky, and malevolent ones, as by Jair Bolsonaro and Kim Jong-un. In either case, these advances relate directly to the other disciplines which also offer new insights on leadership.

New research builds on past discoveries. The critiques of economic orthodoxies – place-blind public policy, the market knows best, and the Treasury knows best of all – do not release left-behind places from genuine economic fundamentals. These places cannot catch up by retreating into nostalgia and parochialism. Their future economies will be built through a step-by-step discovery of how their workforces can become more productive.

As the human sciences have advanced, they have become more complex: they show that many effects that were previously the exclusive domain of individual disciplines are due to interactions across subject boundaries. This opens the distant possibility of an integrated human science that would bring the predictive and normative power of better models to bear on a myriad of baffling human problems, some of which have only recently been noticed once previously neglected patterns were explored.

Until that time, we need something more modest: provisional answers that attempt to integrate the new advances but focus on much narrower questions of practical urgency. Instead of single-discipline models that give precise answers that are badly wrong, we need integrated models that confess to imprecision but are roughly right. The two questions we must answer are those posed by those left behind: Why did we fall behind? How can we catch up? Left-behind places need something that enables them to move beyond the economic orthodoxies that have held them in thrall.

A new idea on trial

Reflecting an old interest, I had agreed to give the keynote speech at a conference on conflict at the Department of War Studies at King's College.* Two weeks before I spoke, Vladimir Putin ordered the invasion of Ukraine. Inescapably, that became my subject, so I checked the forecasts made by the conflict modellers: they were unanimous in predicting with a confidence approaching certainty that President Putin would swiftly crush Ukraine. My immersion into those pathbreaking advances across the human sciences was already sufficient for me to grasp that the predictions were wrong: though precise, they were derived from bad models. I stuck my professional neck out and told a surprised audience that Putin would not succeed.

Not only was I prepared to predict that Putin would not win the swift victory expected, but there were grounds for believing that Ukrainian President Zelensky might do more than merely survive; his country could even win. He was an excellent communicator and pulled off several tactical masterstrokes, the first, his heroic commitment to remain in Kyiv, giving him a moral authority. His next masterstroke was to know what he could do and what he couldn't: in the terminology of social psychology, he has a well-calibrated meta-cognition. He knew he could shame Western leaders into sending armaments. He knew he had earned the moral authority to call on men of fighting age to enlist in their local militias. He knew that as a Russian speaker from Eastern Ukraine he could bring together a Ukrainian people who had been bitterly divided by

---

* My book *Wars, Guns and Votes* (2009), summarized some of that work.

language and politics. He knew that nightly broadcasts to Ukrainians would be reassuring. He knew his limitations: he lacked the
military knowledge to plan resistance from the centre and so he
devolved the resistance to local militias.

His third and crowning masterstroke was to reframe this empowerment of the militias not as a weakness the Russians might exploit but
as something that gave Ukraine three crucial advantages. The local
militias' knowledge of their terrain was far superior to that of the Russian soldiers. As each militia experimented in their tactics, Ukrainians
would learn rapidly what worked most effectively in particular contexts. Zelensky's opponent was a vain man over-confident in his
military expertise who was surrounded by sycophants too fearful to
give him honest feedback on setbacks. His inept micromanagement
would demoralize Russian troops. In contrast, as the Ukrainian militias figured out what worked and their local successes were celebrated,
it would generate a gulf between the morale of the two armies.

President Zelensky and I had seen the same objective data as the
orthodox models. But we had transposed them into a reality that
the modellers had all missed. Imprisoned in a precisely wrong model,
they had confidently mistaken Ukraine's distinctive advantages for
overwhelming disadvantages. President Zelensky combined sufficient confidence to act on his initial insights with the modesty to
realize the need to learn rapidly. In combination, his ideas formed a
well-crafted sequence of actions: they fitted together like the steps
of a spiral staircase. His self-sacrifice had won enough trust from his
fellow Ukrainians to persuade them to mount it. As they ascended,
not only did each stair lead them closer to their goal of repelling an
invasion but, as on a spiral staircase, it progressively revealed a transposed perspective on the familiar scene below. People began to see
long-familiar features of their locality, their nation and its history
with new eyes. Distinctive features that had previously been viewed
as disadvantages could be reassessed as advantages that Russia lacked.
Some localities discovered their factories were critical to Europe's
auto-industry. Nationally, it was revealed, Ukraine had become a
granary for the world. New evidence revealed why Ukrainians could

not trust Putin any more than Stalin: archaeologists unearthed the mass graveyards of Stalin's genocidal hatred of Ukraine.

I realized that many of the stairs on Zelensky's spiral staircase – self-sacrificing leadership, devolving agency and communicating a hopeful yet credible strategy – were broadly applicable to other daunting challenges. Benefits such as Ukraine's re-evaluation of its distinctive features as advantages led to changes in behaviour that could be applied to an economic agenda as readily as a military one. They could transform the economic prospects of supposedly doom-laden left-behind places as decisively as they had the supposedly doom-laden military prospects of Ukraine. The spiral staircase is a rudimentary model compatible with remarkable recent advances across the human sciences that are pertinent to left-behind places. I set them out in the next chapter: instead of a precise but wrong economic model, the predictions of the new fused model are roughly right. That 'roughly' cautions that this book is a guide, not a textbook.

As with conflict, a misplaced confidence in a bad economic model might discourage a search for patterns in the data that are incompatible with it. I will set out the evidence that was waiting in plain sight. It shows the brutal consequences of those mistaken economic dogmas. More ambitiously, I'll show that the many places around the world that suffered collapses from which they fully recovered did so by using strategies encapsulated in the image of a spiral staircase. Their strategies succeeded despite being incompatible with market orthodoxy. Currently, a few of the left-behind places that have been diverging from the rest of mankind for decades are in the early stages of similar recoveries. The spate of global crises has made them precarious. Those of us in successful places have a modest supporting role, but, mired in our orthodoxies, as yet we are not meeting it.

This book is a celebration of the ingenuity and courage with which poor places around the world transform their prospects. It sets out a new economics of place-based transformation – the principles and practical steps by which these triumphs have been attained. In the coming chapters you will be plunged not only into the struggling places that opened this chapter, Colombia's Atlantic-Caribbean, Zambia's Copper Belt and England's South Yorkshire, but into transformations already well under way. Bangladesh, once destitute, has metamorphosed into a fast-growing Emerging Market; Spain's Basque region, once separatist and torn apart by terrorism and division, has become a national jewel; and Somaliland, a neglected little country in a conflict-ridden region, has quietly forged a cohesive and peaceful society.

Although each of these societies is unique, they are bound together by a common intellectual thread: *shared agency* and *rapid learning*. Shared agency – the secret of Somaliland – depicts the astute steps through which people come together around a shared purpose. Rapid learning, exemplified by China under Deng Xiaoping, depicts pragmatic experiment and willingness to learn from elsewhere.

That triumphant story is told in Part II, which is the heart of the book. But in Part I the tone is very different: it is the story of how damaging ideologies and the politics of greed impeded these triumphs. In doing so they avoidably blighted millions of lives.

The next chapter describes how those ideologies emerged, and how they are now being demolished by research-led revolutions. The two following chapters set out astonishing new evidence about two globally significant processes that to date have barely been noticed: *Hidden Despair* (Chapter 3) reveals the looming global poverty problem of the 2030s; *Hidden Privilege* (Chapter 4) reveals its counterpart, the emergence of a new class in high-income countries that is so favoured as to be a new aristocracy.

Pain before pleasure; anger before celebration.

PART ONE

Spiralling Down

2.

New Revolutions, Crumbling Orthodoxies

Cocooned in its self-confidence, a powerful centre has imposed uniform policies on the left behind. That mindset is no longer intellectually tenable: it has been countered by insightful recent research across the human sciences. A good starting point is the discovery of the syndrome of fragility.

Disrupting Dr Pangloss: the syndrome of fragility

We now know that, far from autonomous recovery, once a place loses its core industries, self-perpetuating decline is the norm. To understand why, imagine two dinghies sailing on a breezy day. One sails on, but the other is hit by a gust of wind and capsizes: the crew doesn't know how to flip it back upright. When the wind drops, the sails of both dinghies are vertical: one pointing to the sky, the other to the seabed. In scientific terminology, they are *locally stable equilibria*.

When the wind picks up, the crew of the upright dinghy sails on, steering to its destination. But the crew of the capsized dinghy is left clinging to it, drifting aimlessly with the current. The initial setback of capsizing has repercussions which feed back and make it worse: this is the essence of a *syndrome*.

The changing location of workers and investment across a country is analogous to those dinghies. If a city loses its core industries, it capsizes; more fortunate cities sail on. Investors watching from the shore are judging which city has the better opportunities. They invest in the dinghy that has stayed upright: that accentuates the divergence. The crew of the capsized dinghy start blaming each other for capsizing: they become too disputatious to figure out the technique of working together to flip over the boat. As they waste their time in the water, the divergence widens further. Their strongest swimmers abandon ship, and some join the crew of the upright dinghy.

People living successful lives in prosperous places often misunderstand the decline of less fortunate places. They assume that either the places or their people must have something wrong with them. If it is the places that are wrong, the people should leave. If the people are wrong, then they need to change. The political right often wants to assign individual responsibility for failure; the political left often prefers to change entire societies through re-education.

Orthodox economics shares these misperceptions but goes one step further by introducing market forces as the remedy, insisting that if investment is moving from the capsized city to the one that has stayed upright it is a good thing. It must reflect a more efficient allocation of capital. Similarly, when workers relocate in response to widening wage differentials between cities, they will become more productive. The traditionalists get worried only if workers are *not* leaving: perhaps it is because the incentive of wage differentials is being muted by over-generous public handouts.

Yet far from remedying the syndrome, market forces accentuate it. They can work well enough for modest purposes like matching producers with consumers, but they cannot cope with the vastly more complex task of determining the best future distribution of thriving cities around a country. Whether a city thrives hinges on expectations about a vast array of future decisions. Will local government grant planning permission? Will central government provide funding? Will laws that have become impediments to investment be changed? Will civil society organizations like trade unions and charities be supportive or disruptive? Will Tesla set the future of vehicles, or will Elon Musk's vision of cars as battery-powered computers-on-wheels be countered by European Union-financed innovations in the combustion engine motivated by the need to save jobs? Quite how market forces are supposed to guide these disparate behaviours to a uniquely efficient spatial pattern of cities around a country is mysterious even to the truest believers in the powers of the market.

The mystery deepens when we look at the concept of path-dependence. The journeys of the two crews – their paths – have diverged: their destinations depended upon that initial, unpredictable puff of wind. The contrast between these two crews, one merrily sailing off while the other drifts with the current, captures the essence of *path-dependency*. To cling confidently to a belief in the inevitability of the ideal outcome is a defiant act of faith in a mistaken orthodoxy. Friedman's analogy of the economy as strings on a harp was both a neat image encapsulating a model and a retreat from science into faith.

The syndrome that left-behind places enter when they lose their core industries is a chain of interactions: the loss of economic opportunities has compounding social and political effects. Men lose their jobs, families collapse, people self-medicate on drugs and kids grow up in broken homes. A term recently introduced for this chain of interactions is the 'syndrome of fragility'.[1] Rather than believing that the miracle of market forces leads inevitably to renewal, investors recognize that faced by the collapse of a place's core industries, the price mechanism alone is impotent. While prices are the essence of the market forces invoked by Friedman, they cannot possibly coordinate the decisions among politicians, civil society, financiers, firms and households necessary to achieve renewal. Investors are more realistic than Friedman: they expect that an economic collapse will be persistent. They shift their money to the places that did not suffer collapse – the upright dinghies. Collapse creates adverse expectations which then become self-fulfilling.

The left-behind places in the UK and the US provide stark warnings that spiralling down can take hold anywhere. The initial cause of a collapse is often unrelated to decisions taken in the region, as happened in Pittsburgh and South Yorkshire, where the steel industry collapsed in the early 1980s. Pittsburgh's population halved: it became a left-behind place. But it did eventually renew itself: it is now rated the twelfth most successful American city. South Yorkshire also became a left-behind place, but the reaction and the outcome were very different. Although unemployment soared, people didn't leave. Nor did the region renew itself: its economy spiralled down to become the poorest region in England. Accounting for these differences is a good starting point for understanding public policy towards left-behind places everywhere.

In South Yorkshire, as everywhere in England, there was a complete reliance upon market forces, with no active public policy. The steel industry was killed by a national macroeconomic policy introduced in the early 1980s which hit export-based manufacturing all over the country. Overall, twenty places suffered severe declines. Studying those declines enables us to test the rival predictions about behaviour: the Panglossian model versus the self-fulfilling expectations of divergence postulated by the syndrome of fragility. Only one of the twenty places revived: the others succumbed to persistent decline. Even worse for the economic orthodoxy, the exception, Corby, revived because it was so severely hit that both local and central government were compelled to intervene.[2] Sustained public intervention in Corby, abhorrent to the market fundamentalists, reset expectations and saved the town. The recovery worked in practice, but instead of being studied it was ignored because, according to the theory prevailing in Britain's Treasury, it should not have worked.

The damage to the steel industry in Pittsburgh and South Yorkshire was exceptional owing to coincident blows. In 1980 both countries had new governments, under Ronald Reagan and Margaret Thatcher, that had adopted Friedman's monetary ideas, causing sharp appreciations of their currencies that made their steel uncompetitive on world markets. At the same time, the South Korean government was pouring money to pump-prime a rival steel industry. Significantly, the German steel industry survived the onslaught of Korean competition because Friedman's ideas did not take seed in Germany. The steel regions were able to invest their way into remaining competitive, with the support of government money and private finance. Germany's steel industry didn't decline; Pittsburgh's collapsed, but the city then attracted new high-skill firms; South Yorkshire's steel collapsed and the area failed to attract replacements. What accounts for these three different outcomes? Germany not only had active national public policy, but both the money and the decisions on how to use it were devolved to regional and city governments. In Germany and America, both public and private finance had long been devolved to cities and regions, and both countries had built strong civil institutions, like universities, deeply embedded in the community. Only in England could none of these features be found.

Disruptive psychology

Just as a sailboat and a local economy have two equilibria, so do the organizations in which we work and which shape many of our opportunities to lead a meaningful life. Recent research in social psychology suggests we are not the greedy, selfish, rational individualists imagined by most economic models. Evolution has equipped us to be an exceptionally pro-social species, willing to forgo our individual interest for the common good of our community. Given the opportunity, these natural instincts come to the fore. If our workplace encourages us to form teams that have the freedom to solve problems together, we not only earn a living but find our work worthwhile. But treated badly, watched by a hawklike boss and given no scope for initiative, we can be dragged down. We become that greedy, selfish individualist that orthodox economics assumes.

More astonishing, this new research has shown that most of our decisions come from the collective mind of our community – the stored wisdom of its experience. Within these collective minds, some nuggets of knowledge are highly specific technical solutions to tasks that people have faced, or *cognitive gadgets*. Societies that lack those gadgets crucial to prosperity will either stall until they have reinvented them or learn from those that have.[3]

In losing their core industries, left-behind places often lose the organizations that gave people meaning. Pittsburgh and South Yorkshire had been communities-of-place with which workers and owners identified. The steel firms had been communities-of-work where conflicts between workers and owners were softened by mutual pride. The Bessemer process of forging steel called for skill and judgement: workers became participants in the majestic drama, analogous to alchemy, turning ore into shining steel. Workers and bosses had been able to come together for attractive common purposes. An instance was the founding of South Yorkshire's first university. An endowment was raised by a collaboration: the steel unions organized a levy through which members each contributed a week's wages, and the total sum was matched by a large donation from the Firth family, which owned the largest steel company.

In South Yorkshire, the powerful combination of place-based and work-based attachments was weakened by the nationalization of the steel industry in 1967, which shifted the locus of decision-making from managers and workers in South Yorkshire to politicians in London. By 1980, South Yorkshire's steel workers joined a high-profile national strike against the new Conservative government. The strike was commercially ill timed, coinciding with the new competition from Korea. While the immediate impact of the centralization and politicization of decisions was to accelerate the demise of the industry, its enduring legacy was to sour labour relations in the region. The fate of the region's other core industry, coal, was a more extreme version of the saga of steel. During the energy crisis of the late 1940s, big coal mines had all the social purpose and glamour of steel.[4] Nationalization started earlier, culminating in 1984 in a year-long, intensely politicized strike; as with steel, it accelerated decline and dramatically soured labour relations.*

* The Thatcher government was determined to get revenge on the National Union of Mineworkers for its successful strike a decade earlier which had humiliated and defeated the previous Conservative government. Thatcher won the battle and rapidly closed Britain's coal industry.

With the collapse of its core industries and the loss of pro-social firms like Firth, the few firms attracted to South Yorkshire brought low-skill jobs. They came only because premises were cheap to rent and desperate people were willing to take tedious work at low wages. Call-centre and warehouse work was well suited to the degrading model of close monitoring linked to incentives. The composition of firms shifted from raise-us-up to drag-me-down; from communities-of-work to hierarchies-of-humiliation. Inevitably, local attitudes to private business became broadly hostile. Although Pittsburgh had the local resources to renew itself, other capsized American cities succumbed to the syndrome and became left behind. In a few, the entire workforce became rootless, a tragedy vividly captured in the book and film *Nomadland*, in which older nomadic workers in search of temporary employment have lost any connection to a settled urban centre.* Such total eclipses did not happen in England because social protection, though modest by European standards, is better funded than in America. People could survive by combining publicly funded benefits with a low-wage job. As a result, most chose to stay in the place where they belonged.

Social psychology has provided us with a credible account of why capitalism can generate both thriving communities-of-work in egalitarian and devolved societies such as Denmark and ugly hierarchies-of-humiliation in places like South Yorkshire. It also explains why as a place starts to decline the local community tends to fragment as people set about blaming each other for the failure. The small nation of Wales, with only half the population of Denmark, illustrates this sad process. Wales is even poorer than South Yorkshire. My Welsh colleague David Tuckett and I conducted a series of interviews among a cross-section of Welsh society in 2020.[5] We found widespread dissension. The public sector blamed Welsh business,

---

* The film was a low-budget production by people who felt passionate about what had happened. Triumphantly it went on to win the Best Picture at the 2021 Academy Awards.

which reciprocated by complaining about the Welsh government. There was also mutual antipathy between regions. North Wales still has many speakers of the Welsh language and has successfully lobbied the Welsh government to make learning it a condition for job recruitment. In South Wales, where Welsh speakers are a minority, this is seen as an impediment to job creation. The Welsh government invited me to Swansea to address its All Wales Economic Summit. The many attendees from Swansea had their own explanation for their city's problems: favouritism towards Cardiff, the neighbouring city, 44 miles away. Wales had become fragmented into reciprocated antipathies that have impeded people coming together to forge a strategy to address their difficulties.

A short step beyond mutual blame is self-blame: people internalize the notion that they have been overtaken because they or the place where they live are in some way inadequate. We extended our interviews to South Yorkshire and talked with teachers to get some insight into how schoolchildren saw their situation. This is a typical account of their attitudes: 'The South thinks we're thick. OK, so we're thick, so what's the point of trying – we'd fail.' Many of these schoolchildren are the descendants of the people who pioneered the Industrial Revolution. The region includes the world's first industrial factory, recognized by UNESCO as a rare World Heritage Site. But instead of people taking pride in their heritage, it has been shredded. With it has been lost the innovative self-confidence of previous generations.

A further short step beyond self-blame is the loss of faith in your own agency, or, in the parlance of social psychology, *learnt helplessness* or *learnt dependency*. The most appalling instance I have encountered is Haiti, a society traumatized in the eighteenth century by slavery: in 1804 its people heroically overthrew their oppressors, and this should have been the foundation of an enduring sense of pride. Instead, Haitian society plunged into other forms of tragedy. Learnt dependency is a despairing inertia in which people deny themselves all agency. They view their problems as entirely due to forces vastly more powerful than themselves. A Haitian student volunteered an example: a common assumption among Haitians is that if they fall sick, it is because a malevolent neighbour has put a spell on them: agency lies with magic. When hurricanes and earthquakes strike, politicians and senior civil servants with decision-making power wait passively until foreign agencies fly in with the resources to help them recover from disaster. Haitian people are hard-working and resourceful: in the USA and Canada, they are highly successful. But as in South Yorkshire, the society's spirit has been crushed by despair.

Sometimes, even exceptionally fortunate people moan to the world about their powerlessness: by trivializing a serious condition, they devalue it. But those most prone to that loss of faith in their own agency are weak groups assaulted by powerful ones. The best-researched example is the left-behind places of America, where it manifests itself most tragically in deaths of despair, as documented by Anne Case and Nobel Laureate Angus Deaton. Among the left behind, life expectancy is falling. Stanford social psychologist Greg Walton has analysed the precise sequence of thoughts that traps people in learnt dependency: they interpret every setback as being due to overwhelmingly powerful forces ranged against them and conclude, like the Yorkshire schoolchildren, that there is no point in trying. It nests within and illustrates the syndrome of fragility in which low expectations are self-fulfilling. They provide a justification for abandoning effort which, unless countered, then entraps people even more.

Social psychology also accounts for social *fragmentation*. If the place where I live is devoid of companions and my workplace is a hierarchy-of-humiliation, my sense of community withers away. Once the good times are gone, all that is left is to grieve for the loss of the past. The resulting attitudes in left-behind America have been analysed in two sociological studies. Arlie Hochschild focuses on the sense of desolation and loss felt by the people experiencing frag-mentation,[6] while Eric Kaufmann documents and condemns its ugly consequences, among them hostility to racial minorities and immigrants. These are two sides of the same tragedy: people bewildered by a loss of the community that gave their life meaning look for scapegoats.[7]

Back in left-behind England, a vignette from my hometown of Sheffield captures the sense of loss that Hochschild encountered. When the city's John Lewis department store closed in 2021, the local population went into mourning: flowers and tributes were stacked by its door, like at a gravestone. This exceptional display of loss over a shop reflected the reputation of John Lewis as being the best employer in Britain. Under new, aggressive management, which ultimately closed the Sheffield branch, the firm had repudiated this tradition, dismissing loyal, long-serving workers. The flowers were emblematic of John Lewis's profound decline from Britain's most admired community-of-work to the shop's closure, once it had become a hierarchy-of-humiliation.

Sometimes, the response to loss explodes into collective anger, frustration and irrationality. The humiliation of a community can trigger collective antipathy towards successful groups. I think of these as rebellions against authority: *mutinies*. This behaviour is found around the world, but America and Britain offer globally significant spectaculars.* By 2016, London and its hinterland had become exceptionally prosperous while every other region of England had been left behind. A referendum was being held, ostensibly on whether to remain in the European Union or withdraw. All three national political parties advocated Remain, and London itself voted heavily Remain. Every other English region voted Leave. The extent to which the region had been left behind was a good predictor of the Leave vote. Yet the vote was not primarily a mutiny against Brussels, which controlled a mere 1 per cent of Britain's national income: it was a mutiny against London, which controlled around 40 per cent. Later that year, an equivalent mutiny by the left-behind regions of the US resulted in Donald Trump becoming president. Both Brexit and the arrival of Donald Trump in the White House

---

* Later in the book I will describe a statistically rigorous analysis of the same phenomenon in Kenya.

were acts of self-harm for left-behind regions. The damage was widespread, but heaviest in the regions that mutinied. Who should be held responsible for this folly? The answer to that question takes us to a further set of disruptive ideas: the revolution in moral philosophy.

Disruptive moral philosophy: Contributive Justice

The responsibility for mutinies of despair does not lie only, or even primarily, with the mutineers. It lies with the powerful people who presided over the decades during which inequalities were allowed to widen without correction. That negligence is why so many places became left behind.

Brexit and the 2016 American election were preceded by angry debates of sorts, but what they lacked was any genuine dialogue that engaged everyone on equal terms. A true dialogue flows back and forth between equals who aim to understand each other: it is not an abusive shouting match between the angry weak and the contemptuous powerful. An analogy is the game of ping-pong: the act of participation implies mutual acceptance of the rules. The rules of dialogue preclude abuse and presume a mutual willingness to search for common ground. Even when it cannot be found, there is a mutual duty to understand and appreciate the validity of the other person's perspective.

Dialogues build a common understanding of a situation, enabling a society to forge a common purpose and devise an agreed strategy for achieving it. Rousseau was the first social scientist to realize that evolution had inclined us to cooperate: his notion of the Social Contract was that by agreeing to do so people had reaped the reward of catching stags instead of rabbits. But Rousseau got no further. David Hume and his friend Adam Smith added the decisive step of *mutuality*: unlike a real contract, reciprocity was not enforced by the state but by relationships of mutual trust. The crucial role of reciprocity has been developed by Michael Sandel of Harvard in *The*

Tyranny of Merit (2020). He introduces the concept of Contributive Justice: fairness demands that everyone in a society has a duty to contribute what they can towards that common purpose. Both self-respect and the respect of others are earned. And for that to be feasible, everyone, including the weak, must have sufficient agency to be able to contribute.

The weak, like others, can contribute in multiple ways. They can bring their voice to the dialogue, sharing the life experience of left-behind places with those more fortunate. The powerful must silence their own over-loud voices, listen to the voices of the weak and honour the heroes of the weak, rather than trumpet their own. Crucially, the weak can join in a common purpose by making material contributions to it, as displayed magnificently by the steel workers who volunteered a portion of their wages to found Sheffield University. But for that, the powerful must ensure the weak have sufficient income to be able to do so: Yorkshire's steel barons were willing to pay their workers a living wage.

The weak mutiny when the powerful are not prepared to step up. As Michael Sandel recognized, in Britain, America and some other societies the successful have been contemptuous of the weak, such as the working class, disdaining their concerns and their values. Thereby, they have been confronted by the costly whirlwind of polarization. In a polarized society, the weak reject any obligation to contribute to the whole.

Supporting evidence for the decline in American acceptance of mutuality comes from the ingeniously simple device of Google word-counts in the media. The ratio of me-to-we describes a U-shape during the twentieth century, so the start of both the twentieth and twenty-first centuries was a time of selfishness, while mid-century American society became more communitarian. Unfortunately, since 2000, it has spiked to an unprecedented concern with the self.[8]

Perhaps the shattering lessons of two world wars have now receded, and that helps account for these swings. In both Britain and America during the First World War powerful businessmen were unwilling to make material sacrifices. By the 1920s their greed had been immortalized in the phrase 'hard-faced men who had done well out of the war', but nothing changed and failures cumulated: in Britain by 1926 the General Strike; in America by 1929 the Great Crash, followed globally in 1931 by the Great Depression.

Transformational political leadership began in America in 1933 with President Roosevelt's New Deal, which recognized that government interventions in left-behind places were essential for social cohesion. After the attack on Pearl Harbor, a new consensus freed America from isolationism and spurred further interventions in the economy. In Britain, the cohort who became adults in the 1920s but were too young for political power until the 1940s had learned from the disastrous selfishness of the powerful that they themselves would now have to make sacrifices to support social cohesion. Once at war, in both America and Britain, this cohort set to work in both government and business. In Britain, food could no longer be imported, so scarcity was handled by rationing. With everyone entitled to the same amount of food, despite it being a time of war, working-class people ate better: national nutritional standards actually rose. Both that and the New Deal were Contributive Justice in action.*

Post-war, the chance events of elections propelled two humble men to leadership. In America, Truman had been dismissed as the sure-to-lose nobody who had been Roosevelt's sidekick; in Britain, Churchill had dismissed Attlee with the quip: 'he has much to be humble about'. Yet they left an astonishing legacy: the United Nations and NATO, which laid the foundations for security; the IMF, the World Bank and the GATT, which laid the foundations for prosperity. Attlee and Truman, both modest men who came to power at a time of crisis and uncertainty, achieved much, despite having to manage what is now recognized as radical uncertainty.

---

* This is the precise antithesis of the mounting deaths of despair currently happening in the left-behind communities of America during a period of rapidly rising national affluence.

The rediscovery of radical uncertainty[9]

Radical uncertainty is the challenge posed by a problem to which there is no known solution: the situation in which Attlee and Truman found themselves. One of its implications is that most of the solutions we find for such problems are unlikely to work for ever, and this was true of the triumphs Attlee and Truman achieved.*

In the economic sphere the two leaders relied on the Keynesian idea that full employment could be maintained by complex forecasting models: government knew best. After thirty years of full employment, the oil-shocks of the 1970s triggered stagflation and Keynesian ideas were abandoned in favour of Milton Friedman's counter-revolution, which replaced government-knows-best with the-market-knows-best. Market-worship died a similarly embarrassing death during the Global Financial Crisis of 2008/9, when frantic and intellectually bereft policymakers reached back to Keynesianism to avert global collapse. But in 2022, Keynesianism revealed the limitations that had doomed it in the 1970s, as unanticipated inflation rapidly changed expectations in job markets.

In the political arena, the successes of Truman and Attlee persisted for longer. The triumphs of social democracy in health care, pensions and welfare programmes survived at least until the Reagan–Thatcher years, and in some respects longer. But by 2023, as

---

* The game of chess illustrates the limits of knowability. Its rules are crystal clear: just thirty-two pieces and only two players. The real-world problem of how to revive a left-behind place is vastly more complex: it depends upon the interactions between the social, political and commercial decisions of thousands of people. Yet even chess is too hard to be solved: we will never discover the unbeatable chess strategy because there are more possible game plays than atoms in the universe. An AI algorithm asked to find the perfect game would be running until the end of time. By chance, two of my students had been world chess champions: from them I learned that while AI can now beat even the best players, a good player who combines judgement with AI always defeats AI. Evidently, even in the simple setting of chess, there is an irreducible need for human judgement.

fiscal crises due to the cumulative shocks of COVID, climate and the war in Ukraine engulfed beleaguered governments, the world was again awash with uncertainty.[10]

Research on radical uncertainty proposes an agenda for action, not a howl of woe. But it does require a very different approach from the known and bounded world of market absolutists. Its core messages are to build robustness and resilience, while taking three practical steps to find out what looks to be working.

To build robustness and resilience, short-run cost-cutting needs to be abandoned in favour of sustainability. An impressive example is how the Swiss government dealt with the accumulating shocks of the early twenty-first century. Their objective was to ensure that they could always guarantee essential supplies for the coming months. The key step was to identify the 200 Swiss firms that were procuring these essentials and summon their procurement executives to a meeting. The executives were told that they would now be responsible for the safety of Switzerland, both individually and collectively. They would meet regularly and should organize themselves into whatever teams they thought best. The Swiss government was relying on the social psychology of creating a peer group with a clear purpose: no procurement executive would want to be the weak link who lost the respect of the others. Supply chains become more robust through duplication and built-in redundancy, which implies accepting inefficiency. They become more resilient by investing in the capacities to be flexible in the face of disruptions.

Just as there are techniques to develop robustness and resilience, faced with an unfamiliar new problem there are ways of swiftly finding out what works well. We can study others who are facing the same challenge. We can organize parallel policy experiments and track how they turn out. And we can shift our mindset from the deductive reasoning of the economics profession to working backwards from the surprising things now happening to figure out what might be going on. Economists try to prove causal propositions. But syndromes often have such complex and mutually reinforcing effects that this is not practicable for real-time policy responses. The same syndrome of spiralling down gripped Pittsburgh and Sheffield: in Pittsburgh the mayor and the governor ignored the passive message of deductive economics, used their deep knowledge of the local context to spot potential solutions and persuaded key people to try them out. That mindset is *abductive reasoning*: neither the mayor nor the governor could prove that their efforts would work, but their city revived. The Treasury inferred deductively that market forces were the right approach in Sheffield, and they cannot be proved wrong. But nor can they be proved right: in conditions of radical uncertainty, proof is elusive.

Mindsets make a difference

Winning the trust of key people in Pittsburgh was vital to the strategy for renewal, but trust is not something that economists are well equipped to understand. The profession's workhorse human, *Homo Economicus*, embedded in most macro-modelling, is too congenitally selfish to be trustworthy. But leaders can build trust, and here the different national responses to COVID in Denmark, America and Germany are revealing. In March 2020, as the dangers of catching COVID became known in the West, Mette Frederiksen, the Social Democrat premier of Denmark and a single mother, addressed her fellow Danes. She acknowledged that she had no medical expertise, and that not much was yet known about COVID. But since the danger came from contagion, she argued that all Danes had a moral duty to protect their neighbours. The retired should stay out of the way of busy working people, while those with children should keep them from inadvertently endangering their grandparents. Contemporaneously, but in contrast to that moral message of 'protect your neighbour', Americans were rushing to gun shops to buy handguns. 'Shoot your neighbour' revealed the low levels of trust in fellow citizens that had been a legacy of decades of pervasive *Homo Economicus*. The German chancellor, Angela Merkel, also opted for *Homo Economicus*, but the country's very different gun laws protected the society from America's fate. The limitations of *Homo Economicus* in Germany emerged later, when the vaccines were developed. Chancellor Merkel tried to persuade Germans that it was in their individual self-interest to get vaccinated: they would then be less in danger of dying if they caught COVID. But by then social media had infected many people around the world with concerns that the vaccines themselves carried risks, and Germans were no exception. A significant minority of Germans concluded that their individual self-interest was simply to work from home and self-isolate. They would be safer without the vaccine. In consequence, the German population had a significantly lower rate of vaccination than other parts of Europe, never reaching the critical threshold level for effective containment. As to the outcomes of these three different COVID strategies, new analysis by the research department of the IMF measures excess mortality due to COVID from January 2020 to the end of 2022. Denmark had the lowest overall excess deaths of any significant OECD society.* In Germany, *Homo Economicus* turned out to be over-confident: self-isolation had too many flaws to be effective.

These contrasting approaches to *Homo Economicus* were only one aspect of differences in governance. The exaggerated faith in markets that came to dominate Anglo-American economics never took root in continental Europe. Nor, in America, was it allowed to kill the chances of reviving left-behind places. With both political and economic governance devolved to states led by governors and cities led by mayors, some left-behind places like Pittsburgh used their powers of local agency to take measures which must have been anathema to orthodox economists. In Britain, the Scots gained local agency, but they spectacularly misused it. As oil prices jumped from 1979 the oil off the shores of Scotland triggered a contest for votes between the Scottish Nationalist Party (SNP) and the Scottish Labour Party (SLP). The SNP slogan 'It's Scotland's oil' appealed to voters' self-interest, but by chance, from

* Only a few tiny societies like Andorra did better.

1997 to 2010, Britain's prime ministers and finance ministers belonged to Scottish Labour. They countered the SNP by creating a new Scottish government and parliament, into which they poured powers and money. To no avail: in 2010 the SNP took control and threw money around in a high-risk strategy of winning a once-in-a-generation referendum for independence. The result was narrowly against independence, but the legacy is that Scotland is now spectacularly broke. Devolution is not a panacea, and Scottish devolution freakishly contrived to result in irresponsible governance.

The Treasury's iron rule increasingly applied only to England and Wales. Hence, uniquely in the vast expanse of North America and Europe, only there did left-behind places experience the toxic combination of local impotence and path-dependent decline. The culprit was a powerful, distant and over-confident Treasury which from 1980 adhered to its market orthodoxy almost uninterrupted, regardless of which political party was in power.*

During those decades, the evidence that the decline in England's regions and Wales was internationally exceptional became increasingly apparent. Not only were some once-broken places in North America reviving, but the same was happening across continental Europe. The most spectacular example was East Germany. At the time of German reunification in 1990, East Germany was far poorer than South Yorkshire. Thirty years later, now part of a combined Germany, the region had renewed so rapidly that it was far more prosperous than South Yorkshire. German policies had differed profoundly from those of the Treasury. Once the Berlin Wall fell, the burning priority became how to renew the East. A centrally planned society, all decisions taken in East Germany had been concentrated in the government ministries of East Berlin. Neither the region's cities nor its businesses had built any capacity for decision-taking: they were merely junior bureaucrats implementing ministerial directives. In contrast, despite increasing

* The brief exception was the reversion to Keynesian demand stimulus, 2009–10.

centralization in London, South Yorkshire still had public institutions with some long-standing autonomous capacity, like its universities, and a business community of some 20,000 local firms. In the former East Germany all this had to be built from scratch. But the Germans had two advantages the left-behind regions of England lacked: effective national political leadership and pertinent national institutions.

Chancellor Helmut Kohl decisively seized the moment. His political masterstroke, which horrified Anglo-American economists, was to announce that the East German mark would be linked with the West German mark at parity; orthodox economics advised a deep discount on the East German mark, which would have made its economy competitive at the expense of impoverishing its workforce: the skilled would have flocked to the West. Under Helmut Kohl's terms, East Germans gladly embraced unification because it offered the prospect of a West German lifestyle without leaving the places they regarded as home.

Kohl saw that market forces would not revive East Germany: discounting the dogma of market fundamentalism, he realized that if employment was not to collapse, West Germans would have to pour public money into the East. Persuading West Germany's prosperous and powerful of the moral necessity of showing solidarity to their weaker fellow citizens in the East was Kohl's outstanding achievement. By expressing it as a moral commitment, he depoliticized it. He instituted what he called a solidarity tax, which essentially redistributed wealth from West to East. Despite periodic changes in the political parties holding power and their chancellors, it was sustained for the next thirty years. It was huge: an annual transfer of around €70 billion.

The institution that would effectively manage the wealth transfer was a national public bank that had been created in 1948 with the intention of rebuilding infrastructure and enterprise post-war. For both these purposes, the crucial design feature was devolved decision-taking. For infrastructure, the bank loaned huge amounts to regional and city governments which were then left to determine their own priorities. For enterprise, it loaned huge amounts to firms to rebuild key sectors of the economy.* Both activities contravened the principle of 'the market knows best'. Once reunification became the priority, the bank was simply repurposed to revive the East.

The contrast with UK Treasury policy towards England's left-behind regions is stark. The infrastructure agenda was determined not by local governments but by Whitehall's ministries. Alone in the OECD, England's regional governments were not permitted to issue bonds to finance infrastructure or anything else. Everything to be spent by a local government or even by another Whitehall ministry had to be pre-approved by a Treasury fixated on controlling public spending through its annual budget. Any money unspent by year-end would be forfeit: one implication was that any strategy beyond a single year was pointless, so no capacity for it was developed – in the regions, in the ministries, or even in the Treasury itself. Short-termism was hardwired into all public decision-taking. As for support to business, in 1945 Britain's Labour Party announced it would rebuild the 'commanding heights' of the economy.[11] But in contrast to Germany, the vehicle was nationalization and the creation of state-owned public enterprises such as the Coal Board. The term 'nationalization' was misleading. Often, the organizations being 'nationalized' were already in the public sector but had been run locally. The more accurate description was 'centralization'.†

Post-war America has not had the same need to rebuild, and in contrast to Britain its trade unions had never committed to socialism and nationalization. For nearly thirty years, American business had generated millions of mid-skill jobs around the country. They had enabled middle America and left-behind places to prosper as never before. Or ever since: in 1970 Milton Friedman publicly stated

---

* For this it used its private sector arm, DEG.
† Examples were universities, which by the 1960s were largely run from Whitehall; hospitals, which were public but locally run until 1948; and the probation service, which was localized until 2013, briefly privatized, and then centralized under Whitehall in 2019.

that the sole duty of a business CEO was to make a profit. Endlessly repeated in business schools, by the 1990s the advice was parroted by a generation of MBAs who had risen to run major companies. By the 2020s their greed-sodden behaviour had made many young Americans as hostile to capitalism as the people of South Yorkshire are.

Both the American mutiny that produced Donald Trump and the British mutiny that produced Brexit were legacies of policy mistakes that began around 1980. Though contemporaneous, the American and British mistakes were different. America turned into a devolved plutocracy; Britain turned into a centralized bureaucracy. Each initiated a downward spiral: the plutocracy plundered; the bureaucracy blundered. America's super-rich used their wealth to increase their political power, and their political power to increase their wealth. Britain's exceptionally over-centralized bureaucracy inevitably faced mounting failures, to which it reacted with further centralization.

In neither country did the safety mechanism of political competition work very well. The parties of the left, Democrats and Labour, had each been captured. In America, a bizarre legal ruling gave businesses the same political rights as citizens – including freedom of speech.* This fulfilled every lobbyist's fantasy and, in consequence, the cost of election campaigns exploded. To match the campaign fundraising of the Republicans, the Democrats needed to court their own super-rich: liberal New York bankers and West Coast tech bros. The super-rich shifted the party's agenda towards their own

---

*In 2016, a Supreme Court with an in-built pro-business majority decided that corporations had the same political rights to fund political campaigns as persons: the contributions of the super-rich even became tax-deductible. Campaign contributions and costs exploded, crowding out candidates lacking name-recognition unless they had sponsorship from the super-rich. This Supreme Court decision, which precipitated the degeneration into 'one dollar, one vote', had been imagined by the Supreme Court in the 1870s and considered to be fundamentally incompatible with American democracy (see Collier and Kay, 2020).

concerns. As a result, both major parties ignored the (already) left behind.

In class-ridden Britain, Labour had traditionally represented the concerns of the working class, but by the 2019 election its members were overwhelmingly young, educated middle-class people in the South-East. England's left behind were overwhelmingly not in the South-East; they were older, working class and had not been to university. Suddenly the left behind had no one to speak for them, and so they shifted their political allegiance.

After watching over three decades of widening economic divergence, the British government conceded that *private* investment in left-behind regions was too low. Ostensibly, it addressed the problem by establishing the British Business Bank (BBB). By 2021, it was even willing to concede that the Treasury's obsession with annual budgeting had resulted in *public* investment being too low as well, and its solution was another bank: the National Infrastructure Bank (NIB). But these were gestures, not solutions. They gave the illusion of action while disguising the painful reality of which Helmut Kohl had made Germans aware: restoring the left-behind places required large increases in taxes. The gestures were pitifully tiny, and their purposes confused. The British Business Bank has not had the scale and, perhaps until a change of leadership in 2022 not sufficient appetite, to reverse the spiral down of Britain's regions. Similarly, the National Infrastructure Bank has a balance sheet of only £22 billion and a staff of 127. The German equivalent, KfW, has a balance sheet of €500 billion and a staff of 7,600. The National Infrastructure Bank has a fudged mandate that combines the clear commitment of a transition to net-zero carbon emissions with a vague nod to regional balance: that could easily be interpreted as lending the same amount to every region rather than enabling the poor regions to catch up.

The advantage of public development finance institutions such as the British Business Bank, the National Infrastructure Bank and Germany's KfW is that they can target nationally determined objectives like narrowing the grossly unequal economic opportunities between regions. They can achieve these objectives by pump-priming growth in places trapped in spiralling down. Commercial financiers observing places trapped in the spiral walk away, whereas the public interest is precisely the opposite. Britain at last has these public institutions, but to date they have manifestly lacked the heft needed to achieve their objectives.*

There is now clinching evidence of failure: the collapse of Bank North. The inadequacies of London-centric finance had induced new banks better rooted in the regions to challenge them. Bank North was the most prominent, a nation-wide bank for the regions outside London. Instead of outmoded symbols of prudence – an imposing office with a pillared entrance – it put its money into recruiting local bank managers made redundant when London banks switched to algorithms run from headquarters. Algorithms have a modest role, but they are no substitute for experienced judgement based on local knowledge. Armed with this expertise, Bank North was able safely to offer five-year loans to local firms. Its intimate knowledge of a firm's business plan and management enabled its loans to be larger-for-longer: this made them far more attractive. Able to tap into this huge unmet demand, the quality of Bank North's growing loan portfolio was recognized as exceptionally high. Consequently, it had gained approval from the Bank of England in record time. Similarly, it had attracted private investors and was hugely attractive to the local governments of left-behind regions. A credible estimate of the benefits of opening a branch in South Yorkshire found that in the first five years it would generate

---

* But the BBB is rightly fearful of public criticism that it is 'wasting taxpayers' money'. During COVID, it opened a Futures Fund to protect around 1,200 innovative SMEs hit by the temporary shock. Unsurprisingly, by 2023, 83 of these firms had failed: the criterion for success are the long-term returns on the portfolio. Yet even the *Financial Times*, Britain's only financially literate news source, reported this as 'UK Taxpayer faces losses after companies backed by Futures Fund fail' (24 January 2023). Governments have failed to build a financially literate population.

around 20,000 jobs.* Recognizing these benefits, the cash-strapped regional government of South Yorkshire had been willing to invest £3 million of equity in return for its presence.† Yet despite this, Bank North was left to collapse. It did so because in the summer of 2022 Whitehall generated unprecedented chaos in financial markets, including four different finance ministers, three different prime ministers and wild swings in public policy. In such circumstances, private investors hunkered down, sterling collapsed and Bank North was unable to attract enough private finance to complete its funding round by the end of September 2022, the arbitrary deadline imposed by the Bank of England before policy chaos set in. Opportunities like this should have been golden for the British Business Bank: an acknowledged public benefit, financial support from a regional government, and utterly exceptional circumstances in which the need for publicly supported national investment was self-evident. Instead, the British Business Bank refused even to consider financing Bank North, and so it collapsed. Ironically, since, an Estonian bank has bought Bank North and is recapitalizing it. Now owned in Estonia, it has been able to bypass British misgovernance: I expect it will flourish.

Incompetent public decisions contributed to a miserable economic performance. According to OECD data, in 2023 Britain was the only one of the G7 nations in which national income has still not recovered to pre-COVID level. As to regional equity, England, other than London, has barely recovered from the hit of COVID,

---

* The estimate was made by my colleague Professor Colin Mayer, the former Director of the Saïd Business School at Oxford, based on standard ratios of investment to employment in British SMEs and the Bank North business plan for volume of loans.

† Revealingly, the primary difficulty that officials faced in providing this support was that, as with the Treasury, their criteria for estimating the public benefit were almost ludicrously inappropriate. Initially, the employment benefit generated by Bank North was restricted to the few managers and the other staff it would directly employ, thereby excluding the effects of its £500 million planned loans.

whereas London's GDP was over 4 per cent higher. Nor is the situation getting any better.[12] The regions are spiralling down, as predicted by the syndrome of fragility. The evidence from these aggregate numbers complements emerging stories of persistent public errors: how much more is needed before the blinkered Treasury begins to question its orthodoxy?

The most distressing aspect of these mistakes in governance is the failure to learn. The Treasury ignored the lessons of Germany's successful support for its steel industry; of Whitehall's own success in renewing Corby; of Pittsburgh's success in having the power to forge civil society strong enough to renew itself; and of West Germany's success in igniting fast growth in East Germany. The pattern of not learning from mistakes is persistent: if this is merely a *failure-to-learn* we are adrift in a ship of fools. More credibly, it reflects a *refusal to learn*: an active denial of a reality too uncomfortable to be faced. It is the condition known in psychology as *cognitive dissonance*.

How did this dismal situation come about? Thanks to the contributions of Nobel laureate economist Roger Myerson of Chicago, we at last have a convincing account of the link between highly centralized power and the abuse of power. His work is a paean for devolved and democratic governance in which local political leaders are directly accountable to local voters rather than to centralized scrutiny. In Germany, devolved government has worked exactly as Myerson predicts: the most successful regional politicians get noticed and rise to national office: such was the path taken by both Helmut Kohl and Germany's current Chancellor, Olaf Scholz. It also worked in America – Presidents Carter, Clinton, Bush and Obama all rose from regional prominence. Only Donald Trump broke this pattern, owing to his celebrity. Recent political science has more to say on power. A key advantage of democracy over autocracy is fewer extreme outcomes. While a benign autocracy can speed up necessary change – making the proverbial trains run on time – a malign one leads to unspeakable catastrophes.[13] There is no democratic equivalent to the 60 million deaths attributable to Hitler, Stalin and Mao.

Unfortunately, Britain has developed a unique form of democracy which meets neither of Myerson's conditions. Not only is power extremely centralized, but the electoral system is grossly unrepresentative. Members of Parliament are elected by first-past-the-post voting, which results in it being concentrated in a two-party duopoly. Centre parties attract votes but win very few seats. Either of the political parties in the duopoly can consequently win a majority in parliament with only around 40 per cent of the votes. Worse, the leaders of these two parties are selected by their paying members. Only a tiny minority of voters pay to join them, with the extremes of opinion on the far left and far right heavily over-represented. These paying members form a tiny selectariat – barely 1 per cent of all voters. The only power that British democracy allows the remaining 99 per cent of us is to choose which of these two selectariat-chosen leaders will rule over us. Worst, once a leader has a majority in parliament, they face only negligible constraints on how they use power. Almost uniquely, Britain has neither a constitution nor a second legislative chamber; the House of Lords is a powerless embarrassment. No other high-income democracy comes close to these cumulative deficiencies. The nearest analogies are in Latin America, where governments repeatedly find themselves facing Brexit-style mutinies. In 2022 there were fifteen elections in Latin America. All resulted in mutinies which ousted the incumbent government, regardless of whether it was on the left or the right.

Power that is over-centralized, over-confident and under-restrained is not trusted by citizens, so those who hold the power cannot rely on the citizens' willing compliance in its objectives. It has too much *formal* power to win the informal power conferred by social cooperation. It finds itself frustrated by widespread non-compliance with its commands. Its instinctive response is to escalate confrontation by resorting to greater coercion. We see this spectacularly with President Putin's war in Ukraine. Convinced that he knows best, the only diagnosis of his failure that avoids cognitive dissonance is that others are disobeying his orders – precisely the conclusion Hitler reached in 1944, and for the same reason. Putin's solution has been to dismiss his generals and impose mass conscription on his citizens. As families bribe officials to get the documents that exempt their sons, he cracks down on his own bureaucracy. As young men flee over the borders in response, he orders their closure. As border guards take bribes to let people cross, he sees a further target for punishment. As people distrust his reassurances and turn to independent media for news, he imposes censorship, which inadvertently confirms their doubts. This downward spiral of formal power into impotence is an echo of what happened in Communist-run East Germany. The Stasi constructed an intense and all-pervasive system of coercive scrutiny: everybody spied on everybody else. It left East Germany impoverished, and despite the regime's fixation on remaining in power, it collapsed like a house of cards. The weaknesses of centralized power in Putin's Russia are perfectly captured by Ilya Krasilshchik, a censored Russian journalist: 'think how they are going mad over their own powerlessness'.[14] Sadly, even after these setbacks, Putin has been able to fall back on three advantages. He can draw on the vastly greater manpower that Russia can afford to lose in combat; he is now getting material support from China and North Korea; and he can rely on the dysfunctions and distractions in major Western democracies that have curtailed the material and financial support needed to counter them.

What accounts for the behaviour of the plutocrats who have controlled American public policy and the bureaucrats who control Britain's Treasury? In the US, a scholarly study by Amy Chua, a professor at Yale, showed that the super-rich had been so self-serving for so long they had not only destroyed the post-war sense of togetherness but as role models for selfishness have reset the purpose of influence for other American social groups as being to gain privileges.* Chua depicts the nightmare Michael Sandel feared and predicted. Doug Rushkoff, a noted lecturer on the media, described a bizarre dystopia when during an address to some of the super-rich

* See A. Chua, *Political Tribes: Group Instinct and the Fate of Nations* (2018).

in Las Vegas he was asked: When American society collapses, our super-yachts will take us to remote safe havens, but how then do we incentivize our security staff? When Rushkoff advised the high rollers to build a relationship with their guards by asking about their families, he was dismissed with eye-rolling disbelief. The super-rich knew their collective behaviour was catastrophic and that their years of selfishness had put their relationships with their staff beyond repair.[15]

In the UK, the bureaucrats in the Treasury are distinctive in part because of their exceptional power. Unlike in other countries, their ministry combines a Ministry of Finance and a Ministry of the Economy. Its entrants are young people recruited directly from the top universities. Being an economics ministry, many of them are economists, who bring with them the fashionable ideas learned from their professors. Since the 1980s, that has meant market fundamentalism. If the market knows best, then public policy must be not only place-blind but blind to sectors or ownership. Moreover, growth of GDP will be maximized by avoiding any industrial policy or any favouritism towards British-owned firms. The growth of GDP can benefit everyone in the country: in the jargon, it is Pareto-efficient.* Alongside market fundamentalism, for a while another fashionable idea was monetarism: inflation was directly linked to increases in the money supply. Monetarism soon self-destructed and was abandoned even by the Treasury, though not before it had done damage. But it became increasingly important in the IMF as its 1980s vintage recruits nurtured on monetarism rose in seniority and led negotiations over the terms on which poor left-behind countries could borrow.

Although the Treasury notionally combines two functions, it is dominated by the annual event that defines life for people in finance ministries around the world: setting the annual budget. As Budget

---

* Diane Coyle is a rare wise voice who argues with devasting logic that since Pareto efficiency is indifferent as to whether poor people end up losing from a policy that increases GDP for others, it is unethical to use it as a criterion.

Day approaches, politicians and staff see themselves as the only bulwark protecting taxpayers against wasteful spending and inflationary deficit-financing. The Treasury's enemies are the other Whitehall ministries and local governments around the country, all viewed as reckless spenders. Finance Ministry staff see themselves as a small band of heroic warriors desperate to kill spending proposals to limit expenditure as close as possible to revenues. This underpins the instinct to control all public spending on a year-by-year basis. It requires scrutiny before authorization; authorization before spending; and the reclaiming of all money not spent by the year-end.

But no Ministry of *Economy* should behave in this way. In Britain, the consequence has been that nobody within either Whitehall or local government is tasked with longer-term economic strategy. The Treasury sets an example of parsimony to the spending ministries by squeezing its costs. It hires junior staff and overworks them until they move on: it has a very high turnover rate. And because the young people hired come from top universities, they tend to be over-confident. This is how twenty-five-year-olds find themselves tasked with assessing and, usually, rejecting proposals from specialist ministries such as education, and localities like South Yorkshire, without being equipped to make good judgements.

Given the exceptional power of these Treasury bureaucrats and the deficiencies of British democracy, they need to be reasonably representative of British society. The sharp end of Treasury policies has been felt by the North, which has fallen behind other regions; by the working class, which has fallen behind the middle class; and by those who do not go to university, who have fallen behind in valued skills. So it is reasonable to ask how well represented these groups are within the Treasury. There is indeed good international evidence that as once-neglected communities gain representation, their fortunes improve. Could the persistence of the brutal policies from which these three overlapping groups suffered be due in part to social exclusion? Belatedly, we can now answer this question: since 2023 we have reliable mirrors of the beliefs and social backgrounds of the people who have run Britain's Treasury from a mass survey and interviews by Sam Friedman and Aeron Davis.[16] The results are extraordinary: the deficiencies of Britain's democracy, though exceptional, are outclassed by its unrepresentative Treasury bureaucracy. It is far more socially exclusive than any other part of the civil service, and wildly unrepresentative of Britain's population,. Northerners are systematically under-represented: recruits are skewed to those who grew up in London. The working class are also grossly under-represented: the parents of recruits mostly went to university and then worked as professionals. Those without a degree are rare: whistleblower evidence suggests that for most recruits the issue is not whether they have a degree but whether it is from Oxbridge.

Once recruited, information on past performance is disallowed, so promotion depends heavily upon good connections. Only one in ten Treasury officials have working-class origins, and they seem to miss out on the insider tips by which the socially confident off-spring of professionals mount the 'velvet drainpipe'. This graphic term was never mentioned by working-class interviewees but was frequently cited as the path upwards by those from the middle class.

There is no need for the Treasury to be so exclusive. America's public bureaucracy manages to be broadly representative of its population, and on those aspects of diversity to which the Treasury has paid attention it has been able to change its composition quite rapidly: the shares of women and ethnic minorities have rocketed. The failure better to represent the three social groups that have borne the brunt of Treasury policies can only be interpreted as deliberate: neglect of something so crucial has been a conscious choice, not an oversight.

The lethal combination of deficiencies – power that is both exceptionally centralized and exceptionally unrepresentative – has resulted in mounting failures that cumulate in political crisis. Currently, one of the burning crises is that nearly half of British teenagers are assessed as so anxious and depressed they need support from mental health services. The Treasury is tasked with doing something about it, but it dares not delegate the choice of action to public officials who know more about the problem. When the Treasury's junior employees find themselves landed with such tasks, they will fail. In Denmark, using the same criteria, one in six teenagers are anxious and depressed. The Danes have long realized that public money needs to be spent on an integrated range of services such as schools, childcare and clinics, and that it needs to be focused on the youngest children so that by their teens they are resilient. The Treasury has had no such realization.

The equivalent Whitehall anecdote to Rushkoff's story about some of America's super-rich comes from a whistler-blower – Jonathan Slater. Recently retired as Permanent Secretary at the Department of Education, he attributed Whitehall's dysfunction to its spectacular disconnect from context-based practitioner knowledge. This was compounded by the habit of rapidly rotating civil servants and ministers around departments before they had time to gain even minimal expertise. Slater grew up in a southern middle-class family, went to a good southern private school and a good university, yet came to see himself as an *outsider* because he had not been to Oxbridge. If Slater is a Whitehall outsider in this hermetic little world of civil servants and the political class, what chance the left behind?

The failures mount inexorably. Britain has bumped down the international league tables even on the key number by which the Treasury judges itself: national income per head. By 2023, fourteen countries had overtaken Britain, and the latest forecast is that Poland will overtake it by 2027. And Britain has also bumped down the ranks of measures which reflect how citizens judge their own lives: the life chances of their children, the strength of their community's social capital and the dignity of their work.

In October 2023, just as I was finishing this book, Angus Deaton's *Economics in America* was published. Building on his work with Anne Case, Deaton shows that for most Americans the economy has not been delivering a good life; growth has been captured by the privileged. (In Chapter 4, 'Hidden Privilege', I set out a corresponding story for Britain.)

But Deaton's fundamental message is a critique of economics for having become unmoored from the study of human welfare. By insisting on methodological purity, it has retreated from the big questions. The discipline is at last changing – he celebrates 'a great ferment of debate', with many economists now challenging ideas that have long been accepted; in a *mea culpa*, he includes himself. He argues that economics needs better acquaintance with other human sciences like sociology and, above all, philosophy. The task is urgent because unlike in the post-war decades, those who have lost from economic change have gone on losing. We do not know why, but the likely menu of policies to address it takes economists into what he admits is 'uncomfortable territory' for many orthodox economists, such as place-based policies.

And now, back to that agenda: as you read on, you will see how much of what I say chimes with Deaton's critique. Americans, Britons and all societies with left-behind places can learn from the ideas reviewed in this book. They bring some oxygen into the claustrophobic little world of orthodox economics and liberate public policy from beliefs that have repeatedly failed.

I'll begin with disturbing new evidence on the pace at which, world-wide, the left behind are diverging from the successful.

3.

Hidden Despair

In the decades since 1990, the international economy has become more integrated – 'globalization' – yet people's economic circumstances have become more varied and erratic. In some places people's incomes have surged, most spectacularly in China. But alongside this unprecedented prosperity for some there is a contrary process: a widening patchwork of places and communities that have fallen behind. Where are they?

For many people reading this book, the answer used to be 'elsewhere'. The left-behind *countries* indeed became concentrated in the poorest parts of the world: Africa and Central Asia. The latest evidence reveals the grim reality that, as a group, these poor countries are still falling behind the rest of mankind. Countries like Malawi and Mali, long poor by world standards but once modestly prosperous relative to their own past, are now diverging faster than ever.

But many *communities* within middle-income countries are also falling behind – like the people of Barranquilla in Colombia. Collectively, the middle-income countries are now known by the upbeat designation 'Emerging Market Economies': technological innovation and global market integration have worked well for many of their people, but not for everyone. On average, they are rapidly catching up with the lucky billion living in the advanced economies: alongside the spectacular success of China, many other countries like Colombia have prospered as never before. But within Colombia a divide has opened. The coastal regions were once as prosperous as the capital, Bogotá. As global opportunities changed, Bogotá has boomed while they have fallen far behind. Their brightest young people leave, and those who stay feel that their home region has become marginalized. That experience is repeated in many Emerging Market Economies around the world. Such divergence breeds despair – and despair breeds anger.

As the next chapter will reveal, precisely the same process of divergence alongside prosperity has spread even to some of the richest countries in the world. Here, I focus on a disturbing and shaming message which has barely been noticed.

The poorest countries are getting poorer*

Created in 1944 to finance post-war reconstruction and development, the World Bank is by far the largest public international agency in the world. By 1973, when the need for reconstruction had receded and many newly independent countries had become members, its revised goals were spelled out by its president, Robert McNamara. The Bank was 'to accelerate economic growth and reduce absolute poverty'. Its entrance lobby encapsulates this with the message 'our dream is a world free from poverty'.

A crude interpretation of this goal used by the World Bank is an annual headcount of how many people are living on less than $2.15 a day, the amount deemed necessary to avoid hunger. This is a very conservative measure of the Bank's performance – it could be met even if all the poorest countries were to fall further and further behind the rest of mankind. But even on this inadequate measure, prior to 1990 the Bank was failing. The pre-1990 picture is no longer in dispute. For each of those three decades, on standard statistical measures the incomes of poorer countries were diverging from richer ones. When I first worked on this problem of global

---

* This section is based on J. Cust, P. Collier and A. Rivera-Ballesteros (2023), 'Are the poorest catching up?', World Bank Working Paper WPS10622. It represents work by a statistical team at the World Bank and draws on the latest data from both the IMF and *The Changing Wealth of Nations*.

divergence in 2003, I found that within it there was a further problem which had not been noticed. A group of sixty poor countries concentrated in Africa and Central Asia but with pockets elsewhere had not managed to ignite economic growth and were gradually falling behind everyone else. They had a population of about a billion people in total – I termed them 'the bottom billion'. China and India had initially been much poorer than most of them, but from the 1980s China had started to grow rapidly, and from the 1990s India and Latin America had also taken off. While in 1990 these three regions had still dominated statistics on global poverty, they are now favoured by investors as Emerging Markets and by 2035 their problems of mass hunger will be a thing of the past. It was due to their growth that global poverty began to decrease – probably for the first time in human history. But that success did not extend to the bottom billion. As a group, their incomes continued to diverge from the billions in the Emerging Market countries and the lucky billion in rich ones.

The divergence of the bottom billion continued until 2003, when the world prices of natural resources began a decade-long boom so exceptional it became known as the *super-cycle*. Because the growth process had never ignited in the bottom billion, the exploitation and export of their natural resources had become their predominant form of engagement with the international economy and so the super-cycle boosted their income. This was their Golden Decade, lasting from 2003 until 2014, when prices tanked; prices have since been highly volatile. Post-2014, the world economy entered a period known as the New Normal.* For the bottom billion, the New Normal looked very similar to the Old Normal, that long period until the Golden Decade during which they had fallen behind.

Pulling this together, I distinguish three periods: the Old Normal, prior to 2003; the Golden Decade, 2003–14; and the New Normal, 2014–19. Only during the Golden Decade did the bottom billion as a

---

* A term coined by the celebrated Egyptian economist, Mohamed El-Erian.

group briefly interrupt the tragedy of falling further and further behind the rest of mankind.

If the trend set in the New Normal were to be sustained, the global poverty count would soon revert to its grim pre-1990 upward march. From 2035 the number of people below that $2.15 poverty threshold – the number of people so poor they go hungry – would be increasing relentlessly. They would be concentrated in very different places from 1990. Replacing China, India and Latin America, the new poor regions are now Africa and Central Asia. Given the World Bank's mission, that prospect of rising global poverty should be galvanizing it into action.

Of course, there are plenty of reasons to doubt those projections, but many are not encouraging. National affluence in the Emerging Markets need not imply that hunger is eliminated – a theme of this book is that left-behind places abound. Also troubling, the crises that began in 2019 with COVID may bequeath enduring damage.*

But we can supplement projected trends with the evidence on changes in national wealth per person, including private assets like houses and public ones like infrastructure. Imperfect as it is, by looking at how assets are changing, we get some guide to how incomes might change in the future. In both the Old Normal and the New Normal the few assets of the bottom billion were effectively stationary, while the assets of the Emerging Markets were growing rapidly – at 3 per cent or more each year. In the lucky billion, they were also growing comfortably, at around 2 per cent.

The people of the bottom billion are radically poorer than the rest of mankind. By 2020, the average assets per head of the lucky billion was half a million dollars. The emerging markets average had leapt to $85,000 and was on track to catch up with the lucky billion within a generation. But people of the bottom billion had less than one thirtieth of those in the lucky billion and their assets are growing only slowly – how can they catch up? Unless there is radical

---

* For instance, in Britain the combination of left-behind places and the COVID shock has resulted in charity-run food banks.

change, these yawning differences in opportunities will widen into two different worlds – most of mankind in affluent societies, a minority mired in frustrated lives. Yet through social media, the two worlds will be in full view of each other.

While this picture is bleak, the core message of *Left Behind* is hopeful. Some of the countries among the bottom billion have found the confidence to think for themselves and are thriving. As role models to other neglected places still demoralized, and as a guide to how international policies need to change, their experience is invaluable. Just as the prospect of a return to rising hunger should galvanize international action to avert it, so this means of learning rapidly how to do so should have been centre stage. Yet neither has happened. Instead, owing to a combination of stale ideologies, confusing statistical evidence and distracting shocks, the danger and how to address it have been overlooked or ignored.

Cognitive dissonance?

The data used above were generated within the World Bank. But after thirty years of declining global poverty, the Bank had lulled itself into the complacent belief that because its mission was consistent with what had happened it must vindicate what the Bank had been doing – the Bank's programmes must be working. The Bank indeed had small programmes in China, India and Latin America, but on any realistic assessment they were peripheral to what had happened. The Bank's main influence, through policy advice, aid and the leverage of receiving policy conditional upon accepting the aid, was in Africa and Central Asia. The statistical results showing that these were precisely the regions where the growth process had *not* been ignited were incompatible with this self-congratulatory assessment.

But when cherished beliefs collide with new evidence, the evidence does not necessarily win. Instead of being galvanized into soul-searching questioning of why its approach to its stated purpose was not working, the Bank decided to change its stated purpose. It would no longer aim for a world free from global poverty and would no longer even measure it. It would simply aim to reduce the number of people living below an income threshold specific to each country. If that number was falling it would declare victory: its programmes in that country must be working. This measure was sufficiently undemanding that most programmes even in Africa and Central Asia would get a pass grade most years – everyone could relax. To avoid a blighted career, a staff member assigned to one of the countries not currently getting a pass grade would simply need to shift to a different country as fast as possible. Since everyone would be playing this game, the most junior staff would end up working together with the least able ones on the most difficult countries.

A premature celebration?

Coincident with the Bank's adept sidestepping of its own disruptive evidence, high-profile statistical studies offered reassuring messages of celebration. Not only was poverty falling, but the poorer the country, the faster it was catching up. This happy world was blessed with its own technical term: 'unconditional convergence'. Can such rigorous work by some of the world's most distinguished economists be misleading? Unfortunately, it can. But of course, rigour must be matched with rigour. Rather than clutter up *Left Behind* with a lengthy statistical detour, I refer you to *Are the Poorest Catching Up?* (Cust et al., 2023). However, I can give you a sense of how 'unconditional convergence' became inadvertently misleading. It was due to biases in samples, biases in time periods, and measures which answer the wrong question.

The bias in sample arises from the demanding data requirements of the elaborate tests used – they end up systematically over-representing countries with good statistics and therefore good governance. Unsurprisingly, such countries also tend to be growing fast. Another bias arises from China and India. For most of the long period for which the studies estimate trend growth rates, India and China were still catching up with the global average income. This gives the misleading impression that the poorest countries *as a bloc* are growing faster than those less poor. Only now that China has decisively overtaken the global average will the same statistical measure begin to bias the story in the other direction.

A more complex bias is that the fashionable statistical measure of trend growth rates makes an implicit assumption that there is a common global growth process which has become more benign through the decades. In fact, there are two different growth processes, one in the countries which have ignited their domestic economies, and one in those that haven't yet done so. Further, there was a super-cycle in 2003–14 which temporarily boosted growth in the latter group and happened near the end of the long period the studies consider.*

As to the question being addressed, the studies were providing answers to the beta-divergence question 'What is the trend in this pooled data up to 2015?' Since there were two different trends in process, the pertinent questions were why a large group of countries had been falling behind for many decades and what should be changed in consequence.

Embarrassingly, the happy answers to the wrong question were published just as many of the poorest countries were diverging faster than ever as the poly-crisis ripped into them.

The shock of the new?

Both the bleak overall picture and the evidence from heroic exceptions warranted decisive and timely action. Instead, what arrived was the poly-crisis. COVID-19 struck in January 2020, followed by climatic shocks, acute international tensions over Taiwan, the war in Ukraine and the conflict between Hamas and Israel. It became a world dominated by uncertainty in which governments needed to take reassuring actions that restored confidence.

---

* The statistical measure is beta-convergence. It appeals to economists because it pools a large data set and enables them to establish a trend, period by period.

In the lucky billion these exceptional shocks were cushioned by drawing down a little of the enormous national wealth they had accumulated over previous decades. The Emerging Market economies also had some scope to do the same, although global capital markets proved to be fickle. The bottom billion, with so little wealth on which to draw, had no domestic cushion and were largely frozen out of global capital markets. If ever there was a time when they needed some support from the rest of mankind, it was during this period.* Yet it has not been forthcoming. On the contrary, the future of the bottom billion has fallen further down the ranking of global attention.

Nor is the shock prospective bright.[1] In late 2023 an estimate of future damage caused by an increasingly erratic climate by Swiss Re, the world's largest insurance company, found the costs skewed heavily against Africa, favouring the temperate high-income countries where costs would be lower. Yet again, the lucky billion would live up to their name.

Schadenfreude?

Clearly, as the foremost global institution, the World Bank should be aiming for global convergence: that is its essential mission. The countries that have fallen behind to become the poorest should be growing faster than the other groups. That they have not, save for the Golden Decade, should be reason for soul-searching and re-assessment at the Bank, reinforced by reasonable concerns about the adverse prospects of the poorest. Such soul-searching is indeed what the International Monetary Fund (IMF) did in 2018 while

---

* In May 2023, the meeting of G7 Finance Ministers warned of rising uncertainties. Although they probably had US interest rates in mind, a few months later the unanticipated war between Hamas and Israel proved their larger point. By the time of the IMF–World Bank Annual Meetings in October 2023, the international situation had deteriorated so badly that a commissioned report issued there was entitled 'The world is on fire'.

under the direction of Christine Lagarde. Through an independent assessment of its performance, it found that in fragile states only one in seven of its programmes of support and advice were succeeding. This triggered a major research programme, published in 2021.[2] But in addressing the persistent slow growth of many countries in Africa and Central Asia, the IMF was handicapped by a change in leadership and its restricted mandate. The mandate for this problem was held by its bigger sister – the World Bank was where the buck stopped.

But big sister was engrossed in the cumbersome internal process by which it might redefine its purpose to something easier to achieve, and change its measures of poverty so that rising *global* poverty would not even need to be reported. Before it had finished this nefarious process, international anger at its failure to respond to the poly-crisis boiled over and reached its Board of Management. The Bank was correctly judged to be dilatory in disbursing funds that could have enabled the governments of the poorest countries to prevent their economies imploding. In February 2023, in humiliating circumstances, its president was forced to resign.

This might have galvanized the Bank to put itself through the same soul-searching the IMF had. Instead, it appears to have galvanized it into speeding up the implementation of its plan to change how poverty was measured. The new president, Ajay Banga (an American from the private sector), promised the governments of the lucky billion what they most wanted to hear: he would magic up the money for all their priorities.

Left-behind places in Emerging Market Economies

Colombia is one of the most successful Emerging Market Economies in Latin America. But Barranquilla, capital of the Atlantic-Caribbean Region, is all too conscious that it has seen better days. It once felt modestly prosperous but has now fallen behind the other parts of the country that are booming. In June

2022, Colombia held a national election, which was tense, close and polarized. Ostensibly the battle was between the incumbent pro-business party of the right and a pro-worker opposition candidate from the left, the result being a narrow victory for the left. Yet the real cleavage was not left–right: it was the widening gulf between booming regions and left-behind places. Enough voters in regions like the Atlantic-Caribbean swung behind the candidate of the opposition party to give him that narrow victory.

Colombia is emblematic of what has been happening across Latin America. The election in Colombia was one of the fifteen in Latin America in 2022 in which the incumbent party lost regardless of whether it was on the left or the right. In all these countries a localized initial economic shock had been compounded by further economic decline. And the adverse psychology of localized discontent amplified it. The story of Barranquilla is representative of what has been going wrong across Latin America, and indeed in many other Emerging Market Economies.

Barranquilla was once Colombia's gateway to the Caribbean and the US because of its harbour at the mouth of a river. But then the city was hit by a natural shock: the estuary began to silt up because of erratic rainfall upstream. This was the random puff of wind that capsized the city while leaving other parts of Colombia unaffected. As Barranquilla, the region's core city, started to decline, the entire Atlantic-Caribbean area was dragged down with it.

What happened next was driven by the adverse dynamics of social psychology. Economic decline relative to other parts of Colombia triggered a blame game: rivalries, fragmentation and despair. This in turn fed into local politics: as in South Yorkshire, the local governments in the towns and cities of the region blamed the government of Barranquilla. Its decline aroused all the petty, hostile narratives typical of towns and rural areas towards a core city: it was supposedly corrupt, incompetent and greedy.

These psychological reactions to decline contaminated local politics, which became too distracted to focus on solving the underlying problem: the estuary was silting up. There was, in fact, a straightforward solution. Regular dredging along the length of the river would have cost a fraction of the mounting economic damage. Dredging upstream required a partnership between all the local governments through which the river ran: each would bear some of the cost, as would the city of Barranquilla itself. But instead of cooperating, each local government found itself trapped by its own short-term interest: the collective response was mutual distrust instead of a recognition of mutual interest. They lacked any viable model for cooperation.

Remarkably, facing the region on the other side of the Atlantic Ocean was a similar group of rivalrous governments that share the Mano River – Liberia, Sierra Leone and Guinea. While they were no more trustful of each other than are the local governments of the Atlantic-Caribbean Region sharing the Magdalena River, they had discovered a work-around. It was to create a shared institution, the Mano River Union. It had well-crafted rules and good leadership: despite not trusting each other, they all trusted their institution. It was potentially a cognitive gadget for the local governments of the Atlantic-Caribbean, but they were unaware of it.

Lacking this crucial knowledge, their inability to dredge the river was only the beginning of the political problems triggered by adverse psychology. Within the region, not only did localities fall out with each other but conflicts between businesses and workers were exacerbated. As productivity fell behind that of the more prosperous regions of Colombia, trade unions understandably demanded that wages keep up with those in these more prosperous regions, whereas businesses understandably argued they could not afford to increase them. Hostile, stereotyped old narratives were revived: local businesses were exceptionally greedy; local workers were exceptionally aggressive. Owing to the adverse economic shock, the region needed a boost to investment, but these stories had the opposite effect: local firms shifted expansion plans to places where worker productivity was higher, and firms from elsewhere were deterred from coming by the region's poor reputation.

Most crucially, at the national level politics turned against the region. In Colombia political power is highly centralized in the capital, Bogotá. The capital and its region were booming thanks to mining and oil. They had the resources and institutions to renew the Atlantic-Caribbean but neither understood its problems nor had sympathy with its plight. Being deep in the interior, the Bogotá region is unfamiliar with river systems, and yet again, hostile narratives provided a convenient alibi for inaction: the Atlantic-Caribbean region was thought to be incapable of addressing its problems, so public money would be wasted.* There are ways of reversing such downward spirals that have worked. But they all involve people in left-behind places like the Atlantic-Caribbean accepting that they need to come together, claim agency over their problems and explore options for dealing with them.

Emerging South Africa?

During the grim decades of apartheid, South Africa was an Emerging Market Economy in which extreme polarization between a prosperous minority and a left-behind majority had repeatedly provoked mutinies. Supported internationally, the majority black population was eventually sufficiently powerful to force political change. Wisely, the president and leader of the ruling Afrikaans Party, F. W. de Klerk, realized that he had to make concessions, and magnificently, the leader of the oppressed majority, Nelson Mandela, realized that crushing the Afrikaans was neither materially advantageous nor morally right. The pair received the Nobel Peace Prize.

Mandela had the wisdom to recognize that economic policies would be critical for the transition to an equal and prosperous

---

* Colombia and Britain are both extremely centralized, and the parallels between Bogotá's disdain for the capacity of local government in the Atlantic-Caribbean and Whitehall's disdain for local government in the north of England are unsurprising.

society: there was already massive structural unemployment among the rapidly growing black workforce. He had the modesty to recognize his limitations: he knew no economics and so could not tackle that problem. Having overseen the existential uncertainties of the peaceful transition of political power, he stood down at the first opportunity, leaving South African society with a prestige far greater than its economic size. South Africa qualified as Africa's only member of the G20 and so became the global spokesman for the continent; its leaders inherited from Mandela a potent and valuable global moral authority.

The challenge of generating millions of productive jobs for black workers was daunting: it depended on businesses in South Africa and internationally having the confidence to scale up investment. Also daunting were the psychological and political aspects of the transition. The psychological imperative of victory in a long and brutal moral struggle against oppression was to redistribute income from the prosperous Afrikaans and white English-speaking communities to poor black ones. The political imperative for the senior ranks of the African National Congress (ANC), which had been the organizing force behind this struggle, was for advancement into positions of authority and influence. The three objectives led to tensions. Would the ANC prioritize the interests of future black workers or those of its ageing leadership? If the ANC squeezed the profits of Afrikaans- and English-speaking firms and the wages of skilled white workers, would they emigrate? Would global manufacturing businesses that could invest in China, or global agricultural businesses that could invest in Brazil, invest in an uncertain and potentially hostile South African environment?

As with the dilemmas faced by Barranquilla, there were international answers which might have been useful. But rather than being studied and resolved, the dilemmas were denied and postponed. President Mandela's successor was Thabo Mbeki; he was well intentioned but over-confident in his abilities and lacked any experience in business. He had not been Mandela's preferred candidate but had been chosen because his father, a fellow senior

ANC member, had made way for Mandela following his release from prison.*

President Mbeki built on some of Mandela's successes. As decades of barriers that had denied black people opportunity were lifted, institutions such as the Reserve Bank and the Ministry of Finance were strengthened with talented people the equal of any in the G20. Mbeki also oversaw major improvements in living conditions. Politically and psychologically, this was essential: in mega-slums like Soweto in suburban Johannesburg people were living in squalid conditions. The chosen strategy was to relocate slum dwellers to decent new houses with a plot of land, which to be fiscally affordable were located far out from Johannesburg. While this demonstrated that the ANC was committed to serving black interests, it reduced the job prospects of those who had been relocated.† People could have been rehoused closer to work, and it was the responsibility of political leaders to think through the trade-offs.

Mbeki introduced pensions. Inadvertently, this compounded the youth unemployment problem. Surveys found that pensioners were supporting their unemployed grandchildren, many of whom chose to retreat into inactivity more commonly associated with learnt helplessness. In Kenya, young people were being energized to reach the global cutting edge of coding skills: why not in South Africa? Mbeki was learning, but not about jobs. From the wilder shores of social media, he picked up the idea that AIDS was not caused by HIV. This led to a public health disaster in a society ravaged by the disease.

---

* American analogies of the presumptive entitlement of political dynasties would be the Bush family dynasty among Republicans, and among Democrats the support for Edward Kennedy during the Primaries for the 1980 election against the incumbent Democrat President Jimmy Carter, a peanut-farming outsider. In Britain, the nearest equivalent would perhaps be the three generations of the Benn family in Labour cabinets.

† South Africa was not the only middle-income G20 government to make this mistake. Mexico City built housing estates so far away from the centres of work that they inadvertently condemned the occupants to premature retirement.

Submerging South Africa?

As his failures mounted, Mbeki became vulnerable to challenge from rival ANC dynasties. The most politically astute was Jacob Zuma, who with his wife built a nationwide patronage network. The result was a formidable vote-mobilizing machine within the ANC which Zuma used to oust Mbeki. Once president, Zuma and his cronies had so much power they could manipulate economic policies however they chose. He could use his power to redistribute the nation's wealth to reward his clients in the patronage network. Or he could use it to grow the economy and generate job opportunities for young Africans. But he couldn't do both: he faced the Paradox of Power, a well-understood aspect of political science.[3] To grow the economy he would have to reassure businesses sufficiently that they would invest, and for that he would need to build checks and balances that limited his power. Given his prior record of campaigning, businesses feared being outcompeted by crooked firms that paid bribes or being pillaged by unchecked abuse of power. Zuma could have fixed the problem by limiting his power, giving businesses clear rights of justice in courts and establishing tax administrations that were visibly independent of ANC authority.* Instead, he did the opposite, placing cronies in key positions and forging an extraordinary partnership with the Guptas, a shady business duo based in India who are currently wanted by Interpol. He succeeded in building an effective machine to loot the economy. Its epicentre was the state electricity monopoly, Eskom: as its assets were stripped by Zuma's avaricious cronies, power cuts, once unknown, escalated. By 2023 they averaged twelve hours a day and, according to the Reserve Bank, cost South Africa about $20 billion a year in damage.[4]

By the end of Zuma's tenure, business investment had plummeted and unemployment had rocketed. In the election for his successor, Zuma's patronage network was inherited by Madame

---

* The technique by which fears that political power will be abused are allayed by demonstrating the independence of tax decisions is an application of the concept of Signalling, developed by Nobel laureate Michael Spence, albeit very different from its initial uses.

Zuma.* Her opponent, Cyril Ramaphosa, inherited the Mbeki wing of the ANC and tapped the mounting frustrations of economic failure. By a narrow margin, Ramaphosa won, possibly aided by some patronage deals of his own.

Once in power, he attempted to reform Eskom, appointing a new chief executive, André de Ruyter, brought in from the private sector. De Ruyter was astounded by the extent of the looting, especially in the coal industry, which had become 'a feeding trough'. He recommended a straightforward solution: rapidly expand private-sector generation of green energy from wind and solar and hive off electricity transmission from Eskom. The Minister of Energy, a Zuma ally who controlled the coal industry, saw this as a mortal threat to his interests. In an extraordinary turn of events, he invited de Ruyter for coffee, which turned out to be poisoned with cyanide. Lucky to be alive, de Ruyter reported the crime, yet it was not properly investigated, nor was the minister suspended: indeed, he was allowed to dismiss de Ruyter. Exasperated, the poisoned and dismissed chief executive went public with his story: he was promptly threatened with imprisonment for treason.

At the same time, Zuma's corruption had been brought to court. But when sentenced to jail, Zuma incited his cronies to open revolt: the port of Durban was torched in riots.† As he had done over de Ruyter, President Ramaphosa retreated: Zuma was not jailed. These indications that corruption in the high echelons of the ANC enjoys impunity are a dangerous twist in South Africa's decline from having been a global moral authority.

Emerging Russia?

Russia, once in both the G20 and the G8, has decayed much further. President Putin has succeeded far beyond Zuma's dreams of

* By then she was his ex-wife, thanks to an amicable divorce which avoided any legal conflict of interest.
† There are clear parallels with Donald Trump's incitement to rebellion to frustrate the transfer of power to President Biden.

avarice, to become reputedly the world's richest man. Like South Africa, Russia began a hopeful transition from economic and political collapse; although it failed, its path from hope to tragedy has been very different.

As in South Africa, by the mid-1980s its economy was collapsing. In apartheid South Africa business confidence had evaporated in the face of internal mutiny and external pressure. In the Soviet Union it was due to the mounting absurdities of central planning as ministries in Moscow sent incompatible and unmeetable directives to state-owned enterprises hundreds of miles away. A privileged elite of senior and elderly party members – the selectariat – had their dachas, apartments, cars and little luxuries, but for most Russians life was dominated by queuing, as shortages had proliferated.

Mikhail Gorbachev, who like Mandela received the Nobel Peace Prize, brought Russia and the West together, recognizing that the divide between party privilege and worker misery was unsustainable. Believing that state ownership and central planning could compete with capitalism in the marketplace, he opted for Perestroika: opening state firms to international competition. Faced with the prospect of competing with imports, the managers of state-owned enterprises were more realistic – and pessimistic – than Gorbachev. They behaved like a giant version of Eskom, looting their doomed enterprises in league with criminal gangs which were already thriving on the black market created by shortages. Managers gave the gangs licence to pillage the produce and equipment of their factories, which the gangs then sold through their existing marketing networks. The profits were shared between the gangs and the managers.*

President Gorbachev knew that the Soviet Union rested on an

---

* The brilliant BBC series *Russia 1985–1999: TraumaZone* (2022) gives a graphic account in a collage of film clips taken by locally based film crews both of the failings of the communist system and the difficulties of introducing a post-communist market democracy. Russia is still paying a huge price for communism more than three decades after it ended.

unsustainable imbalance of power in which Moscow-run Russia ruled over many alien societies that aspired to autonomy. The empire had been assembled during the violently expansionist autocracies of the tsars, and Lenin and Stalin. Gorbachev's policy of political liberalization, Glasnost, was his counterpart to his economic liberalization, Perestroika. It freed the countries of the former Warsaw Pact, but within Russia the price was a coup attempt in 1991 from factions in the army and the KGB.

Submerging Russia?

Neither Mikhail Gorbachev nor his successor Boris Yeltsin knew any more economics than Nelson Mandela: they sought advice from American academics. Unfortunately, this was at the peak of ideological certainty about the miracle of the market. Disastrously, they were urged to privatize everything as swiftly as possible by distributing tiny shareholdings in each company to each citizen. The aspiration was noble: the gulf between privileged party members and neglected workers would be closed by an equal distribution to all citizens: each would become owners of a tiny share of the nation's wealth. Nobody would be left behind as the Russian economy 'leapt across the chasm' from communist shortages to a new, better market equilibrium. The aspiration was noble, but the strategy was over-confident and mistaken. The outcome was a further massive boost to the gangsters, as rich crooks used them as agents to buy up individual shareholdings in companies very cheaply. People were hungry, desperate and had no idea about the true value of the bewildering pieces of paper they had received. They sold their shares cheaply to buy food. The rich crooks bundled them up into controlling holdings in a company. Never had so many been fleeced of so much national wealth by so few: the Golden Fleece took on a new meaning.

A new, far more dramatic divide had opened between the privileged and those left behind: the oligarchs had arrived. As it dawned on Boris Yeltsin that he had been duped into authorizing this plunder, he descended into despairing alcoholism and unpopularity. The oligarchs needed a more electable replacement and settled on Vladimir Putin, who combined practical experience of political campaigning in St Petersburg with years of training in the KGB. There, he had learnt about the sinews of hard, coercive power within the state. Once a judo champion, he had mastered the game's psychology of turning an opponent's strength to his own advantage while finding and exploiting weaknesses.[5] As president, he turned these techniques on the oligarchs themselves. One by one, they were threatened: get out of politics and cut me into your wealth, or else. Since the oligarchs each had their own well-armed gangs, some thought they could face him down. Quite quickly these challengers were jailed or murdered.

Putin replaced non-compliant oligarchs with people he had known a long time and who were totally dependent on his patronage. Sometimes he went to extraordinary lengths: when frustrated by the failures of his claimed military expertise, which he blamed on his generals, he turned to the owner of a St Peterburg restaurant whom he had known for years. Yevgeny Prigozhin himself became a minor oligarch through owning the Wagner Group, a psychopathically brutal gang of mercenaries. Gangland is often depicted as kill-or-be-killed, but more commonly its pattern is kill-and-then-be-killed. By 2023, Prigozhin had accumulated enough enemies to meet his fate.

Mind the gap?

Colombia, South Africa and Russia are all Emerging Market Economies beset by the challenge of helping large left-behind communities. Nationally, Colombia's economy continues to be successful, while South Africa and Russia have become *Submerging* Market Economies. But despite this important difference, none of the three has yet closed the gap between those communities that are successful and increasingly powerful and those that are left behind and increasingly marginalized. In Colombia the task is not in principle daunting: as the nation prospers, it can afford the large public investments that would be needed as one component of breaking the geography of discontent. President Gustavo Petro aspires to that goal, but missteps during 2023 intensified polarization. Some of the gadgets and successes introduced in the following chapters may help him in his struggle to turn it into reality.

The prospects in South Africa and Russia are less rosy: their economies are shrinking, and their ageing leaders appear to view the world through similarly distorted lenses. Fittingly, in 2023, South Africa's Foreign Minister invited President Putin's Foreign Minister to watch a joint exercise by the Russian and South African navies. This gratuitous insult to the alliance of countries opposing Russian military force in Ukraine was revealing. South Africa faces no military threat from the USA or any other member of that alliance but is in urgent need of their economic support to avert further decline. In contrast, Russia can offer South Africa little assistance. Rather than being a calculated move for advantage, the choice may reveal an abiding hostility to the West and the wistful appeal to the glory days of Russian communism. Like Vladimir Putin, top ANC officials are living in the past instead of facing the reality of political, social and economic crisis.

The privileged in both countries will use their considerable power to oppose the investment in the left behind that a transition would need. If the ANC cannot face down its cronies, voters may face down the ANC: its support has tumbled well below a majority. In President Putin's Russia, change is harder to envisage. Kill-and-then-be-killed may turn out to be the fate of Putin, but whoever replaces him might merely be a new face playing the same game.

The lucky billion are spared the fraught transitions of the Emerging Market Economies. But they still need to mind the gap between the communities of the fortunate and those of the left behind. Some have failed to do so.

4.

Hidden Privilege: Diverging Life Chances

America and Britain are highly unequal societies. But as with all emotive terms, inequality needs to be handled carefully. The standard statistical measure – the Gini Coefficient – fails to capture what most people mean when they lament that our societies are unequal. Compare a student at Oxford – or Harvard – living on a modest scholarship against a youth of the same age who dropped out of school and is working long hours at Starbucks. The Gini Coefficient will record the student as poorer than the guy who is serving him his coffee. But who envies whom? The student is on course to rise high in a community-of-success; the drop-out is heading for a community-of-humiliation. Income inequalities can matter a lot if they persist over a lifetime but are less significant if they are only transitory, as is likely for those two youths. We need to supplement measures of inequality in current incomes with something more sophisticated – life chances.

Life chances and incomes around the world

Life chances measure whether the children of two adults stuck in low-income jobs will grow up to earn no more than their parents or, at the other extreme, have just as good a chance of ending their lives on a high income as those born into affluence. The scholar who has pioneered the measurement of life chances is Steven Durlauf at the University of Chicago.[1] Like many concepts in economics it has been graced with a technical name, though one less opaque than most – 'inter-generational social mobility'. It measures whether

69

inequalities roll on between generations. Thanks to his meticulous work, the results were updated in 2022 to cover enough countries that we can compare America and Britain with many other high-income societies and a few of the Emerging Market Economies.

Durlauf and his team have also investigated whether inequality in life chances is related to inequality in current incomes. In twenty-two countries they have measured both forms of inequality. The country with the most unequal life chances in the world is Peru, which also turns out to have among the most unequal income distributions. The country with the most unequal income distribution in the world, Brazil, narrowly exceeding that of Peru, also turns out to have among the most unequal life chances. At the other end of the spectrum, the country with the most equal life chances, Denmark, also turns out to have the most equal income distribution. Perhaps you begin to see the pattern? With the odd exception, the two aspects of inequality turn out to go together. Not just Peru and Brazil but also Chile and Argentina – the only four Latin American countries measured – stand out as being exceptionally unequal on both measures. Conversely, not just Denmark but Norway, Sweden and Finland – all four Nordic countries – are exceptionally equal on both measures.

That unequal life chances and incomes are so closely linked often has a straightforward explanation. If large swathes of the population are excluded from life opportunities, they are unable to contribute effectively to the economy and so have low incomes. Compounding that waste of talent, such exclusion generates frustration, despair and anger – a cocktail that incubates damaging mutinies. Consequently, countries in which governments ensure that everyone has a fair chance of succeeding – no communities left behind – avoid the waste and the damage, and so tend to be more prosperous than those that don't. This has implications for public policy in countries around the world, and for their politics.

That equal life chances and equal incomes are conducive to prosperity should be welcome news to governments with ambitions to improve the lives of their citizens. Wide inequalities are not the price they have to pay for economic growth: to date, they have been most common in the *less* successful middle-income countries. Peru and Brazil, the two stand-outs for gross inequality, are among the poorest of the twenty-two countries on which we have data. Along with much poorer countries, they can catch up with the lucky billion more rapidly by adopting policies well crafted to promote inclusion in the productive economy.

Inclusion is also good politics. The four Latin American countries measured are unlikely to be exceptions to their region. Recall that all fifteen Latin American elections in 2022, including these four, resulted in defeat for the incumbent government – the left-behind communities used the election to mutiny. Conversely, in Denmark, which has prioritized inclusion, the 2022 election resulted in a resounding victory for the incumbent, a Social Democrat. Politicians usually wish to be re-elected and so often find the goal of inclusion attractive. But they seldom know how to craft the policies that make it happen.

Future promise?

The Chinese take justified pride in their astonishingly rapid ascent out of poverty. But the society also has highly unequal life chances and highly unequal incomes. Was this a necessary price for the growth, or is it attributable to other policies?

China in the 1970s had relatively equal household incomes because the entire country was exceptionally poor: other than a tiny elite, poverty was pervasive. From 1978, a distinctive growth strategy was adopted based on breaking into global export markets. In consequence, the needed infrastructure and the growth were concentrated near the ports: less accessible places fell behind. Growth strategies not so narrowly focused on exports manufactured near ports could potentially be more equally distributed around regions. China's spatial inequalities were exacerbated by social policies not intrinsic to growth: entitlements to public services were made specific to where people were initially registered. When millions of workers migrated to the coasts, they and their children lost these entitlements and found themselves at a disadvantage relative to coast-born workers.[2] Together with other distinctive policies, this has bequeathed a legacy of severe social inequality. Life chances are now exceptionally unequal relative to other middle-income countries, worse than every country in the data apart from Peru. Income inequality is even higher than in the US.

China's remarkable escape from the pervasive grinding poverty of the early 1970s was inevitably going to increase social inequality. But policy choices clearly aggravated it: with hindsight, the growth could have been achieved with less inequality. By the early 2020s the phase of rapid growth looked to be over, while the habits and regional differences bequeathed by past policies may prove to be deeply entrenched. Whether China will continue to be a land of promise through the twenty-first century is uncertain. Yet it is so important to understand China's growth process and its consequences as best we can that I return to it throughout *Left Behind*: these are just preliminary remarks.

Like many Chinese, many Americans recognize that their society has unequal incomes but take pride in being *the* land of opportunity. Many Britons like to think of their society as Europe's kinder version of America – a post-colonial Britannia, cool, multicultural and offering opportunities to all who want to work for them. Are these happy beliefs of Americans and Britons justified?

On Durlauf's data, neither country does well. In terms of life chances, Britain has become one of the most unequal countries in the world; America, despite its proud claim, is only a little better – pretty much on a par with Argentina. In terms of income inequality, the US is about on a par with China, while Britain, though less unequal than the US, ties with Italy as the least equal in Europe.[3] American inequality is somewhat compensated by its exceptional prosperity – average income is high (although later in the book this achievement will be heavily qualified). Britain is far less prosperous, not only much poorer than America but also much poorer than Denmark. Inequalities, especially in life chances, look to have made Britain poorer, not richer.

But why are life chances in Britain so exceptionally unequal – tying with Italy as the most unequal high-income country in the world? Thanks to Robert Putnam, we know that in Italy much of it is geographic, due to deep cultural differences between a thriving north and a stagnant south that began in the fourteenth century. But comparing modern Britain with Italy would be misleading. Although Britain also has wide geographic differences, its north now poorer than its South-East, the causes look to be very different – in the nineteenth century there was a net flow of workers to the region now left behind. The causes of Britain's unequal life chances, as distinct from their severity, have been something of a mystery. They could predominantly be due to spatial inequalities, or to some entirely different influences on opportunities.

Why are life chances and incomes in Britain so unequal?

This is a question that calls for research. The organization that has done most to answer it is the Institute for Fiscal Studies. Together with my colleagues Philip McCann and Jamie Walsh, I joined forces with them to push it forward. The results below are the preliminary fruits of that effort.*

Life-chances: rolling biased dice

With such exceptionally unequal life chances in Britain, you might have expected that Whitehall would try to find out what was going

* This section draws heavily on recent work led by Sonya Krutikova and her team at the Institute for Fiscal Studies. See S. Krutikova et al. (2024), 'A preliminary analysis of life chances across England'. I also draw on P. McCann, *Levelling Up Economics*, The Deaton Commission on Inequality, Institute for Fiscal Studies (2023).

on. Instead, it appears to have done the opposite – the data needed to disentangle what determines life chances are very tightly held in different ministries and neither pooled nor released. But at last, the IFS had a breakthrough; otherwise, I would have had less to say. As with global poverty, the details are technical, but I can give you a sense of the progress they have made.

Our method is designed to answer the question: Who is *born lucky*? There are many potential influences on why life chances might differ right from birth, but people rightly view wide differences at the starting line with suspicion. There is also much passionate advocacy on behalf of various small but unambiguously disadvantaged groups such as the neurodiverse and the transgendered, which I support. However, given the exceptional scale of the inequality and the prolonged ignorance as to its causes, the research priority is to identify key weaknesses of British policies which if addressed could improve the futures of millions of people. If geography turned out to matter, it would point to one set of policies. If gender turned out to matter, it would point to a completely different set of policies, since women and men are not concentrated in different regions of the country. If age turned out to matter, perhaps with young workers disadvantaged relative to the retired, it would point to a further set of policies, such as spending more on vocational training and less on pensions. If ethnicity turned out to matter, it would suggest a hybrid: distinctive policies such as racial discrimination in employment, but nuanced by region, gender and age. Some ethnic groups have distinctive profiles in respect of each so addressing disadvantage might warrant support to raise the quality of schools heavily used by particular ethnic groups in a few cities. If all these factors turn out to matter, we need to be able to rank them objectively.

We investigated each of these characteristics. Everybody is a little different and this creates a lot of noise in the data. But to establish policy priorities we group people according to a few salient advantages and disadvantages. To make them memorable I will give them colourful names, which might seem to trivialize the issue. As the evidence reveals that millions of young lives have avoidably been blighted owing to bad policies, any sense of the trivial should recede.*

The most advantaged – Lord Lucky will represent them – is, of course, male and white; he grew up in an advantaged neighbourhood of London – perhaps you might think of Kensington – and now he is working in London. His chances of finding himself in the top 40 percent of all 28-years-olds are a comforting 68 percent.

Before discussing the implications of this privileged life-chance we need to get some more results, changing the characteristics that have the biggest impact on life-chances. An advantage of this approach is that we let the evidence set the priorities instead of our own prior beliefs or passions. In principle, it can reveal uncomfortable realities that have been little noticed or deliberately underplayed. The research is more sophisticated than I have set out, but the curious can check it in Krutikova et al., 'A preliminary analysis of differences in life-chances across England' (2024). Here I summarize what we are finding and begin some discussion of its implications for policy.

Our first changes are two aspects of Lord Lucky's location: we change where he grew up. We pick them because between them they most decisively reduce his life-chances, though the first change is not massive. We are going to give him the same start as his cousin Baron Far-Away, who grew up in Yorkshire and still lives there. Although he may shudder at the thought, and his life-chances do deteriorate, since he now grows up in a favoured neighbourhood within Yorkshire – perhaps a wealthy district of Harrogate – he still has a better life-chance than most 28-year-olds.

But when we change the neighbourhood where he lives from a favoured one to a poor one like the Parson Cross Estate in Sheffield, he is only called 'Lucky' sarcastically. His life-chance of being in the

---

* As explained in Krutikova et al. (2024), our results depict people who were attending school in England when they were 16 and are now 28 years old. Success at that age is to be in the top 40 percent of incomes of all 28-year-olds schooled in England. Conversely, lack of success is to be in the bottom 40 percent. Removing the middle fifth reduces the noise in the data.

top 40 percent when he is 28 is well below average despite the advantages of being white and male, and getting an English education. Perhaps it is quite hard to persuade him that he is particularly privileged?

We can make a similar two-step deterioration in Lord Lucky's life-chances by changing his gender. First, please step forward Baroness Far-Away who grew up in a good neighbourhood of Yorkshire and still works in the region. Her life-chances are worse than her cousin Lady Lucky, who grew up in Kensington and now works in the city (and quite possibly in the City). But the life-chances of the Baroness do not collapse: in fact, the advantage of a good neighbourhood in Yorkshire softens the disadvantage of being female and working in Yorkshire – her life-chances are about par for the entire age-group.

But now we again take that further step. She has grown up in a poor neighbourhood of Yorkshire such as Parson Cross. Meet Miss Misfortune: she has the lowest life-chances of any category in our dataset. Her chance of being in the top 40 percent of 28-year-olds is barely 11 percent. Despite the benefits of being white, of growing up in England and of attending English school, Miss Misfortunate faces pitifully poor life-chances. Were she to conclude that there is no point in trying, her despair would be understandable as well as self-fulfilling.

How to be born lucky

To be born lucky in Britain, you need to ask your parents to endow you with characteristics that in combination give you such a large advantage at the starting line that even at an amble you should win the race. Tell them that you must grow up and work in London. Tell them to ensure that you should grow up male (and stay so). Finally, and if Britain is like America this one is the most important of all, tell them to get a degree. We suspect that in this respect Britain is indeed like America, and we will be testing it on ONS data to see whether it holds up. You can check the results though the regular updates to Krutikova et al., (2024).

As long as your parents have followed these simple instructions, they have earned your future living for you. By growing up and working in Britain your chances of being in the top 40 per cent of earners aged 28 are exceptionally high. The difference between the life-chances of Lord Lucky, 68 percent, and Miss Misfortune, 11 percent, at 6-to-1, is staggering compared to any other high-income country. Her well-founded reason for despair is the counterpart to his well-founded reason for self-assurance. Just as Miss Misfortune's despair inclines her to behaviour which is self-fulfilling, so Lord Lucky's self-confidence reinforces his advantage. To a first approximation, he has been born into a new hereditary caste analogous to an aristocracy.

Doubtless, Lord Lucky and his ilk feel fully entitled to their good fortune. But recall that their fortune is too good to be due to Lord Lucky's genes or his dedication to his work. It is not credible that he is so remarkably smarter than fortunate Danes, Germans or Japanese men born with equivalent characteristics. They do not have anything like a 6-to-1 advantage over the most disadvantaged major group in their societies. Something other than Lord Lucky's brilliant genes or exceptional greed must account for why Britain post-1980 has stumbled into social mobility so low as to be unique among the world's high-income countries. The only credible explanations are distinctive changes in the structure of the British economy, or distinctive public policies. Either might have skewed opportunities towards Lord Lucky. A prime candidate for failing policies is education.

Failing education policies?

In both America and Britain, parental education makes a massive difference. In the US, entry to university is now more likely for a teenager whose measured intellectual ability is in the bottom quintile but whose parents are in the top income quintile than one with the opposite configuration. Entry to a good university is the gateway into any of the professions, leaving open only the high-risk path to successful entrepreneurship for those who lack that opportunity.[4]

Nevertheless, America differs substantially from Britain. The life-chances of Americans are massively affected by race: African-Americans have faced systematic discrimination for centuries. In contrast in Britain, Black disadvantage began mainly with the arrival of the *Windrush* in 1948, so discrimination is more recent. Also in contrast with America, it is softened by the geographic advantage that the majority of Black Britons live in London. In America the opposite has happened: African-American communities are concentrated in left-behind places suffering from the familiar adverse dynamics of spiralling down. America is now well analysed, Britain less so. I will concentrate on Britain here.

In America, if your parents get a degree, that raises your own life chances a lot. In Britain, we know that if you yourself get a degree, you will enjoy much higher earnings throughout your working life. Most people with one are earning £40,000 a year by their late thirties. While at age 22, a minority of young people will gain a degree, at 16 every child in the country is required to take the same set of exams: GCSEs. If you leave school with no higher qualification than GCSEs, throughout your life you will only earn about half what a degree holder earns and your chances of earning more than £50,000 are negligible. But unlike other high-income countries, the crucial parts of the GCSE are uniform, irrespective of how talents and aspirations differ. Performance on a few narrowly defined skills when 16 becomes the decisive gatekeeper for all future opportunities.

For 2024, we have an approximate snapshot of the education profile of people in Britain aged 34, and it paints a depressing picture.* The top third have a degree; the bottom third have virtually no educational qualifications; and a quarter have nothing beyond A-levels – they could expect to earn only around £25,000.

The most glaring British anomaly compared with the rest of Europe is that barely 5 per cent of the cohort had sufficient voca-

* The snapshot was taken in 2016 when these people were 26 years old, but few people in their late twenties continue with their education: indeed, the number of people in adult education has fallen sharply.

tional training for their peak earnings to breach even the modest barrier of £30,000. Due to extraordinary biases in Whitehall's priorities, Britain has spectacularly failed to invest in the vocational skills of its youth. It is still failing to do so.[5]

In consequence, teenagers face an existential struggle: get a degree or be condemned to low lifetime earnings. So, what determines who gets a degree? Fortunately, we can trace back the history of this cohort of 34-year-olds. Those differences between the degree holders and the lesser educated can be traced back to when they were 16 and sat their GCSE exams in the millennium year. Doing badly in the maths exam at that tender age had catastrophic consequences on these children's futures. Evidence suggests some of this was due to nothing more solid than a tick-box approach to credentials when they sought other opportunities. Shamefully, millions of kids still have their fate decided by this single examination. In that millennial cohort, those whose grades were in the top third had around a 70 per cent chance of going on to get a degree. Those in the bottom third had around a 4 per cent chance. Consequently, it is a high-tension exam.* So, what determines who gets the good grades? We can tell from the prior socioeconomic status of those 34-year-olds. Those who had attended fee-paying schools had a 70 per cent chance of getting a degree. Those who had grown up in the most deprived fifth of households had a mere 17 per cent chance.

There is also recent evidence that one of the crucial stages in falling behind is the passage from the child's primary school to their secondary one: the children of the more affluent get into the better-performing secondary schools and so overtake those from poor households who were previously smarter.[6] The most likely means by which the affluent pull off this trick is to buy houses in the catchment areas for the best schools, which are consequently more expensive than in the worst catchment areas. There are simple ways of removing this advantage. The league tables of school performance could be seen only by local education authorities and used for

---

* As I am acutely aware, since in 2024 two of my teenagers are sitting it.

the assessment of headteachers, or the catchment areas could be enlarged and places to over-subscribed schools assigned by lottery. Instead, these grossly biased policies remain frozen in place. In no other high-income country are fates so heavily stacked in favour of the children of the affluent.

Fates are also heavily stacked in favour of children in London. It is quite clear where the greatest needs are to be found. The poorest children are those getting free school meals. But even within this group there is bias. Those on free school meals in London are 40 per cent more likely to get good results in the crucial maths and English GCSE exams as those in the North, and twice as likely to go on to university. Yet the allocation of government funding is perverse: schools in London get more money per student than in any of the poorer regions – indeed, 40 per cent more than the poorest English region, Yorkshire and Humberside. Of course, the cost of living is higher in London, but the best teachers stll choose to be there as demonstrated by the superior exam results and the testimony of the children's commissioner below. The same perverse priorities apply to health care: the places with the highest deprivation, found predominantly in the North, get substantially *less* funding per patient than those with the least, found disproportionately in the South-East.[7] With such an advantage, they have been able to attract better-qualified teachers and doctors. Those advantages are complemented by the abundant opportunities for a London teenager to recognize that a university is a gateway to a high-earning job. They are surrounded by recent role models of success and hear narratives of schooling success as a pathway. Recall that in South Yorkshire, teenagers are dragged down by that toxic narrative 'OK, we're thick'. To quote the Children's Commissioner, 'We have been struck by how many children [in the North] fall back during the secondary years, when children growing up in the areas of greatest need often underachieve. Here hundreds of thousands of children face a double disadvantage of living in a poor community and attending a poor school.'[8]

Not only is government funding perverse, amplifying unequal life chances instead of reducing them, it has been getting increasingly perverse. Between 2009 and 2023, the most deprived secondary schools suffered much larger cuts than the least deprived.[9] The funding of education and training beyond secondary schooling is also perverse: per person, young people from London local authorities are the most favoured, while those from Blackpool and the North Midlands are the most disadvantaged in England.*

Black Lives Matter turned a long-overdue spotlight on the extreme and enduring disadvantages faced by Black youth in America. Due to the pervasive exposure of Britain to American social media, similar prominence has been given to racial discrimination in Britain. In the job market, Black applicants undoubtedly face disadvantage, but in schooling, in contrast to the gross regional biases described above, there are no equivalent biases. In the excessively important GCSE maths and English exams, the most successful of the major ethnic groups identified are the Chinese; around a quarter more of them pass than white British students. The least successful are the African-Caribbeans, with a fifth fewer passing, which may well be a legacy of despair due to 75 years of racial discrimination. Black Africans – whose experience of discrimination is much more recent and may still have the ambition common among recent immigrants, are more successful in exams, being at or above par with the white British majority.

Among the most deprived households – those in which the children are getting free school meals – the ethnic effects are distinctive, which is a warning to delve into the details of results. The chances of white British children are exceptionally low – only 16 per cent continuing to university.† This contrasts with around a 60 per cent rate of university entry for the Black African children on free school meals and around a 30 per cent rate for the smaller group of

---

* See the Institute for Fiscal Studies Press Release, 'Schools serving disadvantaged children have faced the biggest funding cuts', 11 December 2023.
† the data source for all these numbers is government official statistics released by the Department for Education. Here we use the data for 2019 since the 2020 exams were abandoned due to COVID and subsequent university entry was affected.

African-Caribbean children. This is partly because the racial discrimination faced by being Black is somewhat compensated by the advantages of geography: nearly 60 per cent of Black Britons live in London, in contrast to only 10 per cent of white Britons.

Returning to the previous results about life-chances, the effects of ethnicity in England look very different from those in America. In England, if Lord Lucky is of Indian ethnicity his life-chances of being successful at 28 are even higher than if he is white.

Further, the effects of gender are radically different depending on which ethnic group is studied. Bangladeshi men are a large and considerably disadvantaged group relative to white men with otherwise similar characteristics. But Miss Misfortune, the most disadvantaged group in our analysis, is white; if we change her to Bangladeshi ethnicity her life-chances improve by a third to a level similar to Bangladeshi men.

There is an alternative to Britain's model*

The Estonian education system is the antithesis of Britain's, but not because a lot more is spent on it. The differences are in where money is spent and, more importantly, on how education is run.

In summary, the British system is heavily focused on getting children into primary schools when they are aged four, followed by early specialization from the age of twelve on a few academic subjects. The content of education is set centrally and enforced by discipline, exclusion and scrutiny supported by high-frequency national testing and inspections. Estonia's system focuses on professional pre-school for the early years, where children learn to socialize: while Britain spends much less than the OECD average on pre-school, Estonia spends much more. It delays primary school

---

* For a substantial, readable and politically neutral account of the Estonian education system which substantiates all the points made in this section, see Rachel Sylvester, 'Want the best schools in Europe? Try Estonia', *The Times*, 6 November 2023.

entry until seven. Once there, specialization is prohibited until the age of 19, classes are usually mixed ability and unstreamed, and there is an emphasis on activities that cut across subject boundaries. Far from being centrally controlled, the power of decisions over the curriculum is devolved to teachers and headmasters, with virtually no national testing, exclusion or inspections. While British education has become more traditional, Estonia is continuously pioneering innovations such as integrating virtual reality into classes. British schools are trapped in competition over their rank in national league tables; Estonia has no league tables and teachers are encouraged to visit other schools, learn from them and collaborate.

These two education systems are so radically different that they cannot both be right. One common measure of performance is the OECD's PISA test at the end of secondary school education. There are many deficiencies – trivially, in how it is measured, with concerns about biased samples, but more substantively in whether it assesses the right aspects of success. The Estonian Ministry of Education is quite dismissive of it, while its British counterpart is keen to crow about any successes. Yet Estonian schools get the best PISA score in Europe and beyond, beating North America, Japan and South Korea.

Estonian success extends far beyond that. It radically equalizes life chances: the country has the narrowest gap between the children from the top and bottom socioeconomic quintiles in the OECD. But the feature of which the Estonians appear to be most proud is the very high level of well-being among schoolchildren. By this they do not mean 'happiness' – in the words of a headmistress, 'If we wanted that, we would given them ice cream'. Their measure of well-being is the internationally standard ten-point scale of 'life satisfaction'. Sadly, on that measure, British schoolchildren, stressed to breaking by high-stakes testing, come close to bottom.

If education is fundamental to a society's future, Britain's education system looks to be in need of transformation. In Part II, its deficiencies will be set in a larger context: it is a microcosm of larger failures.

Why is income distribution not more equal?

I now turn from unequal life chances to unequal incomes. While Britain has spectacularly unequal life chances, the story on income inequality is less dramatic, albeit still a matter of concern to many people. Having constructed the social groups to measure differences in life chances, we can now look at their differences in incomes. Instead of asking how good are Lord Lucky's chances of starting his working life in the top 40 per cent, we now ask how much he earns. By asking the same question for each of the groups, we can tease out just how much of an earnings advantage each of his attributes confers on him.

At age 28, Lord Lucky can expect to earn almost £30,000. When he meets his impecunious relative Baron Far-Away, he can enjoy the frisson of condescension in noticing the difference made by the extra £6,500 he is able to earn simply by virtue of his parents' good sense in bringing him up in London, where he has stayed to work. His income premium from fortunate geography is thus 28 per cent. Baron Far-Away in turn can condescend to Baroness Far-Away, who is only earning £18,500. Being male has given him the substantial premium of 24 per cent. And, of course, all of them can be disdainful of Miss Misfortune, who is earning only £10,000 and so lives from hand to mouth.

All these people are only 28 years old. Time is on Lord Lucky's side, his peak earnings are likely to be a much larger multiple of Miss Misfortune's.

We can supplement this new evidence on the value of each privilege with other recent evidence on incomes, starting with the unambiguously fortunate: those adults in the top 1 per cent of annual income. As of 2019, there were half a million of them, earning above £130,000. They are predominantly found within commuting distance of London, with its concentration of high-paying jobs in finance, law and government.[10] They could not have gained those jobs without their university degree, which leads us back to the biases in education policy.

The overall message of *Left Behind* is joyful: communities long left behind can catch up. But the tone of this chapter has been far from joyful: its account of Britain's doom-loop of education and privilege has been angry – I think justifiably so. From the next chapter, good news abounds, but first there is one final unhappy fact to be revealed. Over the past four decades, as each of Britain's age cohorts arrives on the jobs market, these anxious jobseekers have faced deteriorating opportunities.

When to be born lucky

In Britain, as in the rest of Western Europe, the three post-war decades were a period of unprecedented rising affluence for almost everyone. But since around 1980, this has faltered. Grouping the data by the decade in which people were born, those born in the 1950s can now be seen as the Lucky Cohort. They were in time to be swept up by that era of widespread affluence. And they managed to get sufficiently entrenched in their good fortune to protect themselves from the choppy circumstances that set in from the 1980s.* We can track two data series that quantify that privilege: male earnings and property prices.

Average male earnings for those born in the 50s soared towards £35,000 when they came to their late forties. They were far more fortunate, age for age, than any previous cohort. But the following cohort, born in the 60s, is earning around £3,000 less in their late forties. Similarly, the cohort born in the 70s is earning less, age for age, even than the 60s cohort. That pattern of deteriorating incomes is sadly also true of the 1980s cohort. As for the 1990s cohort, it is too soon to assess, but they did not enter a healthy economy.

Meanwhile, the rise in property prices has increased wealth gaps between those who own their house and those who rent, and consequently made it much harder for middle-income people born after 1960 to own a house. Age for age, each subsequent cohort has a smaller proportion of homeowners. This has hit the middle-income group hardest – since 1997 the proportion of them owning a house has more than halved. There is an evident interaction with geographic

---

* This was good news for me, but not for most readers.

imbalance, since house prices in London and the South-East have risen far faster than in the regions.

Again, the credible explanations for these atypical and disturbing outcomes are distinctive changes in the structure of the British economy or distinctive public policies, either of which might have skewed opportunities.

As to distinctive changes in the British economy not reflected elsewhere in Europe, a prime candidate is the growth of the financial sector, which was heavily concentrated in London. But distinctive public policies seem likely to be more important. The exceptional concentration of power in London, with government, courts, finance and media all increasingly based there, detached decisions from the local knowledge essential for good judgement.

These policies interacted with the intellectual counter-revolution of the 1980s to generate two explosions, one in regional inequality, the other in privilege. As to regional inequality, England and Wales became the only countries in the high-income world to experience this toxic combination of highly centralized power and bad ideas such as place-blind policy. By 2024, as Philip McCann shows in the Deaton Review, the result was the wholly exceptional divergence of all other regions from London and the South-East.

As to the explosion in privilege, it was ushered in by the intellectual counter-revolution of the 1980s and largely sustained thereafter. The privilege was captured by a new class – the well educated; by a new cohort – those born in the 1950s; and by the privileged region – the South-East. The small group of people who tick all three of these boxes are now retiring. But for these years of divergence, they happened to be running the country. That the gross material privilege now in their laps coincided with their own concentrated political power was perhaps not mere happenstance.[11] As they reach their retirement, the inversion of Wordsworth's youthful celebration of revolution is perhaps an apt epitaph:

> Bliss was it in that dawn to be alive,
> But to be *old* was very heaven!

PART II

Spiralling Up

5.

Leadership

Good political leadership can reverse the spiral of decline, and we can learn a lot from the places that have been transformed by it. Such leadership arrests the economic and psychological forces that drag places down.

Although the initial trigger of decline is usually economic – an adverse shock – the downward spiral sets in immediately as expectations deteriorate. They induce an exodus of investors, the psychology of despair and divisive narratives of blame. Good leaders begin with dramatic actions that reset how people see the future. They shift the expectations of discouraged investors, lift the despair of their inhabitants and counter the narratives of blame with a prospect widely attractive to people previously divided. But they don't end there: they realize their own limitations and so build and motivate teams within public organizations. They then empower them to figure out solutions to problems that initially look intractable.

The rise of Singapore and the near-miss of Tanzania

In the 1960s, two leaders of left-behind places aimed to transform their societies from poverty to prosperity: Julius Nyerere, the founding President of Tanzania, and Lee Kuan Yew of Singapore. Each became the head of government in about 1961 and found himself facing surprisingly similar problems to which each brought similar solutions. Both are heroic figures: that one succeeded is a triumph; that the other failed is a tragedy. Those different outcomes illustrate that all transformational change is subject to uncertainty. Neither Julius Nyerere nor Lee Kuan Yew was in a position to know with confidence what strategy would work. A seemingly minor difference in approach was more important than either would have suspected: it led to spectacularly different outcomes. Julius Nyerere failed in his goal of economic transformation: with immense honour he recognized his failure and resigned. Nevertheless, he bequeathed an invaluable legacy, and for this he was, in my view, a great leader.

Both leaders made personal sacrifices that earned them widespread trust. Nyerere inherited from the departing British colonial governor an imposing official mansion and a Rolls-Royce. He refused to live in the mansion; he refused to use the Rolls-Royce. He set a standard of simplicity and modesty: his moniker became 'the teacher', not 'the big man'. This lifestyle contrasted quite radically with that of many other African presidents.

Lee Kuan Yew's personal sacrifice was more dramatic, but equally effective. By the late 1950s Singapore was not only dirt-poor but had a recent history of deep public corruption. Lee had campaigned on a platform which included tackling it, but to win his campaign he needed money. Not being a rich man, he had been fortunate to be bankrolled by a wealthy businessman, and once elected he rewarded his backer with a public position. To his discomfort, once in that position the man started to misuse it for his own advantage. Lee's choices were limited. If he punished the man, neither he nor anyone else was likely to finance Lee's next election campaign. But if the corruption became public knowledge, people's cynical suspicions would be confirmed. The cautious thing for Lee Kuan Yew to have done would have been to tell his backer to stop abusing his power on threat of dismissal. What he actually *did* was to prosecute him: the backer was convicted and sent to jail. That sacrifice of future campaign finance astonished his sceptics: it established that he meant what he said.

In their different ways, both Julius Nyerere and Lee Kuan Yew swiftly won their people's trust that their intentions were good. But intentions are not enough: people also need to trust a leader's competence. Most people were very poor and had highly practical needs: housing in crowded Singapore, food and education for their children in Tanzania. Both leaders had the modesty to realize that to provide these things they had to choose well-educated advisers and create a meritocratic civil service. Their dynamism was tempered by realism: they recognized that transformation would be a long haul and spoke repeatedly of patience and mutual self-sacrifice.

With these strategies in place, they set about resetting the ideas prevailing in their polities. The first challenge, a priority for both, was the lack of shared identity among their citizens. Tanzania was an arbitrarily constructed colonial territory: it swept up fifty different tribes, many languages, several religions and various races. Its core was a vast territory with major port cities on Lake Victoria and the Indian Ocean. Pastoralists grazed wandering herds of cattle. Many farmers practised shifting cultivation to allow plots to lie fallow for years, ranging over land which belonged to the tribe, not the individual. In other areas, farmers planted coffee trees and regarded that land as their own. This whole territory was loosely linked to a semi-independent offshore island: Zanzibar. The island itself had a variety of peoples, but it differed from the mainland in history and economic interests. Forging an effective union between the mainland and the island was hard: Zanzibar managed its own finances and was far more prosperous. As Nyerere recognized, Tanzania was not, in any meaningful sense, a nation. The country's borders had evolved from those of what was German East Africa until 1919 and then Tanganyika under British colonial administration until 1961.*

---

* Britain had become the colonial power because at the end of the First World War, with Germany defeated, the British were granted trustee status to manage the territory under the auspices of the newly created League of Nations. In taking responsibility for the territory, the primary motivation of the British empire had been to ensure that no other power would control the coast, potentially threatening the shipping route to India.

Singapore, despite being small, was even more fractured. The country was made up of three different groups – Malays, Chinese and Indians – all highly suspicious of each other. Most dangerously, there were two rival ideologies. From China, Maoist Marxism had a considerable appeal, while across the Pacific the USA offered the prospect of harnessing the alluring new products of its consumer society to the parliamentary democracy the British had bequeathed. Like Julius Nyerere, Lee Kuan Yew saw these bitter divisions as a fundamental impediment to progress and resolved to use the post-independence moment to bring people together.

Both leaders used their powers of communication to reset their citizens' ideas about identity. In Tanzania, tribal identities were downgraded; in Singapore, ethnic and ideological identities were downgraded. In their place, they tried to build a new shared identity. Lee Kuan Yew supplemented communication with micromanagement of public housing. Realizing that owing to the salience of race, each ethnic group preferred to live within its own community, he ensured that anyone who wanted public housing would find themselves with racially different neighbours.

President Nyerere took the process of building shared identity so seriously he devoted his first year in office exclusively to promoting the narrative that people were now first and foremost Tanzanians, not a member of a tribe. This idea was reinforced by powerful actions such as the introduction of a common language taught in all schools and used in all documents and discussion.

Ultimately, both leaders hoped that changing people's sense of identity would encourage them to concede a little self-interest to contribute to larger purposes. But humans are creatures of habit, guided by our collective minds. If asked to be less self-interested, we ask ourselves why now? And why me? Both leaders came up with compelling answers. As to why now?, they seized on the unique moment of Independence. To that they added a frisson of urgency. Nyerere was explicit about it. He told Tanzanians that they must run where others walk: the need to catch up is universal to the concerns of the left behind. For Lee Kuan Yew the urgency arose not from opportunity but from threat. The country only existed because it had been thrown out of a federation with Malaysia. Having been expelled, it found itself surrounded by enemies: Singapore's very survival was at stake.[1]

The why me? question was the more challenging. Having themselves made sacrifices, both leaders asked other privileged people to do the same. Julius Nyerere created two vanguard groups. The political vanguard were the people who satisfied demanding requirements to join his political party: the only one he permitted. He opted for a one-party state not to ensure his own power but because he was a realist. He saw that the only basis on which rival parties could form were the inherited tribal and religious identities. Competitive party politics would make it impossible to build shared identity. Multiparty politics would need to wait until shared identity was firmly established. His other vanguard was a new cadre of senior civil servants, whom he recruited on the basis of their exceptional educational performance. They would have considerable power to take decisions: again, he was a realist, recognizing the pressures that they would be under. With power over appointments and contracts, their relatives would expect favours: strong traditions of loyalty to family would trump any nascent loyalty to the new nation. So, he made their appointment subject to a rule that they could not work in their home region. They would have no relatives knocking on their doors.

Lee Kuan Yew came up with a vanguard approach that was broadly similar. Although he left other political parties in place, he set bounds on dissent. His civil service approach was also fiercely meritocratic. Singapore being a city-state, he could not post people away from their home area, but he addressed the temptations of dishonesty. The pay for ministers and top civil servants was gradually raised to a high level by international standards. His rule of thumb was that pay should be set at two thirds that of similar jobs in Singapore's private sector. But in return, those at the top were personally accountable for their conduct and the quality of their work: corruption and weak performance invariably resulted in dismissal.

These strategies succeeded in changing people's identity. For Tanzania, the evidence is surprisingly concrete. The border between Tanzania and Kenya is a straight line drawn on a colonial map that sliced arbitrarily through East African societies. The same tribal mix characterized each side of the border. This created the ideal conditions for a natural experiment: could people living in the same village but from different tribes cooperate? The key public good in a village is a well: everybody uses it, but to keep working it needs to be maintained. This gave rise to a simple collective-action problem: could the community muster the social pressure to curtail freeriding? On each side of the border, some villages were inhabited only by a single tribe, and in such places social pressure should work readily enough. But other villages were multi-tribal congregations of people who had settled there relatively recently; here intertribal tensions might frustrate cooperation. No Kenyan political leader followed Julius Nyerere's example of attempting to reset identities away from allegiance to tribe. In 2001, when this research was conducted, despite nearly forty years of nationhood, on the Kenyan side of the border people lacked a sense of shared identity. In tribally mixed villages people were unable to cooperate. In contrast, people in the Tanzanian multitribe villages saw their salient identity as Tanzanian: they were surprised that the researchers might think anything else of them.*

For Singapore there is also unambiguous quantitative evidence: the Ministry of Community measures social interaction. They found that the divisions which Lee Kuan Yew had faced between rival races and rival ideologies had by 2018 long been overcome: everyone indeed thought of themselves as Singaporean. Indeed, they were very proud of it.†

---

* The research on which this discussion is based was treated more fully in *The Bottom Billion* (2007), and was led by Ted Miguel.
† I discuss these results more fully in *The Future of Capitalism* (2018). The civil servant who shared these data with me had become worried because he was finding a new and very different disconnection – between well-educated high-earning

Both leaders built trust in their leadership and a new sense of shared identity among their citizens. But those achievements were just necessary preludes to their ultimate objective: building common purpose for economic transformation. Citizens now knew that everyone in society was hearing and trusting the same message, which made such coordinated action easier.[2]

Lee's and Nyerere's ambitions were to enable their societies to catch up with more prosperous countries. To achieve them, they wanted to change not only people's sense of identity but how they understood their world. One key but tough message was that only if people accepted belt-tightening would the state be able to finance investment. In turn, only this investment could make everyone better off. The strategy depended on widespread compliance, which people might reasonably doubt. Both leaders felt justified in implementing it through forced savings. In Singapore, wages and farm incomes were held down by public policy; in Tanzania, the price at which the government bought export crops like coffee was set far below world prices so that the state could bank the difference. As a political strategy, squeezing living standards to make room for collective investment took courage and skilful communication.

Their skill in political communication was in setting this demanding idea in the moral context of common sacrifice for a better common future. Their own moral instincts had led them to the idea that Michael Sandel's philosophy later elevated into Contributive Justice. They cast it as a new mutual duty: everyone had an obligation to comply. By leading from the front with their own sacrifices, Nyerere and Lee had earned the right to call on others to make modest sacrifices for the common good. As with all willing compliance, they understood that the main force policing mutual generosity would be the gentle pressure of social approval.

---

insiders and the less-educated, lower-earning outsiders. This was the 'peeling off' of the successful which was the focus of that book. That, however, is largely a rich-world problem; much of the poor world still faces the fragmented identities that these two leaders successfully surmounted.

What happened? Lee Kuan Yew's transformation in Singapore was spectacular. In the span of a single lifetime, living standards rose from being pitifully low to being among the highest in the world. This is testimony to his inspiring leadership and team-building, astutely combining the powers of commander and communicator. He was not afraid to use his power of command boldly to face down privilege. Through his powers as communicator, he wove an increasingly dense web of reciprocal obligations.

Yet tragically, even though he adopted an apparently similar strategy, Julius Nyerere failed. The squeeze on individual consumption was successfully implemented. The savings were channelled by his new civil service into public investments. But instead of this leading to an increase in income as in Singapore, the opposite happened: the economy imploded. Lee Kuan Yew used the collective sacrifice for investments that positioned Singapore to enter global markets. At the time this was an unconventional approach to development. Julius Nyerere followed the prevailing received wisdom of the 1960s and invested in industrial import substitution. Partly owing to unlucky timing, this strategy rapidly proved ruinous. As foreign exchange was pre-empted by imports of capital equipment for industrialization, the economy was starved of essential supplies like oil needed for all forms of activity. Production collapsed in both industry and agriculture. With it went the credibility of the president's claim that shared sacrifice would lead to a better future. People saw that across the border in Kenya farmers were becoming better off, while Tanzanians were hungry and their shops empty. With the narrative of shared sacrifice for future prosperity discredited, the mutual obligation to sacrifice lost its rationale and moral force. The contrast between the public rhetoric and the grim reality was devastating for the vanguard, the civil servants and party bosses who were supposed to exemplify the new virtues. Living a lie taught some of them to use their positions opportunistically. The government tried to cushion falling consumption with price controls, but this led to acute shortages. The shortages provided public officials with tempting opportunities to profit by abusing their power. Unrestrained self-interest was unleashed and public corruption among officials grew explosively. As the vanguard continued to spout the official rhetoric while some of them were seen to be fleecing ordinary people, cynicism set in and became endemic. No subsequent Tanzanian leader has yet been able to restore the trust that Nyerere had won by his exemplary life of sacrifice.*

The rise of Botswana

While Julius Nyerere's strategy of transformation failed, another African leader of an initially impoverished society succeeded spectacularly. At Independence in 1966, Botswana was so underdeveloped that it lacked any large town: until 1965 it had been administered from the South African city of Mafeking. Sir Seretse Khama, the founding president of Botswana, set a high standard of ethics and competence. The diamond-mining company De Beers asked the president for permission to prospect for diamonds. They explained that Botswana was a good prospect for a strike. The president immediately saw the potential dangers of divisive disputes. To pre-empt them, he went round all the clan leaders asking a question. If diamonds were discovered, should they belong to the clan on whose territory they were found, or should they be shared by the entire nation? Clan leaders realized that if the neighbouring clan found diamonds and kept them, while their own clan found nothing, they would fall far behind their neighbour.† As a result the clan leaders all opted for sharing the diamonds wherever they were found. A further detail showed Seretse Khama to be not just a wise

---

* In March 2021, owing to the death in office of the incumbent, Vice-President Samia Hassan became the first female president of Tanzania. At the time of writing, she is on track to restore public trust in the economic competence of government.
† Perhaps more alarmingly for the clan leaders, when the members of the unlucky clans challenged the 'finders keepers' rule as unfair, they would be revealed as having agreed to it.

leader but a great one. Based on earlier searches, De Beers had told him that there were diamonds under the territory of his own clan. In putting nation before his clan, he showed exceptional moral leadership.

Seretse Khama anticipated the potential jealousies from disputes over the ownership of diamonds and pre-empted them. He soon needed to do so again. A resource discovery brings the potential to be a rocket or a curse. If much of the early revenue is used to invest in the future, it enables rapid growth without pain. There need be no belt-tightening, such as Lee Kuan Yew and Julius Nyerere had to per-suade people to accept. Yet the prudent use of resource revenues also requires persuasion. In its absence, the discovery of resource wealth may tempt maverick politicians to promote a seductive narra-tive: We're rich, so we don't need to work any more. Seretse Khama anticipated this risk precisely. He found and repeated a narrative-plus-image so compelling that every Botswanan came to accept it: We're poor, and so we must carry a heavy load. People could readily relate to the idea because it described their own lives. But its implica-tion was that revenues should be used prudently for a step-by-step climb out of poverty. That mass understanding was the social bed-rock for the practice of using the revenues from diamonds to accumulate assets. Khama was wise to pre-empt misunderstanding. A rival populist politician indeed came up with that seductive incite-ment to consume rather than invest. But because Botswanans had accepted Seretse Khama's proposition, they dismissed him as a clown, re-electing the president and then his preferred successor. Quett Masire also exemplified the modesty, self-deprecating humour, scrupulous behaviour and good judgement that define good leader-ship. He in turn promoted a good successor: Festus Mogae. When he stepped down as president, he received the coveted but seldom awarded Mo Ibrahim Prize for African leadership.[3]

Inspired by these fine leaders, motivated teams of public officials invested the diamond revenues, but since Botswana was small, dry and landlocked, there were not many commercially attractive opportunities locally. Instead, revenues were invested abroad in a

Sovereign Wealth Fund, or locally in education and infrastructure. Consistent with prudence and integrity, all local spending was subject to strict discipline. A professional estimate of the likely social rate of return had to be undertaken and only those projects that met a threshold were approved. It all worked sufficiently well for Botswana to become the fastest-growing economy in the world. It is now the highest-income country in Africa, having overtaken South Africa, once celebrated as one of the fast-rising BRICS.[4] It has a well-educated population, a good university, a lovely and well-functioning capital city and a thriving tourist industry.

The rise of China

When Mao Zedong died in 1976, he left a society that was huge but impoverished. About 60 million people had died as a result of the disastrous strategy known as the Great Leap Forward: China was the global centre of poverty. From the ensuing power struggle, Deng Xiaoping emerged as China's new leader. He was a provincial politician who kept his strong local accent. Perhaps this inclined him to devolve agency from Beijing. But his most important influence was an early visit to Singapore. He was stunned by the prosperity that Lee Kuan Yew had so swiftly achieved. It persuaded him of the superiority of a market economy over central planning and led him to experiment with Shanghai as a prototype for a new national approach. Thus began the most significant instance of transformational leadership in human history.

It began with the demise of Mao's over-centralized personality cult.* Deng Xiaoping's priority was to build a capacity in Chinese society for rapid learning. Every five years, he and the other top

---

* I learned what follows in China from discussions with the vice-minister in charge of the government's think tank, the DRC, long after Deng had ceased to be president. Having checked it with those more knowledgeable, I believe it to be accurate, but I am not myself a China specialist.

managers agreed a limited number of goals for the state to achieve. They combined social and economic aims, such as reducing infant mortality while raising worker productivity. Crucially, Deng and his fellow managers admitted that they didn't know how to achieve these goals. His audience were a tiny vanguard: the top forty young Communist Party stars. They were an educated meritocracy even more selective than that in Singapore. They were told that they would each be posted as the local Party Chief in one of the forty regions of China. Their job for the next five years would be to achieve the goals set. The ambitious new Party Chiefs faced a classic instance of radical uncertainty. They were going to be judged on a task nobody knew for sure how to accomplish. The normal response of a bureaucrat when faced with such a problem is to minimize the risk of failure: play safe by doing nothing. Like Seretse Khama, Deng had anticipated how others would react to his challenge, and he added a caveat. If they had not got anything under way in the first six months, they would be recalled and dropped from the elite cadre. This introduced an incentive for action. The outcomes of the forty experiments were then carefully monitored. A success was not understood to necessarily offer a solution that would work everywhere in China: the context might be distinctive. Instead, those who were failing were told to go and look at the successes and judge whether there was anything useful to learn from them. Over the five years, patterns of success emerged and were scaled up. At the start of the next five years, the process was repeated with new goals and a new cadre. The approach was sustained for forty years. The model contained a sequence of three steps. Communicate a common goal; devolve agency to teams so that society learns from experiments in parallel; then hoover up these experiences and share successes. It propelled a billion people out of mass poverty at a globally unprecedented rate.

In tandem with the pragmatism of learning by experiment, Deng fostered a moral narrative. It called for collective sacrifice of consumption for a common purpose, like that pioneered by Lee Kuan Yew and Julius Nyerere. Astoundingly, people tolerated an unprecedented squeeze on individual consumption for an entire generation. They could see that the economy was growing rapidly, but this could have induced impatience rather than compliance. The annual sacrifices accumulated, enabling around half of the country's income to be saved and invested. That transformational collective sacrifice was presided over by the state, but much of it was chosen by households themselves. People willingly saved for a pension rather than spending their money immediately. This capacity of the Chinese government for toughness is sometimes interpreted as reflecting an advantage of autocracy over democracy. But an alternative, which I find more credible, is that China's people accepted a distinctive common purpose. Rather than sacrificing only for their personal future prosperity, they did so in part to avenge China's past humiliations. There had been a century of these, inflicted by the British, Portuguese and Japanese empires and then compounded by the dominance of the USA since 1945. People knew their society had been the Central Kingdom for two millennia and wanted to regain a strong China in which they could take pride. As people saw that the strategy for rapid economic growth was working, the practical legitimacy of the government was reinforced by this evidence of its competence. It made the implementation of the high savings rate easier.

*Regional divergence in Russia**

By 2000, shortly after the Russian presidency changed from Yeltsin to Putin, the three regions of Kaluga, Voronezh and Ivanovo began to diverge. All three had become depressed after heavy industry collapsed owing to economic liberalization: they were spiralling down

---

* I would like to thank Anna Volynets, my former graduate student, for these Russian case studies. Anna is an experienced leader in economic policy research and analysis and advises governments on economic development.

into poverty and mass unemployment. New governors came into the regions, but through very different processes.

Part of President Yeltsin's legacy had been that governors were elected. The people of Kaluga chose Anatoly Artamonov, a local man who had started as a worker, rose to direct an agricultural firm, then studied and gained a doctorate in economics. People trusted him as a modest man with good intentions and proven competence. He and his team had campaigned on the goals of renewing economic growth and improving the living standards of everyone, albeit they were uncertain how to accomplish them. Their strategy was to build on whatever advantages the region might have, while piloting experiments to see what worked. As a legacy of its industrial past, the region had a skilled workforce who were now mired in poverty. It had good transport logistics and was well located for Western Europe. An early experiment was a new zone for an automotive cluster. They borrowed to prepare the site, updated regional investment law and introduced a standard tax regime favouring industrial parks. As it started to succeed, Artamonov's team worked with firms both individually and as a group to address problems, such as launching an Automotive Training Centre that rapidly upskilled over 10,000 workers. With that success, over the next decade they repeated the model with eleven other specialist parks. Unemployment fell, median income rocketed and, despite the tax concessions, revenues soared. To ensure that the benefits were widely spread, Artamonov created Community Councils with elected local members and authority to allocate some of the budget: this was an instance of his more general policy of devolving decisions to the lowest level at which they could be accomplished.

In Voronezh, Kulakov also came to power through a regional election. But in stark contrast to Artamonov, his previous experience had been as head of the Federal Security Service Directorate. Habituated to using his authority to manipulate decision processes, he applied it to his own election and continued in the same style in his decision-taking. Kulakov simply copied some aspects of

Kaluga's approach but without considering the distinctive context of the Voronezh region. Over-confident, he disregarded experiment. He established his own regional investment corporation, raising money and scaling it up despite mounting evidence of mismanagement. The economic outcome was dismal: his fund ended up going bankrupt and, despite the region's significant agricultural and industrial potential, Voronezh went into a deep economic decline. More fundamentally, the regional election had been insufficient to compel the governor to feel accountable to local people: he had simply pursued his own interests. His style of governance had resulted in citizen disengagement from public policy.

In 2004, elections for the post of governor were abolished by President Putin. While in most regions Moscow re-appointed the governors who had previously been elected, some regions received governors who were new to the region. Such was the case with the governor of Ivanovo region, Mikhail Men. A musician and philosopher by training, he had made his political career in Moscow and had never lived or worked in Ivanovo. Once in post, he announced that he would develop Ivanovo, but did not trouble to learn about the region's potential competitive advantages or adopt an incremental approach. Instead, he drew on his intimate knowledge of the Moscow elite. He decided to use the region's budget for a project to attract them as visitors to Ivanovo. But their visits did not lead to the envisaged improvement in the welfare of Ivanovo citizens: gross regional product per capita fell to barely half that of Kaluga.

Neither in Ivanovo nor in Voronezh were the governors in fact responsible to the people of the regions. Men, appointed by Moscow to Ivanovo, looked for the approval of those who empowered him. The centre-knows-best approach adopted by both these governors failed. On the economic and social indicators, both regions fell further and further behind Kaluga. In Voronezh, the performance of an election had proved insufficient to persuade a governor to feel accountable to the people of the region and led to the same overconfidence and disregard for context as in Voronezh.

The rise of Rwanda*

In 1994, in the face of genocide, a Tutsi group of exiles invaded Rwanda from their temporary home in Uganda and defeated the army of the extremist Hutu military government. Their leader, Paul Kagame, was a brilliant military tactician whose talents had been spotted at the US Army's General Staff College. Like Julius Nyerere, he thought that the priority was to build a new shared identity that transcended tribal identities and that free multiparty elections would make it impossible.

For once, a natural experiment tests this idea because Rwanda has a sister country, Burundi. The two were united during the period of colonial oppression, under Germany until 1918 and then under Belgium until their Independence. Their populations had the same ethnic split between a minority Tutsi group and a majority Hutu. Post-Independence, by the mid-1990s, both had plunged into ethnic civil wars, but in Burundi the crucial difference was that in 2000 the United Nations brokered a peace deal and a new constitution, the Arusha Accords. In one giant leap, Burundi found itself with power-sharing and multiparty democratic elections: the West's confident

---

* In 2022 Rwanda became embroiled in the toxic and polarized atmosphere of British party politics. Owing to its welcoming approach towards Muslim refugees, it was adopted as a darling by Conservatives who neither knew nor cared anything about the country but wanted to send irregular immigrants there if their asylum applications had been rejected. This ugly instrumental use of a poor country for political convenience was inevitably pilloried by Labour supporters, who, despite knowing little more than their opponents, gilded their critique by depicting Rwanda as a brutal place in which anyone arriving would be endangered. Confusion was deepened by some naive journalism. In Britain, it has become an issue on which people 'knew' what to think before they encountered evidence. This is a pity since there is so much to be learned from the attempt to reverse the downward spiral that culminated in genocide. I delve deeply into it based on long, first-hand knowledge of the country. It is a prelude to my critique of over-confident and naive international public policies exemplified by the implosion of Afghanistan and the Sahel.

formula for success. By then, Rwanda had recovered from the catastrophic ruin of genocide, and the two countries were neck and neck: both desperately poor, with per capita incomes of $850. Yet two decades later, despite electoral democracy, Burundi had plunged into repeated conflict, incomes had declined even further, by around 10 per cent, and it is now the poorest country in the world. Compounding this disaster, the Rwandan Hutu gangs which had moved to the Democratic Republic of the Congo were left without effective restraint to pillage, rape and massacre the local population on a massive scale.* In contrast, despite continuing rule by Paul Kagame and his team, incomes in Rwanda had tripled: it had become one of the fastest-growing countries in Africa, attracting refugees both from neighbouring Burundi and distant Afghanistan. This divergence does not imply that autocracy is better than democracy. Rather, it suggests that these conflict-ridden situations are highly complex and sensitive to context. Simplistic solutions like that leap into electoral democracy are misplaced. Julius Nyerere's doubts about sequencing elections before building shared identity look to have been vindicated.

One skill of a good commander like Paul Kagame is to set an overall strategy, select and motivate his officer core, and then devolve operational control to them in a cascade of responsibilities. Recognizing that his expertise was military, not economic, he looked to past economic successes that could be emulated: he settled on Lee Kuan Yew's Singapore and, closer to home, Mauritius, once itself as poor as Rwanda, yet growing so fast that by 2023 it was the richest country in the African Union. Like Lee Kuan Yew

---

* See N. Nunn and R. Sanchez de la Sierra, 'Why being wrong can be right: magical warfare technologies and the persistence of false beliefs', *American Economic Review*, Papers and Proceedings, 2017. While here I use this article for its evidence on Hutu militias, it is also important for the concept of self-fulfilling beliefs. In Part I, I showed how such beliefs could be damaging – trapping communities into spiralling down. In Part II it is equally valuable for the more hopeful purpose of spiralling up. It shows both analytically and empirically that even new beliefs that are objectively false can enable a community to lift itself up.

he groomed an elite cadre of public servants and often sent them to Mauritius to learn. As these teams experimented and found workable strategies, they gained the confidence to think for themselves. Each year the top 200 public officials were summoned to an army camp, where all of them, including the president, slept in tents and lived on army food. Each official had to report on whether they had accomplished the goals agreed with their superiors. Failures were tolerated as long as there was something useful to learn from them, and significant success would pave the way for merit-based promotion.

As in Tanzania, an early priority was to reset Rwandan identity. In the weeks before the genocide began, extremist Hutus using the regime's radio station, Mille Collines, broadcast a message of ethnic hatred that played off the competing identities. Rwanda is mountainous, its population scattered among the hills, so on the blind side of the hill people were unable to hear the message of hatred. On those sides, the rate of genocide was significantly lower than on the sides that received the broadcasts: state narratives of hatred had worked. For a generation President Kagame replaced the divisive ethnic message with one emphasizing a common Rwandan identity. He too used radio messages, and again research found that on the side of the hills receiving that message people are significantly less likely to identify themselves as Hutu or Tutsi.[5]

The new government tried to build willing compliance by finding some interest that both Hutus and Tutsis had in common and asking them to contribute to it. They were realists: the purpose had to be attractive, the ruling elite themselves had to contribute a lot, and what they were asking of others had to be very modest. The contribution from the ruling elite to this and many other common purposes was cumulatively massive and fiercely resisted within the ruling party. The decisive struggle was in 1998, between two factions. One wing of the party wanted to use the newly acquired power to benefit themselves and other Tutsis. Paul Kagame's wing argued that such an approach would end in a Hutu uprising and another genocide. Only if everyone benefited from the shared gains of rapid growth would society be stabilized because then people would realize that they had too much to lose by revolution.*

Rwanda had not only suffered genocide: it was landlocked, heavily populated and lacked natural resources. It did not have the growth opportunities of Singapore, China or Botswana. Yet over the next twenty-five years it indeed grew rapidly, overtaking Zimbabwe and fully catching up with Uganda, itself growing quite rapidly. At times the rate of poverty reduction even matched that of China. How it was done shows a pattern of carefully selected goals, chosen to benefit the many.

For the capital itself, the goal was that Kigali should be beautiful, green, clean and uncongested. It was to be a city in which residents could take pride. In that, it would contrast starkly with the cities of neighbouring countries. The government encouraged all residents to help in modest ways. One Saturday morning each month they were asked to clean the streets of their neighbourhoods and keep the city looking attractive: many chose to take part. To ground the activity in Rwandan culture, the president infused an old concept of coming together in common purpose into this new goal.

But the government was well aware that since the ruling Tutsi-dominated elite were necessarily living in Kigali, it was vital to distribute other gains from economic growth around the entire nation. They used the vehicle of health care and set a goal that there should be a clinic within reach of every community – so that Rwandans did not need to travel to the teaching hospital in Kigali. The clinics had to provide a wide range of services. The crunch came with the delivery of fresh blood. Without that, transfusions and all related activities, like maternity care, would be safer in Kigali. The only known means of distributing fresh blood across Rwanda's

* I learned this directly in private discussion with a multi-ethnic group of Rwandan students at Sciences Po in Paris, where I was teaching. Some of them had witnessed these disputes. I got to know some of them well, and had the whole discussion been stage-managed from Kigali, individually, they had ample opportunity to tip me off.

inadequate road network and hilly terrain was by refrigerated Land-Rover. When the Finance Ministry costed it, they realized it was prohibitively expensive. Necessity drove innovation: they solved the problem by delivering blood by drone.

Drones had been pioneered by Amazon in Silicon Valley and the Pentagon in Washington, but neither had thought to use them for blood delivery. Amazon used them to deliver packages, the Pentagon to kill terrorists, and neither spotted the potential for health care in poor countries. Nor did an expert health team at the World Bank. Clever as they were, they did not know as much as the home team about Rwanda's geography and political imperatives.

Drones were not the only Rwandan innovation. As in much of Africa, the rights to own land were contested. Once, land had been allocated by chiefs to people for farming: their continued right to the land depended on using it for that purpose. European concepts of land ownership were overlaid on this history. But to invest in an office block or a factory, a firm would need a secure title of land ownership that could not be challenged by a chief or someone claiming to have farmed it. Until this was sorted out, it would deter investment and all the new jobs that would have followed. The World Bank advised mayors and ministers how to address the problem. Their solution was the standard Anglo-European process: land surveyors would chart the plot on which the property was to be built; courts would adjudicate any disputed ownership, where lawyers would present the case for each side.

But in Kigali alone, thousands of plots would need to be adjudicated, and Rwanda had very few surveyors, judges and lawyers. The process would be prohibitively costly and take years. The workaround was again ingenious, harnessing the technology of GPS and mobile phones. For the simple purpose of delineating a plot of land, the long and rigorous training of a fully qualified surveyor was no longer necessary. A large cadre of recruits were quickly trained to use a mobile phone to demarcate the coordinates of the plot. But the key role they were taught went beyond that modest skill. It was to go into a community and gather a crowd around them. The crowd would resolve ownership disputes on the spot. The process was quick. Not only in Kigali but across the entire country, land rights were clarified in just three years. It was also cheap: the process cost $6 per plot. But above all, it was fair: voices of poor people had a far better chance of being heard in a community discussion than in a court which advantaged the rich, who could afford to hire lawyers.

Drones and land rights were innovative, but the most astonishing achievement was how Rwanda broke into tourism. The objective was daunting. Tourism is very sensitive to perceptions of danger: following murders of some tourists by terrorists in Egypt and Tunisia in 2015, the tourist industries of both countries collapsed. In the wake of the 1994 genocide, around the world, Rwanda had been associated with violence. Compounding that problem of a poor image, most tourists want to lie on beaches in the sun. Rwanda doesn't have any beaches and receives a lot of rain. Other than beaches, most tourists to East Africa want game parks with the Big Five – elephants, lions, giraffes, rhinos and leopards. Rwanda didn't have game parks or any of those animals. Its one advantage was gorillas, but only tiny numbers of tourists could view them.

The government's strategy was multifaceted. The image of violence had to be changed. Kigali needed to look good and feel safe. By collective efforts such as the monthly clean-up, it became so.* Although big game had long been hunted to extinction, since they had once lived wild in Rwanda they could be brought back, so new game parks were filled with game brought from neighbouring countries. Thanks to competent governance and low corruption, the animals survived well. Rwanda now had something to attract tourists. But the breakthrough came when someone with knowledge of American taxation joined the team planning the tourist strategy. Americans attending work-related conferences can charge travel against tax. If the conference venue is exotic, a short holiday can thereby be piggybacked on to tax-subsidized travel. So Rwandan tourism needed conferences. The government invested in a

---

* I have walked across the city alone at midnight, entirely safe.

spectacular conference centre and convened global events. The annual meetings of the African Development Bank, the African Union, the Commonwealth Heads of Government Meeting and its equivalent for the Francophone world were all hosted there.

At last, there were good reasons for tourists to be tempted by a trip to Rwanda. Still, to fly there was difficult until the government opened the skies to airlines, started its own airline, Air Rwanda, and eased immigration processes. Then tourists would need hotels, but Rwanda barely had any. The team saw that they were catering for three different markets. This had clear implications for the hotels they needed. Small numbers of wealthy people who wanted to view gorillas were price-insensitive and would want luxury. In the middle, the conference-cum-game park trade was price sensitive but would expect reliable American hotel brands. A third market was commercial travel from neighbouring countries. Kigali could be a local version of Dubai, enabling businesses in countries whose cities were congested and dangerous to do deals while having an enjoyable time. These people would be unwilling to pay for international hotel standards that they did not need and could not afford.

For the first two markets the government enticed some of the big-brand hotel chains to franchise prestige operations. Alongside them, for the low end of the conference trade, the local business market and global young backpackers, it encouraged cheaper local hotels.

The final step was to get the news out. When I took my son to watch his team play Arsenal in 2018, Rwanda was unmissable. Around the stadium the slogan 'Come to Rwanda' rang out, as it did on the players' T-shirts. An audience of millions watches the games so buying that advertising was expensive: some NGOs condemned the Rwandan government for wasting money.* Assessed by the number of tourists, it was far from wasteful: by 2019, the year before COVID hit, Rwanda had become one of the most visited countries in Africa, breaking into a promising, job-intensive sector.

---

* Perhaps NGO pressure might have been better directed at the millionaire footballers who could have stumped up to pay for it?

Teams of clever, motivated public servants had evolved integrated, long-horizon strategies for health care, land rights and tourism.* Each called for training Rwandan workers in new productive skills – nursing in a clinic; using GPS to take the coordinates of a plot; cooking in a hotel; running a game park; driving a bus. They needed training facilities, but to avoid inflation budgets were brutally tight. Kagame was faced with tough choices: on his military authority, the army's main training facility was repurposed for civilian use. On apparently disparate issues such as international transport, urban planning, game parks and marketing, different teams of public officials worked together, pursuing a goal with panache and persistence while working with the grain of economic opportunities.

Why leadership works

Lee Kuan Yew, Julius Nyerere, Deng Xiaoping, Seretse Khama, Governor Artamonov and Paul Kagame came up with their strategies instinctively. Like Volodymyr Zelensky, they were not guided by academic research. Even if they had sought it, until recently there was none to guide them. Even now, many orthodox economists would dismiss their successes. Trapped in the conviction that the market knows best, they would explain away each of these transformations as being due to some coincident shifts in market conditions. Until recently, all the social sciences were uneasy with the proposition that the character and skill of leadership mattered. We can now do better: the successes of the teams these leaders built can be linked to their specific actions, with each link between an action and its effect backed up by research. Their key actions fall into three broad

---

* The high calibre of Rwandan public officials became widely recognized around the continent. As I was finalizing *Left Behind* in late 2023, Claver Gatete, who had gained wide experience through a series of important economic appointments, was elected head of the UN Economic Commission for Africa.

categories: resetting ideas, building new winning coalitions and deploying the arts of inclusive governance.

One idea that these leaders tried to reset was to build shared identity. An international team of social psychologists has concluded that 'a group of people with a shared identity will always have more power than a group without it. History is made . . . by those groups whose energies have been galvanised by leaders into the most coherent social force.'[6]

Leaders also tried to reset prevailing customs. They created vanguards and gave persuasive answers to the implicit question of why the privileged people included in them should be the first to contribute to new common purposes. Recent advances in experimental game theory show that early self-sacrificing behaviour by the privileged is effective and crucial in resetting social norms.[7]

These two acts, creating first a new shared identity and then new norms of behaviour, were well-chosen initial priorities. What the leaders grasped instinctively is now demonstrated in experimental game theory.[8]

The COVID crisis called for people to change their behaviour to avoid spreading the disease. Since this was a matter of life and death, a large and distinguished group of academic social psychologists summarized what the profession had learned about how leaders can induce behavioural change. Here it is, condensed into a few linked propositions that reinforce the argument that public leadership can be valuable:

> Experimental studies clarify what leaders can do to promote trust leading to cooperation. A priority for leaders is to create a sense of shared social identity amongst their followers . . .
>
> A large body of research suggests that people tend to prefer leaders who cultivate a sense that 'we are all in this together.'
>
> . . . In part, such leadership gives people a sense of collective self-efficacy and hope . . .
>
> More importantly, though, it provides a psychological platform for group members to coordinate efforts to tackle stressors.[9]

A final type of evidence comes from credible counterfactuals. Julius Nyerere's Kenyan counterpart, Jomo Kenyatta, did not seize the moment of Independence to reset identities. Forty years later, Tanzanians could cooperate across ethnic divides and Kenyans couldn't. Within a decade, the costs of division among Kenyans had escalated disastrously. The evidence comes from an ingenious randomized controlled trial conducted in a modern flower-packing factory. Each day, managers randomly assigned packers along the conveyor belt and paid them all a bonus reflecting the number of flowers packed. Sometimes, the packers at the beginning and end of the line would be from rival ethnic groups, such as Kikuyu, Kalenjin and Luo. When this happened, the team at the beginning of the line, who determined how many flowers were placed on it, often used this power over those at the far end to reduce everyone's bonus: their delight in hurting their helpless rivals outweighed the cost to themselves. The initial phase of the study took place just prior to brutal ethnic violence in which more than a thousand people were killed following the 2008 election. When it was repeated post-violence, this vindictive behaviour had got much worse. By neglecting Julius Nyerere's wise strategy of building shared identity, the divisive identities bequeathed by colonialism were still unhealed.[10]

Public leadership can also succeed in forging new coalitions which overcome opponents keen to maintain the status quo. Deng Xiaoping won the support of enough key people in the Communist Party and the military to defeat the Gang of Four. Paul Kagame won the struggle within the ruling party to govern in the interest of the majority of the population rather than just the Tutsi elite. Seretse Khama built winning coalitions first for equal sharing of diamond revenues rather than finders keepers, and then for prudence rather than instant gratification. Lee Kuan Yew built an extraordinary winning coalition that spanned the once rival racial groups and the once rival workers and businesses. That coalition held together for decades, enabling the government to implement improvements and experiments in its strategy without significant opposition. Julius

Nyerere's coalition fell apart only once his bureaucratic elite were tempted into plunder.*

Each leader followed an instinctive strategy. They drew on a common menu of four instruments by which leaders can govern: the arts of inclusive governance. One of those instruments, the most evident, was *effective communication* with citizens. A second was to *pronounce and enforce new rules*. A third, more complex instrument was to *create effective institutions*: public organizations each with a mandate and budget for a specific purpose, and a staff motivated to fulfil it. Transformation depended on a high-calibre civil service within which there were a multiplicity of specialist institutions. Overarching these three instruments of governance was the fourth, an *active authorizing environment*, the group around the top of government which could deploy the presidential roles of communicator-in-chief and commander-in-chief to communicate effectively and create new rules and institutions.

Julius Nyerere, Lee Kuan Yew, Seretse Khama, Deng Xiaoping, Anatoly Artamonov and Paul Kagame each inherited a desperately difficult situation. They were not aspiring to sanctity: they were practical leaders, some of whose actions breached contemporary Western standards of individual rights. All of them have been criticized accordingly and my assessment here is not an apology for them: like all leaders, they made mistakes, but they were arguably better than most at learning from them. *In extremis*, Julius Nyerere heroically accepted that he had failed, and took the responsibility for it. What cannot reasonably be doubted is that all of them aimed to transform their societies for the better, all but Nyerere succeeded, and even his legacy of shared identity might now prove decisive.

Could they have done better, caused less harm to those who suffered and achieved larger successes? One purpose of this book is to distil the lessons of good leadership and put them in the larger

---

* Each of these struggles created enemies who often became 'stressors' in the sense of Van Bavel et al. (2020), meaning people who cause division and impede the process by which people come together around a common purpose.

context of enabling left-behind communities and societies to catch up. But critics need to find other leadership teams in comparable situations which did better. They won't find them in Burundi.*

This chapter has demonstrated that leadership can be transformational and has given instances of how good leaders have used the arts of governance to reset ideas. But transformation can also come from below: ordinary people doing extraordinary things can reset ideas and may even be able to deploy the arts of governance.

---

* Criticizing these leaders as not meeting some hypothetical absolute standard of perfection is at best self-indulgence. A basic tenet of radical uncertainty is that aspiring to any permanently perfect goal is an intellectual mistake: the human condition is a quest into the unknown. To imagine that one's own current ideas encapsulate that perfect goal belongs to the innocence of youth. To avoid this charge, critics of these and other leaders must propose an alternative that would have been feasible in the context and would most likely have produced better outcomes.

6.

How Places Renew from the Grass Roots

The catalysts through which left-behind places restore themselves from the bottom are a few people with no pretensions to leadership who begin to inspire many others. Their stories are uplifting, in part because they are heroic struggles that overcome the forces of the downward spiral by courage. But if we fixate on the heroes, these successes appear exceptional. In fact, successful grassroots processes abound, but their most common habitat is in places with thriving economies. There, they amplify economic success and widen its beneficiaries. Because they are common, they have been well studied: there is an impressive and often inspiring literature that delves into how these bottom-up processes happen. But similar processes are now working in places whose economies have only recently started to catch up. These are less studied and even more pertinent for people in left-behind places.

The notion that success could be driven from the bottom up was first proposed by the eighteenth-century Anglo-Irish philosopher Edmund Burke. He wanted political change: the government of George III regarded him as a traitor for supporting American Independence. But he was wary of violent revolutions, seeing that they easily got captured by extremists. His alternative was for change to progress by widely shared participation: millions of people coming together in a myriad of small purposeful groups. He captured the idea in the phrase *little platoons*.

Burke's twenty-first-century successor is the Harvard sociologist Robert Putnam. He coined the now widely used phrase *social capital*. It captures the idea that habits of sociality become a valuable asset. Places that lack such habits will tend to be poorer. By characterizing them as an asset, two related economic concepts come naturally to mind. An asset is accumulated by a process of *investment* which generates a sustainable *return*. In his example, Putnam's emblematic little platoons of value are choirs. Directly, their purpose has no material benefit: the people who join a choir simply enjoy singing together. But in choosing to do so they are accepting limitations on their behaviour: they are expected to turn up at the right time and sing their assigned part. Their reward is that by doing so they can participate in generating a sound and an experience unattainable as individuals. Putnam was excited by indirect benefits of this behaviour that were much more material.

During the Renaissance, choirs became very popular in the many city-states of central and northern Italy. Putnam argued that thanks to their choirs, the inhabitants of these cities learned how to cooperate for a common purpose across the differences of family, guild and status that had divided medieval society. In contrast, the cities of southern Italy were pawns in a highly centralized empire ruled by a small militarized group of Norman-descended conquerors. In medieval times, the Normans had maintained a monopoly of violence and built infrastructure beyond the scope of the warring little city-states to their north. Their state had flourished while the city-states had floundered. But like all empires, the Normans were predatory and bitterly resented by their subjects. Their top-down empire lacked the popular legitimacy to build common purposes. Its successes had not been sustainable: the society had spiralled down into distrust and decline. Further north, with the habits forged through choirs, the Italian city-states had accumulated social capital: the capacity to conceive and unite around initiatives that increased and widened access to prosperity. As each successful initiative opened up further possibilities, through this bottom-up process the northern city states' economies began to spiral up, surging past those of southern Italy. In the 1850s Garibaldi redrew the political boundaries, creating the new country of Italy. But that was not enough to reset the two divergent spirals, which continued. Among the regions of present-day Europe, those former city-states remain among the most highly productive, while southern Italy languishes as a perennial recipient of support programmes from the EU.[1]

Paul Harris and the power of community in America

Later in his career Putnam co-wrote *The Upswing* (2021), which applied the concept of social capital to America.[2] It is already widely recognized as his magnum opus. Just as he had celebrated the un-heroic little platoons of choirs, now he had another equally unlikely emblematic catalyst of social capital. Paul Harris slayed no dragons, nor was the civic organization he launched a warrior in the league of grand causes. He was a modest man who persuaded other modest people to make incremental improvements to their local communities. His genius was not in the grandeur of his objectives but in the clever design of a process. His organization was so suc-cessful that the cumulative scale of the thousands of small improvements which it initiated is astounding.

Paul Harris grew up in a small town in Iowa, a place with a strong sense of community but only limited opportunities to excel. Chi-cago was then the magnetic great city of mid-western American aspiration; being a young man brimming with talent, he decided to take his chances there. He got a good job and did well for himself, yet he missed that small-town sense of community. Although thriv-ing, he was lonely: he seemed to be surrounded by striving individualists. By day, he was living for business; returning to his apartment, he spent his evenings in wistful regret. And that is how he might have continued had it not been that one evening in 1904 he had an idea. In this vast city of arrival, he was unlikely to be the only person longing for community. There must be others like himself: his business persona kicked in and he took action. He booked a meeting room and put an invitation in the local newspaper. His hunch had been right: 200 people showed up and he announced the formation of a new club. Clubs must have rules of membership, a protocol, and he had thought carefully about what was expected of anyone choosing to join. He had created *an effective institution*, not an instrument of government but a cooperative within civil society.

The purpose of his club would be for successful local business-people to join forces to contribute to the local community. Although Chicago was a boomtown, not everyone was doing well. Acute misery abounded, cheek by jowl with affluence. The club would bring the talents and resources of the successful to reduce that misery. Those not interested in this purpose should join a different club. Having made that clear, Paul Harris knew that those choosing to sign up at least went along with his purpose. But as to the depth of their commitment, he was a realist. Neither his prospective members, nor he himself, were saints. Unlike the leaders discussed in Chapter 5, once the club was up and running, he could not issue commands. There would be no leader: all members would have equal responsibilities. But like some of those leaders, he anticipated likely temptations and added defences. His protocol banned deal-making: he created *rules, enforced by social pressure*. To emphasize that all members had equal status as contributors to a common purpose, the venues of their meeting would rotate. To enshrine that principle at the heart of the organization he named it the Rotary Club.

His new Chicago club was so successful that it was imitated in other American towns. Soon these local clubs came together for a national conference. Today, the Rotary Club is an international organization with millions of people who come together around concrete practical local improvements that benefit the less fortunate. Their meetings do not quicken the blood – student dorms are not adorned with images of Paul Harris. But the lives of millions are a little better thanks to him; his legacy was the equal of the most admired celebrities.

Chicago was not the only thriving American city where grass-roots local energies accomplished the sort of welfare now mostly regarded as the responsibility of the state. Across the country, in the early decades of the twentieth century, mass primary schooling was achieved by bottom-up local social enterprise that financed schools, community by community. It did not depend on electing good national political leaders. That was fortunate, since during those decades good leaders were not abundant. Social capital did more than schooling and the Rotary Club: it ignited an upward spiral analogous to that in northern Italy.

The Upswing charts the trajectory of social capital using a wide array of indicators. Many are commonly used proxies for the concepts they track, such as cross-party collaboration and bipartisanship. Others are original: Putnam uses Ngram to find the frequency of 'we' and 'me' in all American publications. Amazingly, this vast cultural trawl casts up the same snake-shape as the other indicators. By 1900 America had descended into a trough of individualism: Paul Harris was indeed surrounded by the 'me' society. As social capital deepened in the first half of the twentieth century, it strengthened the economy and encouraged broken communities-of-place to lift themselves out of despair. Another of Putnam's examples is the shift in Protestant theology from individual salvation to the 'Social Gospel', which emphasized community and equality. During the catastrophe of the Great Depression, such shifts countered the powerful forces dragging down even further the many communities confronted by the economic implosion. By the 1960s, the peak of the 'we' society, the ghost-town desolation which had besmirched the face of America had been substantially reduced.*

Crisis as opportunity: West Germany in 1945

These American grassroots successes were self-generated during unpropitious times. But clever *nationwide* policies can create conditions fertile for people to come together. West Germany post-1945

---

* Even at its peak, the 'we' society did not surmount America's appalling legacy of slavery; nor did it address gender inequalities. This is not a limitation of social capital, but of how ideas spread.

illustrates what is possible even in the apparently unpropitious context of cities reduced to rubble, the state discredited, and the country partitioned. This created a 'concatenated crisis', Putnam's term for reversals so severe and extensive that past beliefs are abandoned. In the world of the late 2020s many countries may be facing such crises, so the German experience may be valuable. Like America in 1900, West Germany was at an inflection point in which people expected radical change. German intellectuals such as Werner Richter spoke of *Stunde null*, Zero Hour: not the *end*-of-time Armageddon the Nazis had talked of but the *beginning* of a new era. People were mobilized into teams that cleared the rubble, literal and metaphorical, participating in a practical communal purpose unattainable by individual effort. Fortuitously, US President Harry Truman sought advice from social psychologists on how Germans might embrace a post-Nazi future. Although the discipline was in its infancy, its core advice was already a rudimentary synthesis of the COVID-19 analysis and the ideas of Roger Myerson.* Agency should lie with Germans, not Americans; leaders should emerge through a carefully controlled process of devolved democracy in which only anti-Nazi Germans should be permitted powers of mass communication.† Rapid learning from devolved experiments in parallel would gradually help Germans to renounce the cult of the all-knowing commander-in-chief, replacing it with localized identities guided by communicators-in-chief.

Following four years of such American–British–French direct rule, the new West German politicians agreed a federal constitution in which the motif was devolved agency. Not only did most power lie with regions and cities, it was also to be shared between local

---

* See Chapters 2 and 4 respectively.

† The Allies permitted only people committed to this purpose to enter politics or edit newspapers – they must be on the White List. Even then, initially only local politics was permitted: at the national level, the state was reborn through a bottom-up process. There was no naïve instant leap into democracy analogous to Burundi in 2000.

politicians and local people self-organizing into purposive communities. But those local economies lay in ruins, and so the centuries-long journey of Italian city-states from choirs to prosperity would be too slow. The starting point had to be swift local economic renewal. Millions of people were destitute, violent black-market crime was rife, and the verb *fringen* was coined: 'to steal to feed a starving family'. Cardinal Frings declared such thefts as free of sin. Starving people needed jobs; jobs depended upon local firms hiring workers; and to do so the firms needed to borrow from local banks.

Before the increasingly desperate Nazi leaders centralized finance, Germany had a long history of local banking. But local banking faces a danger: the risk that firms will be hit by a common shock in which they default. As the spectacular bankruptcy of Silicon Valley Bank in 2023 appeared to demonstrate, a bank which lends to the industry in which the city specializes is vulnerable.* Prior to the Nazi state, Germany's central bank had solved the problem by creating an insurance system which mitigated such risks for its banks. After 1945, that was restored.

With both political and banking decisions taken locally, businesses had a strong reason to come together in a locally organized community-of-purpose. The city's business community could speak for the common business interest. To do so, it needed to forge common interests among many different sectors – bakeries, factories and construction companies. This common interest could then become a voice in a city-wide dialogue with workers, local government and banks. A natural consequence of this dialogue was that businesses, banks and political parties found a common interest. While their aims were not identical, they were sufficiently aligned to recognize that by working together for local prosperity they could all gain. Together in a community, local businesses faced the same gentle pressures as if they had enrolled in Paul Harris's Rotary Club. To keep the good opinion of other local firms they

---

* In fact, SVB demonstrated something very different: the dangers of rampant greed. I return to it.

would need to behave well, contributing to the future prosperity of their city, even when it sometimes sacrificed short-term profit.

That benign social psychology of local business soon became a West German cultural asset. At the national level, politicians invested in strengthening it by legislating to give local business organizations important functions. In performing these new functions, the organizations directly achieved purposes which had economic value to their members – a concrete economic return on previous investments in social capital. Moreover, in convening to perform these functions, the organizations were reinforcing their community. Social capital is like a muscle: the more it is used, the stronger it becomes; unused, it atrophies.

Once the economy had strengthened, politicians nationally also encouraged the habits of association purely for pleasure: it was time for choirs and clubs. By supporting local clubs with public money for almost any common purpose, people increasingly participated in the life of their community. Membership in them has expanded considerably since the 1970s, and now covers almost half of German adults.* Within them, people develop habits of sociability. For people with these habits, the next step of helping others – the Paul Harris step – is less daunting.

City by city, these virtuous circles of business and civic engagement – spiralling up – played out in highly practical arenas. One was ensuring that local youth were thoroughly trained in skills that would enable everyone to be equipped for well-paid jobs. German tertiary education has strong links with local business through its prestigious vocational training programmes. It established the norm of training the city's next generation of young people. Executives of a firm that chose to save money by skimping on training would have felt ashamed.

Another concrete consequence of strong local communities has been their willingness to contribute to the physical infrastructure of their cities. Stuttgart, a major city one rank below the national focal

---

* They are known as *Verein*.

points of Berlin, Munich and Frankfurt, exemplifies the mutual support between the business community and the social clubs. The local business community organized and financed the construction of a magnificent civic centre for local clubs, handing it over for the city administration to run once complete. Being well integrated into the city administration, civic society thereby could have its say in how the space was best used.*

The provincial cities of Britain had once been not much different from the German ones. Their local banks had faced the same risks, but the Bank of England chose a different solution. Instead of mutual insurance for local banks, it forced them to merge. By the 1920s, regional banking had been destroyed: in England, there were only five banks, all London-based. In the process, their local knowledge of firms based in the regions was gradually lost. British political decisions also gradually reduced powers and funding for local government. As agency drained away from the cities of provincial England, participation in civic society declined sharply.†
Whereas in Germany the local business community had become an integral part of a civic society, in provincial England it shrivelled: individual firms just lobbied for their own interests. The consequences are painful: as set out in Chapter 4, training of young people for high-skill local jobs has withered away. A pattern of behaviour that is the norm in Germany is exceptional in Britain. The cities and regions of provincial England spiralled down because choices by a small group of civil servants and politicians made catalysing social capital even more difficult than it had been in the left-behind places that had blighted the America of 1900.‡

---

* My grandfather took the train from Stuttgart in 1880 when he left his village to work in boomtown Bradford. Periodically, I reverse his journey, speaking at events in the civic centre and visiting friends and relatives in his village.
† Voting turnout in British local elections is typically in the range of 20–30 per cent. In contrast, in devolved countries like Germany, turnout is 65–85 per cent.
‡ American politicians had the same options for tackling the risks faced by localized banking, but they followed a variant of the German banking insurance system. In doing so they sustained local banking until the 1980s, preserving its

The German post-war experience shows the potential for bottom-up processes to work in highly distressed situations such as those faced by countries left behind.

Bangladesh since 1970

Bangladesh, once the poor half of Pakistan, from which it seceded in 1970, has since comfortably outperformed its once richer sister. The rise of Bangladesh was certainly not due to political leadership. Two rival dynasties, each reputedly corrupt, trapped national politics into a zero-sum mindset. But poor leadership has been more than offset by remarkably strong bottom-up processes. Some have worked at the local level, as in German cities; others have forged nationwide communities focused on specific purposes. Two nationwide civic organizations have become world renowned. The founder of the Grameen Bank, Muhammad Yunus, won the Nobel Peace Prize. BRAC, founded in Bangladesh but like the Rotary Club now international, has become the world's largest NGO.

The Grameen Bank pioneered the approach of lending backed by peer pressure. The very poor people whom Grameen aimed to help had no assets and so could not provide collateral for loans. Grameen relied on its understanding of the distinctive aspects of Bangladeshi village communities. A member of the Grameen team would find a group of five women who knew each other and were working in related activities. They would be offered the chance to form a loan club, which would lend them each money to expand their businesses

---

many benefits. Then, as a result of effective lobbying by the largest banks, under Ronald Reagan America followed Britain down the path of nationwide banks. Soon, big American banks merged into mega-banks that were too-big-to-fail: if they got into trouble, government would have to bail them out. This tempted many of them to sacrifice prudence for profits, leading to the Global Financial Crisis in 2008 and the mega-bailouts. Along the way, the American mega-banks also acquired many of the British banks.

at a modest interest rate without the need for collateral. To get started, two of the five women were given a small loan. If they repaid these loans, all five would get loans on the same terms. This created social pressure from the other three women: it was so effective that default rates were negligible. Once all five women received small loans, the social pressures intensified. Each member of the group became liable not only for their own loan, but for those of any of the other four who defaulted. If the five loans were repaid, they would all be offered larger loans. Faced with this prospect of growing mutual benefit, none of the women wanted to be the weak link. This simple model proved to be replicable on a massive scale. Although the individual gains were usually modest, microfinance enabled millions of Bangladeshi women to expand tiny enterprises, lifting incomes of individuals and entire communities.

Although this wonderful idea has worked well for decades, it might now have been superseded. Algorithm-based lending supported by big data has drastically reduced the costs of lending directly to individuals without the need for collateral. The same prospect of gradually increasing loan size based on accumulating reputation is the incentive to repay. As with group lending, the cumulative benefits are massive. Being able to borrow without collateral enables poor people to survive adverse shocks that would otherwise cause irreversible damage.[3]

BRAC is best known by its initials, even though the words they stand for have changed as the organization has evolved. The constant has been that it is primarily aimed at helping poor women. Beyond that it is an unusual hybrid. The projects range from relief operations following disasters to long-term support for microenterprises. It combines practical on-the-ground interventions with research designed to learn from evaluated experiments. That emphasis upon empirical research done in local contexts most likely accounts for its remarkable success. Few other NGOs have a comparable appetite to evaluate their initiatives.

The randomized controlled trials (RCTs) pioneered by BRAC may be reaching their natural limits. At the time and place of the experiment, and with the same team implementing it, we can have high confidence in the results. But whether that experiment has external validity – whether it would work in a different time and place, or with a different team – is less certain. An attempt to implement a successful BRAC-conducted Kenyan educational reform by teams under the Ministry of Education could not replicate the results.[4] Similarly, just as economists began to learn the use of RCTs from medicine, medics themselves moved away from them. They shifted to learning by comparing how medicines worked in real-world conditions. RCT conditions were sometimes highly artificial.[5] In Kenya, and most other countries, education and health care are largely provided by government. So, if ideas pioneered using RCTs sometimes do not transfer reliably, it is useful to supplement them through the more authentic process of local governments each implementing their own ideas of what might work and learning from each other. Bypassing dysfunctional local governments by means of NGOs may work much better in the short term, but governments are most likely to adopt and scale up new ideas if they own (or co-own) the idea from the design stage onwards.

Overall, Grameen and BRAC helped to lift the incomes and circumstances of poor Bangladeshi women. The returns from investments in social capital among households were matched by an entirely separate process of new social capital among local businesses. The trigger was rapid learning from a foreign firm: for once, globalization really did trickle down. In 1980, a US T-shirt manufacturer searching for cheap labour decided to try Bangladesh. By the end of the first year most of the local workforce had quit, though not because of the low wages and poor conditions. They quit because they had mastered the simple process of making T-shirts, which needed nothing more costly than sewing machines. They had also understood which European and North American retailers were buying T-shirts from Bangladesh – and the Bangladeshi entrepreneurs were quick to seize an opportunity: they could cut out the middleman. They set up their own companies, raising a little capital from relatives, and offered foreign retailers the same quality at lower prices. As with microfinance, this turned out to be a scalable idea: there were millions of young Bangladeshis wanting a regular job, and a vast global market in cheap T-shirts. By the 2020s, the Bangladeshi garments industry, almost entirely locally owned, was employing 4 million people, and exporting $30 billion a year. In the process, the option of getting a reliably paid job had empowered many young women. As the new incomes in the garments sector and microfinance were spent, they opened other opportunities for enterprise: the economy began to spiral up. Wages rose, and T-shirt manufacture shifted to the cheaper labour pool of Madagascar. But with its trained workforce and reliable firms, the Bangladeshi industry was well able to move upmarket, making more complex garments with higher value.

Bangladesh spiralled up: the entrenched mass poverty of 1970 was a thing of the past. By the early 2020s, Bangladesh was a society on the cusp of upper-middle-income status. The politicians barely noticed at first. Soon, however, in a constituency with a thriving garments firm, many voters had a wage earner in the family: the local MP learned to be supportive. Sometimes, the new entrepreneurs stood for parliament and were elected, bringing a new political culture to a country previously accustomed to land-owning dynastic rivalry.

With rising economic prosperity, the strengthening social capital among households and business was fertile ground for a further step up the spiral staircase. This one began with one young man posting an invitation remarkably like Paul Harris did. In 1904, the available medium had been a newspaper; by 2018, it was Facebook. Abir Hasan asked, 'Is it possible to set up a small group of young men and women to discuss policy issues relevant to Bangladesh?' The echoes of Harris continue: Abir was not a scion of the wealthy political elite; socially, he was a product of the new class of people striving to run small businesses. Nor was he from a big city: as a child he had come to newly prospering Bangladesh from a provincial town across the border in India. He was brimming with talent, gaining entry to one of Bangladesh's top universities and from there winning a scholarship to Oxford's Blavatnik School of Government, where I taught him. There he realized the potential power of public policy as a force for good, and that change could come from the bottom as well as the top. Like Harris, Abir's dream was to establish a new objective for his community, not for himself: to create a climate of knowledgeable opinion which could guide public policy. For that, he needed to reach other well-educated young people like himself. As for Harris, Abir's invitation generated a response, catalysing a club, the Youth Policy Forum (YPF). Abir too thought hard about its protocols: political neutrality, mutual courtesy and respect for the views of others. Currently, the YPF has 12,000 members and more than 30,000 followers. Its mantra, 'People, Policy, Progress', neatly encapsulates the principle that public policy should be inclusive. Abir discovered that a group of young, intelligent people wanting to learn is alluring to older people who want to pass on their knowledge. An illustrious group became active as Honorary Fellows: Professor Nurul Islam, the doyen of Bangladeshi economists; Dr Hameeda Hossain, founder of Ain o Salish Kendra; Dr Mashiur Rahman, Economic Adviser to the Prime Minister; and Dr Mohammad Tareque, former Finance Secretary.

The masterstroke was to organize members and advisers into thematic networks. Those interested in climate change or environmental protection join the Environment Network. Those interested in geopolitics join the Foreign Policy Network. There are networks for education, health care, infrastructure for energy, economic growth for jobs, gender, and a grassroots network for taking these discussions to people without the privilege of a university education. Anyone can participate in spontaneous discussions and debates on its Facebook platforms, and the more structured discussions are available to watch on YouTube. YPF has forged partnerships with the media: newspapers now carry well-written and fact-based opinion pieces by its young writers.

It is more than a talking shop: many members are interested in action. A group focused on local development institutions organizes teams to work in villages, where they talk to people about their concerns and aspirations and what could be done to address them. Mentors experienced in fieldwork help people to forge concrete ideas and implement them. This strand of the YPF's work was catalysed by an MP who wanted honest feedback on the issues his constituents were facing. Other MPs quickly realized that this was something worth copying, creating a demand for YPF expansion and linking the organization to politicians. That link generated a further valuable extension, the Governance Apprenticeship programme, through which YPF members do relevant research for MPs, making political debate more evidence-based while learning first-hand about the work of the parliament. YPF has won respect for its expertise: the Minister of Planning has requested it to make summaries of the voluminous Five-Year Plan and 2041 Vision documents to make them easily digestible for MPs. Most excitingly, it is engaging with both government and opposition politicians and providing them with policy research support. YPF is thereby cultivating bipartisan involvement in policymaking – something unheard of in the past politics of dynastic rivalries. Politicians matter, but civil servants are the policy professionals: the Forum has a network for civil servants to learn about new academic research and to teach the young YPF members about their practitioner experience.

This is comparable to the early years of the Rotary Club: explosive organic expansion, devolved agency and a purposive protocol. YPF is already a force for good at local and national levels. And time is on its side: in two decades, this founding YPF cohort will hold senior positions.

How change was catalysed in Basque Spain

The Basque region of Spain has developed a strategy of transformation even more ambitious and far-sighted than the plan for the Rwandan tourist industry; and the grounding in bottom-up, communitarian ideas is unambiguously explicit.

What is now known as the saga of Mondragon began in 1941:

Father José, a young priest with a distinctive moral philosophy, was assigned to a small Basque town. A communitarian, he aimed to turn the little town into a community-of-place in which everyone recognized their duty to contribute to the whole; those with the most should make the first move. As for Paul Harris, one objective of this prospective community must be to raise the conditions of the town's poorest residents. But Father José added another: the little town, devastated by the Spanish Civil War, lacked opportunities and so must generate communities-of-work.

The times are not propitious: Spain has been divided and ruined by the civil war, won by the fascist-sympathizing General Franco. The country is shattered into communists, anarchists, democrats and fascists. Overlying this fragmentation, the Basque region is ethnically and linguistically entirely distinct from the rest of Spain. By the 1940s Basques are divided into those wanting to remain Spanish, those wanting a peaceful political process of secession and those who espouse violence.

Father José spent his first fourteen years in the town educating and training young people who could catalyse the communities-of-place and -work in which he believed. Only in 1955 did he have five people he considered fully equipped to launch the next stage: the five set up a cooperative business, Ulgor, the origins of what grew to become Mondragon.* By 1955, Franco was trying to develop the Spanish economy through an import-substitution strategy not unlike that of Julius Nyerere in Tanzania in the 1970s. Two differences turned out to be decisive. Whereas Father José's strategy devolved agency to small teams, in the Tanzanian strategy agency had been vested in central planners. And while Father José had spent fourteen years training his first small team in business methods, the Tanzanian central planners had neither training nor experience. Franco's import barriers created market opportunities for Ulgor and, true to its guiding philosophy, it kept spinning out

---

* In an echo of the mutual responsibility built into the naming of the Rotary Club, the name Ulgor came from the first initial of each of the five founders.

new cooperative organizations – a savings bank, various manufacturing enterprises, a construction company and a series of local consumer cooperatives. Its objective of raising the living standards of poor people, common to all these independent enterprises, made it natural for them to pool their resources for the common purpose of establishing a training college. Staying true to the norm of helping their poorest members through the sacrifices of the more fortunate, they all raised the wages of the lowest paid above national levels, while paying top management far less than the market rate.

While Ulgor was becoming Mondragon, the Basque region was going through rough times. As in South Yorkshire, between the mid-1970s and the mid-1980s its traditional heavy industries had collapsed, and this was compounded by an upsurge in political violence that damaged the region's international image. But by design, the Mondragon business model was robust, bringing people together in highly skilled future-oriented businesses, all grounded in moral purpose. Further, as Robert Putnam had predicted, the habits of association encouraged by the dual strategy of building communities-of-place and communities-of-work reinforced other forms of social capital. Despite the legacy of fragmentation, people came together in the Basque regional government to seize a new opportunity: New York's Guggenheim Museum was looking for a major new venue. Bilbao, the capital of the Basque region, was scarcely an obvious choice. But the people of Bilbao recognized that it would provide a game-changing transformation of the region's image. Swiftly, the regional government offered to invest €100 million in a new building and to finance its maintenance. The Guggenheim Foundation combined its primary purpose of bringing art to the public with a secondary one of enhancing a community. But while prepared to reinforce a process of transformation, it recognized that as an outsider it could not be the catalyst. It needed reassurance that change from within was under way. Mondragon constituted that reassurance, both directly by what it had achieved, and through the habits which had made its regional government so effective. Opening in 1997, the museum gave a powerful boost to a nascent tourist industry.

Between them, Mondragon, the Guggenheim Museum and a confident regional government transformed the region's opportunities: it is now one of the most prosperous parts of Spain. With 90,000 employees, Mondragon is the largest enterprise in the Basque region, and one of the largest in Spain. It runs fifteen specialized training centres for research distributed around the region's towns, working on locally pertinent technologies. They help to keep Basque businesses at the competitive frontier. The norm that keeps the spread between the lowest-paid and the highest-paid employees narrow is currently below 1:5. This is radically more equal than the 1:300 currently common in the modern Anglo-American corporate sector. A corollary is that Mondragon's top management stays in post only because of its self-evident commitment to the philosophy of mutuality and the responsibilities of privilege. By thinking long term, the organization has not only stayed competitive but accumulated a multibillion-Euro fund devoted to the well-being of its most needy communities. Predictably, it has become hated by the ideologues of left and right, but from the beleaguered Anglo-American centre, it looks supremely attractive.

Perhaps we shouldn't be surprised by the potential for community groups to radically drive progress and prosperity, since the most consequential economic transformation in the history of humanity, the Industrial Revolution, was catalysed by just such a group. The story provides an inspiring example of how social exclusion knitted people together, something that is pertinent for other communities that have faced exclusion.

Quakers and the power of peripheral people

The Quakers were religious dissenters who believed in living simple but purposeful lives in which every member of their community had equal agency, a proposition which collided with the entrenched hierarchy of the Church of England of the eighteenth century. The purpose of the community would be to help others less fortunate, regardless of who they might be. The middle of the eighteenth century was a grim time for poor people, encapsulated in Gin Lane, a famous cartoon of 1751 that depicts drunken women slumped in the street, surrounded by bawling, hungry children. The Quakers determined to apply their ingenuity and acumen to put the gin-makers out of business. Their goal was not the prohibition of gin but providing a new drink that was more enjoyable, cheaper to produce and healthy. Nobody knew if it would work, but their ingenious hope was to find a way of unlocking the potential of the cocoa beans traders were bringing back from West Africa, just as the potential of coffee beans had been unlocked a century earlier. In contrast to coffee, the chemistry required to transform cocoa into drinking chocolate was bewilderingly complicated. With their common purpose, three Quaker families shared what they had learnt from kitchen-sink experiments. Over two centuries later, they are still household names in the chocolate business: Cadbury, Rowntree and Fry. It took over 600 experiments before they hit on the unlikely sequential chemistry. To make cocoa cheaper than gin they drew on their business acumen: although when produced in small volumes it was prohibitively expensive, if manufactured at scale its costs could be sufficiently reduced. Quakers did far more than close Gin Lane, but that gives you a flavour of their contributions to humanity.

Another group of dissenters at the time were Unitarians. They were on a collision course with the Church of England because they denied the theological concept of the Trinity. A crucial early member was Joseph Priestley, a chemist who believed that progress came through experiments that advanced factual knowledge step by step, rather than through grand dogmatic theories. The most celebrated of his many discoveries was oxygen; it transformed the understanding of the role of the heart and arteries and set new norms for how science should be conducted. Becoming a Unitarian clergyman in 1762, Priestley's religious beliefs echoed his science: humane and inclusive. He rejected both the Church of England idea that non-believers were damned and the Calvinist idea that only the predestined would reach heaven. Fortuitously, like the Quakers, here was another excluded group, tightly knit and eager to apply experimental science to socially useful purposes.

Not only were Quakers and Unitarians marginalized by their beliefs, their locations condemned them to being peripheral. Rowntree and Priestley were Yorkshiremen; Cadbury, Fry and many Quakers were from the North Midlands; while political power and social prestige sat in London. The first modern organization to promote scientific inquiry, the Royal Society, had been founded in Oxford in 1660. But it had never been open to dissenters and a century later had succumbed to the patronage of aristocrats. Kitchen-sink science was beneath their dignity. Priestley and Rowntree were not deferential to such pomposity. The North Midlands artist now famous for his depictions of the Industrial Revolution and its key figures, Joseph Wright, felt similarly snubbed by London's galleries. In response, he insisted on signing himself Joseph Wright *of Derby*. By 1831 such irritation led to the formation of a rival to the Royal Society: the British Association for the Advancement of Science. In contrast to its predecessor, it took experimental research seriously, holding annual meetings organized into parallel groups of specialists reporting and comparing new results. It had one rule: those meetings would never be held in London.

Quakers and Unitarians were unlikely little networks of innovation that were the seedbed for rapid learning. The polymath evolutionary biologist Joseph Henrich credits them with driving innovation forward.[6] Quite possibly, similar networks of purposeful innovation have periodically formed in other parts of the world: Sumer, China, Egypt, Persia, Greece, Peru, Mali and Italy all have credible claims. Yet Henrich is right to see these two groups as important because by the 1770s other rare circumstances were already in place. The network of Quakers and Unitarians was the last, and therefore decisive, link in the chain that triggered the Industrial Revolution.

★

The power of little platoons in six entirely different settings – northern Italy since the sixteenth century, early twentieth-century Chicago, post-war Germany, Bangladesh since 1970, the Basque region of Spain since the 1940s and late-eighteenth-century Northern England – encapsulates the idea that modest people can nonetheless ignite processes as inspiring as any claimed by the greatest leaders. The feature that makes them so attractive is agency: these are opportunities open to all of us. Instead of waiting for a great leader, we can join in a bottom-up process of transformation which builds effective institutions supported by enforceable rules and communicates effectively with citizens.

We need to do so, because others are already active in bottom-up processes for less benign purposes. Social media is a technology naively expected to unite mankind. The results in Ethiopia call such hopes into question. Until Facebook arrived, Ethiopia had been growing fast out of poverty. Facebook brought algorithms designed by the most brilliant brains in the world to keep people on the platform in this new African market. The longer the screen-time, the larger the advertising revenue. Frances Haugen, a senior Facebook official turned whistleblower, testified under oath in the British Parliament that these algorithms were *intentionally* designed to feed extreme views. Across America there were many Ethiopian migrants from different ethnic groups, for example the Oromo, the Amhara and the Tigrayans. Unfortunately, these groups often wanted to stoke grievance against minorities living in their home region – the 'stressors' at work again.* Appalling violence broke out as the majority ethnic group in each region, incited by its America diaspora, pursued ethnic cleansing. The ensuing violence displaced 3 million people within Ethiopia. The whistleblower evidence shows that senior management at Facebook knew this was happening but allowed it to continue because it was profitable. It would be tragic if the remarkable potential of bottom-up processes in societies like Ethiopia were to be warped into such perversions.

* See footnote on p. 114.

7.

Inclusive Prosperity

Many of the poorest countries are falling further behind the rest of mankind and are mired in mass poverty. To escape it their workforce needs to become far more productive. In many richer countries, some communities have fallen into hereditary disadvantage. To address it, life chances need to be equalized.

Until the twentieth century neither of these objectives had decisively been achieved anywhere. No society had discovered how the typical worker could become highly productive. Nor had any society been willing and able to redistribute incomes reliably to all who were falling behind. Had our forefathers been told both would soon become feasible, they would have thought it miraculous. Yet nowadays, the miracle of productivity is widespread. The miracle of combining it with redistributions that avert sustained collapses in life chances is less common: the clusters of Nordic and Baltic states and a few in East Asia.

Those of us not fortunate enough to live in these societies would gain from emulating them. Even exceptionally high productivity does not sufficiently compensate for unequal life chances. California is the most productive large region on the planet, but there are entire communities stuck in hereditary disadvantage and extreme inequalities in incomes. Most Californians would have materially higher incomes if their state had the higher Danish level of inclusion, even if the price were to be the lower Danish level of productivity. California is a great place to become a billionaire, as long as you have a thick skin.

Each of these miracles is recent and immensely valuable. We need to grasp the mechanics of how they work. But the process by which

Denmark achieved these miracles required political and social capacities that the Danish state initially lacked: they took decades to build. These two transformations are the agenda of this chapter.

Grasping the miracles

We now know a lot about how to raise average productivity, but much less about inclusion. The miracle of productivity is no mystery. It is a package of characteristics such as economies of scale by which the workforce in all high-income societies became productive. The miracle of *inclusive* prosperity is more mysterious since only a few societies have yet mastered it. Denmark is the most remarkable. It is a bleak, windswept cul-de-sac on the edge of the European mainland, lacking in natural resources. Yet it tops many global rankings. By radically reducing differences in life chances, Danes have freed themselves from the blight of Contributive Injustice, the accusation levelled by Michael Sandel against complacently successful individualists.

The wide gap between the now common miracle of productivity and the still rare miracle of inclusive prosperity arises because the characteristics needed for productivity come with a significant downside risk of exacerbating social exclusion. The research on how the benefits can be retained without the downside of exclusion is recent and scattered, but by learning from it, instead of hindering productivity inclusion can raise it. Social exclusion wastes talent, and the despair and anger due to hereditary exclusion compounds this waste with economic damage felt across the society.

California is exceptionally unequal even by American standards, but what is true of California applies to the rest of America: the average American would be materially better off if America had the lower Danish level of productivity and the higher Danish level of inclusion. Britain has the double disadvantage of being both less productive than Denmark and less inclusive. Like California, Britain is a great place for thick-skinned billionaires, but a large majority of the population would be better off in Denmark.* Social exclusion wastes the potential contribution of many talented people; it is making most Americans worse off than most Danes. These striking facts catch the attention even of the selfish. They also have a crucial implication: although historically the miracle of productivity happened before inclusion, *they are faster when done together*. Left-behind societies can boost productivity by incorporating recent insights about inclusion. Although these societies will need to go through some wrenching cultural changes that raise productivity rapidly, they do not need to tolerate exclusion as the price of prosperity.

The rise in productivity begins with reaping *gains from scale*. Historically, the earliest such gains were technological. Modern economies have moved far beyond them: many gains from scale come from bringing firms together in clusters, as in Kaluga. Two thirds of the world's buttons are made in one Chinese city: by grouping together, button-makers lower each other's costs. But scale comes with many downsides. Workers can feel alienated from the product they produce – a mere cog in a giant process. They can feel alienated from the firm that produces it – a powerless pawn directed by greedy owners and managers. Both are evils: they may also demotivate people, reducing their productivity.

The most successful societies reconcile scale with motivation. Far from feeling alienated from the product, workers in a large manufacturing plant can be thrilled by participating in its grandeur. Workers in Sheffield's giant steel mills and Zambia's huge copper mines took pride in their role – they were not a meaningless cog but a powerful link in a purposive chain.† Far from being alienated by greedy

---

* The technicalities of comparison are that the people in each society are ranked by their household income. The incomes of those with the same ranking in the two societies are then compared. For example, at the 70th percentile of incomes, do Americans, Britons or Danes have the highest income? My use of the word 'average' to introduce the idea is technically the 'median'.

† Fiona Hill, whose father was a miner made redundant by mine closures, writes movingly of his loss of a sense of purpose and self-respect once the mine closed. See *There's Nothing for You Here* (2022).

management, workers can be empowered by being given responsibilities that use their superior knowledge of the here and now. A spectacular example is the prolonged struggle between Toyota and General Motors in the American car market. Once the world's most profitable company, by 2009 General Motors went bankrupt, killed by an innovation of Toyota that it was unable to match.

That innovation was not technical wizardry but inclusion. Toyota's managers dressed like the workforce, ate in the same canteen and eschewed rewarding themselves with big bonuses. Top managers could credibly say 'we' to Toyota's workforce. They used their positions as communicators-in-chief to set the entire firm a common goal of breaking into the American market. It was supported by a clear strategy: Toyota's advantage in the market would be the production of fault-free cars. And for that, top managers needed to give the workforce agency. They grouped the workers strung along its production line into teams – 'quality circles', each of which became responsible for spotting faults as soon as they occurred. By pulling a cord, any worker could halt the entire line and alert technicians to correct whatever might be causing the fault – such as a mis-programmed robot. But stopping the line cost $10,000 a minute. In giving workers the power to pull those cords, managers demonstrated trust. It worked: peer pressure within those teams policed the process that gradually won Toyota a valuable reputational advantage. Even when the CEO of General Motors understood how Toyota had achieved that advantage, he could not match it. After decades in which management had rewarded itself with corporate jets and big bonuses while adopting confrontational, top-down relations with workers, many of those on the production line would have gleefully pulled those cords and brought GM to a standstill.* The CEO of Toyota achieved in the corporate context

---

* The CEO finally ordered the cords to be installed. Recognizing what would happen, and themselves on bonuses, the line managers tied them up: a visible statement of distrust. I wish to thank Rebecca Henderson, University Professor at Harvard Business School, for this graphic example.

what Mette Frederiksen's approach to COVID-19 achieved in the context of governance: people rallied around a new common purpose that they recognized as worthwhile. Toyota was able to devolve the search for faults for the same reason that Mette Frederiksen was able to devolve the containment of contagion: they had governed in an inclusive manner that won trust.

Arguably the main benefit of scale is that it permits *gains from specialization*. That Chinese cluster of button manufacturers is large enough to support highly specialized firms that service the unique needs of the industry. Similarly, within a large firm like Toyota, the thousands of workers on the assembly line can be complemented by small teams of workers skilled in very particular specialisms. Practice enables learning-by-doing: the best eye surgeons for cataracts are in India because operations are organized as a production line, giving them far more practice than elsewhere. Learning-by-doing applies not only at the level of individual skill but to entire firms specialized in making a product. Indeed, the concept was pioneered during the Second World War in the manufacture of aircraft.

As with scale, specialization has a downside. Performing the same narrow task every hour of the day may become tedious. It can also produce overconfidence and skill silos. Overconfidence is a hazard in highly skilled professions: actuaries were over-confident of a model of longevity that was not alert to COVID-19. Even in 2020, with the contagion spreading rapidly westwards from China, their model relentlessly predicted rising longevity. Their consequent actuarial advice to pension funds was entirely misplaced. Skill silos often happen within organizations: each skill is organized into a department that competes for the budget bestowed by top management.* When entire firms specialize but need to do business with each other, skill silos can also shrivel relations between them to transactions enforced only by the wording of a contract.

---

* It was certainly how the World Bank worked when I directed its research department.

The US pharmaceutical industry has both drag-you-down companies like Purdue and raise-me-up ones like Johnson & Johnson. Purdue paid doctors to prescribe highly addictive drugs as painkillers when a cheap, non-addictive generic drug would have been far safer. When the story leaked out, Purdue went bankrupt, but its owners, the Sackler family, have been able to retain the $10 billion they extracted from it. They have been protected from class actions for the redress of addicted people by favourable interpretations of contracts pitched by lawyers highly paid to be persuasive. In contrast, Johnson & Johnson pioneered the approach in which the CEO sets a worthwhile common purpose, devolving and empowering employees to achieve it. The company is one of a handful that have survived as top firms for a century.

The most successful societies manage to reap the gains of specialization without the dross. One of the beneficial side effects of COVID-19 has been that the jobs of ill-paid but essential low-status workers were rapidly reassessed; cleaners and health carers do routine work that can be tedious, but the value of their work was widely appreciated, and they received clear social validation. Similarly, professions and organizations can avoid the overconfidence that leaves them marooned in a narrow mindset. To the credit of the actuarial profession, in 2021 the president of their international association, Tan Suee Chieh, read a critique of their approach to modelling by my colleague Sir John Kay. This led to both of us briefing their membership over the course of the following year, helping to create a new consensus. A large majority recognized that the distinctive purpose of their profession was to ensure that both public and corporate strategies are sustainable despite irreducible uncertainties. This, in turn, led to changes in forecasting practices which built in resilience to a range of credible scenarios such as a further pandemic. Testing a strategy against a range of imaginable scenarios, an approach invented by Shell, is a valuable gadget in conditions of uncertainty.

As firms specialize, they come to depend on each other as suppliers or customers. The downsides of specialization and the need for scale can be reduced by building relationships of trust: European aircraft manufacturers collaborate to make Airbus. It has enabled firms with small national markets to compete with American firms. As firms become interdependent, they need better connectivity: roads, trucks and haulage companies; ports, ships and shipping companies; and airports, planes and airlines.* They need finance, which itself becomes a specialist sector. But more than any of the other requisites for productivity, the financial sector comes with downside dangers now called financialization.

The perils of financialization

At its best, finance is a handmaiden of the firms producing the services and goods needed in a modern society; at its worst it becomes a Frankenstein's monster, predatory on them. Finance firms can get up to mischief – a desire for profit sometimes comes at a social cost. If a financier first buys enough of a company's shares to gain majority control, it can then raise profits by incentivizing the management of the company with bonuses tied to profits. The managers get their bonuses by cutting maintenance and investment, decisions easily hidden in the company's accounts. The cuts are unsustainable for very long, but before this is obvious the financier quickly sells the company on to a pension fund at a premium, reflecting the rapid but illusory increase in profits. This practice is a gadget handy for financiers, but damaging to the firm and the pension fund that buys into it.†

---

* For readers interested in the complexities of finance, from this simple list three implications leap out. Roads, ports and airports are hugely costly, long-lasting infrastructure usually best provided by government. In contrast, haulage shipping and airlines are complex services with intensive day-to-day decision-taking. Their equipment can usually be leased, so they need little finance. These features make the most of these activities better suited to the private sector. Trucks, ships and planes which the transport service companies lease fall between these extremes. They have much shorter lives than infrastructure, but the amount needed for a well-connected economy is still a huge investment.

† This transpires to be the underlying problem at Silicon Valley Bank, introduced in the last chapter. The CFO, Mr Beck, was on a bonus; his CEO, Mr Becker, was

An inflated financial sector drives companies into deception and unsustainability and tempts governments to do the same. Since public debt is underpinned by the power of taxation, governments can almost invariably borrow more cheaply than firms and households. But public debt is a high-profile number that governments like to keep below an announced target. Private finance can disguise public liabilities by complex arrangements such as public–private partnerships, which are often more costly but shift liabilities out of the public accounts. This is a gadget handy in the short term for governments, but damaging and deceptive to voters.*

The financial sector is supremely footloose and so governments compete to attract the high-paying jobs and tax revenues it brings. America and Britain have bloated financial sectors and loophole-ridden tax systems by which the super-rich can minimize taxation. The rich can and do patronize politicians to get policies they like adopted.[1] Since in both the US and the UK finance is the sector that has generated the most billionaires, a further damaging downside is created.† Such fortunes, like the $12 billion of US hedge-fund founder David Tepper and his British equivalent Michael Platt with £8 billion, are commonly judged to be wildly excessive rewards for activities which often redistribute wealth from future pensioners to these individuals. This imbalance discredits the moral foundations

---

on a bigger bonus; both were rewarded if they took more risk. So incentivized, Beck and Becker achieved the grammatically appropriate superlative: SVB went bust.

* Here is an example. Like all police services, the British police need cars, in aggregate costing many millions. There are no published data, but by my guesstimate the stock of police vehicles sums to around £1 billion. Unquestionably, the cheapest way of financing this equipment would be through government debt, paying an interest rate of 3–5 per cent, and most governments finance it this way. But the British police lease most of their equipment from finance companies, the true cost probably exceeding 12 per cent. There are no efficiency savings here and the cost of finance is tripled. But the liabilities have been shifted off the national debt: the government can appear to hit its debt target.

† According to the specialist wealth-focus magazine *Forbes*, as of 2023.

of the practices that have generated high productivity. Politics polarizes between governments trapped into preserving the status quo and populist antagonists who advocate for the financial sector to be eviscerated.

This contrasts sharply with the Nordics, where the financial sector is small enough to be useful. The Nordics have among the highest burden of taxation in the world. Denmark captures 53 per cent of national income in taxation, far higher than either America or Britain, both of which hover around 35 per cent. But in consequence, billionaire Danes have probably contributed something socially valuable. In recognition, far from being seen as contemptible predators, their achievements are celebrated. This even extends to attitudes to inheritance. In high-tax Sweden, those who have amassed fortunes are judged to have paid their dues: they are allowed to pass on their wealth to their heirs tax free.

We need states, but ones that are thick and inclusive

The tantalizing prospect of inclusive prosperity is now within the reach of all modern economies. But achieving it requires a state that captures a large share of the nation's income: the *thick* state. There are plenty of *thin*-state countries, and a few in which the state has disappeared completely. But none of them are prosperous.* There are also plenty of states that are *big* but not thick. They are big only because they are bloated by activities that are socially useless, like make-work bureaucracy. A vicious distortion of thick states are those that are *predatory*. They are controlled by a narrow selectariat that uses the massive power of a thick state to fleece others for its own advantage while subverting all processes of political change to

---

* This is a central conclusion of *Pillars of Prosperity*, by Tim Besley and Torsten Persson (2011). In 2023 their work was recognized as an outstanding contribution of social science by the British Academy.

retain control. Thin states and big states are useless; predatory states are worse: we need thick states like Denmark.

The Danish state is thick and uses its large revenues to be inclusive. Such states sustain their success by combining two reinforcing processes. One is the virtuous circle by which past collective successes due to social cohesion create expectations of future success and so incline people to trust the state's goals. The other is that the equality of life chances makes the most successful people in the society conscious that their children or grandchildren might fall into the poorer half of the income distribution. Since they have normal cares about the future of their children and grandchildren, they consequently favour the high-tax policies necessary for equalizing life chances. That way, if their offspring fall, it will not be very far.[2] Britain and the US have thick states that waste their potential to be inclusive. As a result, the successful know that their children and grandchildren are protected by privilege. These unfair privileges of hereditary success tempt them into disdain and neglect towards the communities suffering hereditary disadvantage. The US now has two distinct groups benefiting from hereditary success: the wealthy inheritors of family money spread around the country, and the educational elite concentrated around those cities with elite universities. The smug moral posturing among these two communities of hereditary success is the unrecognized counterpart to the despairing syndrome of hereditary failure.

The predatory states controlled by narrow interests rather than inclusive prosperity are exemplified by those that were communist. They were hyper-intrusive, interfering in every facet of life, yet despite universally failing their people they clung on to power for decades. North Korea and Putin's Russia are lingering legacies of this vast and tragic twentieth-century experiment.

The big state societies that preside over social failure are now more common than these predatory states. Nigeria has been one of several oil-rich democracies that have spent their oil revenues on a bloated state that confers patronage-ridden privileges allocated by a small but rivalrous political elite. The various factions within it put most of their energies into competing to control the oil revenues, agreeing on only one common elite purpose: keeping taxes low. While in power, they shift their wealth abroad, out of reach of the next regime, in the process draining their country of private investment. Argentina, another big state democracy, also oscillates between rival populist leaders. Lacking oil, they find the public money to spend on their patronage networks by mortgaging the future. Its governments have borrowed huge sums from the IMF, the World Bank and foreign banks: the debts are a huge liability for the next generation. South Africa is a variant of this situation: like Argentina, it is a democracy in the precarious grip of populist leaders running patronage networks. Their strategy has also been to plunder the future, but by neglecting public investment rather than by borrowing.

A key difference between the highly functional thick-state model of the Nordics and these dysfunctional states – some predatory, others just big – is that Nordic governance has not been captured by narrow interests. The Nordic states aim to achieve tasks recognized as worthwhile by their citizens. As much as possible, they are done in partnership with civil society, being devolved to the lowest level of government able to achieve it. As at Toyota, the workforce tasked with each purpose is largely self-policing, motivated by mutual adherence to a goal they hold in common. This enables the state to perform a very wide range of functions effectively. The state thickens for good reason: it reinforces mutuality if many functions are assigned to their public sector.

The benefits of such a wide-ranging state became all too apparent when some Nordic-style countries began to dismantle them: *shrinking* the state. The ideology of shrink-the-state was pioneered by New Zealand in the late 1970s. Its farmers had lost their access to the British market when Britain joined the European Community and adopted the Common Agricultural Policy. New Zealand's government had been panicked into budget cuts that sacrificed policies of inclusion in favour of Milton Friedman's newly fashionable dictum that the market knew best. Invigorated by this English-speaking example and inflated forecasts of what it would achieve, the new ideology swept across the Anglosphere during the 1980s. It became intellectually fashionable to privatize many state functions.* Much of this has not turned out well, especially in conjunction with financialization. The newly privatized state functions had little incentive to pursue the public interest. To rectify the problem a range of new public regulatory agencies was created. The capacity of the state to regulate these activities was wildly exaggerated. The firms knew far more than the regulators and found ways of gaming the rules: narrow interests slunk into power in the Anglophone democracies. Only by being state run could these conflicts of interest have been avoided.[3]

A poor society that built an inclusive state . . . Somaliland

Somaliland is a little-known anomaly. It was once a British colony, the northern neighbour of Italian Somaliland on the coast of Africa's north-east Horn. Upon Independence, each of them was separately recognized by the United Nations. British Somalia became Somaliland, while Italian Somalia became Somalia, but their leaders soon decided to merge so the United Nations re-recognized them as a single entity, named Somalia.† The merger did not work. The unified state was captured by a predatory autocrat from Italian Somalia who sought to centralize control in the capital, Mogadishu, far to the south of Somaliland. The lack of

* New Zealand suffered a poly-crisis in miniature as its thick state administering extensive social protection became unaffordable unless taxes were increased. Unfortunately, the shock coincided with the emergence of a small third party which held the balance of power, and this made the tax increases politically too difficult.
† Precisely the same process of a merger between former Italian and British colonies was mirrored on the other side of the Red Sea, forming the state now known as Yemen.

inclusion provoked a movement in Somaliland for separation. Once the autocrat was overthrown, in 1991, Somalia fragmented into factional warfare and Somaliland seized its opportunity for *de facto* separation. But being legally recognized as part of Somalia prevented Somaliland from receiving aid. The governments of other states could only deal with it via the government of Somalia, as could the World Bank, the IMF, the African Development Bank and UN agencies like the Food and Agriculture Organization and UNICEF. Although one of the poorest societies in the world, it gets no aid. But that extreme neglect also leaves it free of foreign interference.

Meanwhile, Somalia became a humanitarian catastrophe, fracturing into five distinct parts, each beset by warfare and famine. In contrast, Somaliland is at peace, its government is in control of the territory and, though very poor, the state has become inclusive. It is that rare case: a state that has managed the miracle of inclusion but not the miracle of prosperity. It is conceivable that the difference between Somaliland and the rest of Somalia reflects favourably on British over Italian colonialism, but a more credible explanation is that it reflects well on its people, its leaders and their freedom from foreign interference.

The path to an inclusive state began in 2000 with a draft constitution drawn up by elders of the major clans. It was then circulated widely for a lengthy process of citizen consultation, followed by a referendum with a high turnout and overwhelming endorsement. It provided for two legislative chambers – one of Elders chosen within each clan, the other directly elected by all citizens. Legislation would need passage by both chambers and endorsement by a directly elected president. This created robustly inclusive governance: a power-sharing coalition of the main clans with strong checks and balances that guarded against the emergence of patronage politics. Having established effective power-sharing, the top priority was practical security. With no donors to interfere in how the budget was spent, *half of it went on fusing each of the clan militias into an effective national force.* Had foreign donors had power over budget priorities, they would have vetoed such a use, despite its good sense given the context.

Somaliland resembled the Nordics not only in active citizen participation but in a highly equal distribution of income, although this equality reflected not an effective state sufficiently thick to achieve inclusion but an economy so exceptionally rudimentary that the opportunities for high incomes were negligible. The sequential path to multiparty democracy was also astute. The potentially divisive effect of political parties was delayed. They were only permitted to form once the constitution had been approved, the president, Elders and representatives had been elected to the two chambers, and the national army was in place. Reflecting Julius Nyerere's concerns fifty years earlier, only three parties were permitted. The limitation was designed to force parties to organize on the basis of ideas and strategies rather than on clans, of which there were many. With the budget pre-empted by the army, and such a rudimentary economy, the parties coalesced around practical ways of helping the emergence of businesses. For example, Somaliland was predominantly pastoral, its cattle being exported to the Gulf. A common public facility for verifying that exported cattle were disease free was useful. Similarly, by authorizing competing telecoms providers, mobile phones and mobile money made transactions easier and facilitated remittances from Somaliland's large diaspora.[4]

Since Somaliland remains desperately poor, it is not a showcase for the anti-aid arguments common among the libertarians of the political right. But it is consistent with the argument that both aid and democratization are best postponed until the society has found the strength to come together around a common strategy. Oil prospecting off the shores of Somaliland appears to have found commercially viable oil reserves. In Botswana, where Seretse Khama had forged common purpose, the discovery of diamonds provided the no-strings-attached influx of revenues that enabled its rapid transformation. Since the people of Somaliland have also forged common purpose, something similar could now happen in Somaliland.

Small is not always beautiful: Malawi

Like Somaliland, in Malawi the state is too thin to be effective. But in contrast to Somaliland, despite being too thin it has been captured by narrow political interests that plunder the limited revenues it controls. Once an autocracy, in 1994 Malawians ousted their aged ruler, who had been in power for twenty-eight years. It became a multiparty democracy: as one of the poorest new democracies in the world, it began to attract large aid inflows. The new president brought in some admirable ministers. But he overpromised and underdelivered. As a despairing former head of the civil service explained to me, with democracy came one, seemingly petty, change in the line of accountability. The top civil servants in each ministry – the permanent secretaries who authorized spending decisions – had previously reported to their counterpart in the Ministry of Finance. Now they reported only to their minister. The change in accountability had profound consequences: a minister who wished to do so could now plunder the ministry's budget without scrutiny by the Ministry of Finance or anyone else, with predictable consequences. Once a few ministers started to steal from their budgets and live more luxurious lives, honest ministers came under pressure from their own families to do likewise. Only decisive leadership from the president, after the style of Lee Kuan Yew, could have enforced honesty. It was not forthcoming: after a disappointing decade, he died in office.

He was succeeded by President Mutharika, who built a family-based patronage network. His regime was so manifestly predatory that it rapidly became notorious among the donors who were by then financing a substantial share of the budget. As a fig leaf towards inclusive governance, he had chosen a woman, Joyce Banda, as the vice-president, only to marginalize her once appointed. Being excluded from all influence and increasingly vulnerable, she approached me for help, which is how I came to know her. When in 2012 President Mutharika also died in office, it exposed the Achilles heel of his family-patronage system: according to the constitution, she should automatically take over. Peter Mutharika, the dead president's brother and a minister, attempted to override the constitution and mount a coup. With considerable courage, Vice-President Banda drove to the presidency, claimed the office and became an instant darling of the international community. The aid poured in, and the following year President Banda invited me in as an adviser. By then I had realized that to become a communicator-in-chief she would need to convince sceptical citizens of her intentions by some action that sacrificed her own self-interest. I suggested that since her predecessor had been notorious for family patronage, this was the critical fear to allay. She might, for example, emulate the Nordic model. A common Nordic practice has been that assets owned by key ministers are made public. When President Banda brushed this idea aside as irrelevant, I became a little worried. I am no super-sleuth, but a little investigation soon brought to the surface uncomfortable evidence. I quietly withdrew, citizens remained unconvinced of her trustworthiness, and she lost the next election to Peter Mutharika.

Having decided that I had nothing to contribute unless there was profound change within Malawi, I had resolved not to return. But sometimes judgement is tempered by hope. Having read my early work on how left-behind places can reset themselves, a key adviser persuaded the new president to invite me back. The proposal was that I would address a public audience on how society might initiate change, and then periodically return. Initially, the process seemed to be succeeding. A new commission was set up, staffed by a highly capable group of young Malawians. The Minister of Education was similarly impressive, keen to try new, less top-down approaches to teaching and learn from what worked. In the right context, impartial new ideas and evidence can help to catalyse change. They can be picked up either by a president willing to sacrifice their self-interest, or by a wider, bottom-up movement. In retrospect, these conditions were never met, and perhaps my return was an error of judgement. Once I sensed that this president was unwilling to sacrifice self-interest, I withdrew to avoid my participation being misinterpreted as endorsement. Peter Mutharika lost the next election, his opponents forging a united front to oust him.

The new cross-party alliance of an elderly president and dynamic young vice-president at last looked to be the moment of transformation Malawi had long needed. The donor community was keen for me to return. So back I went, but what my wife and I learned was dispiriting. The new politicians were no better than their predecessors. The centre of fiscal plunder had become military procurement, where a veil of secrecy was justified to donors by spurious talk of national security. But while that protected the government from scrutiny by donors and citizens, the plunder was not confined to the Ministry of Defence. By 2022, power had been captured by narrow interests despite electoral democracy: corruption had become pervasive across the top levels of politics and the civil service. A sad lesson from Malawi's experience is that although its incumbent presidents have regularly been defeated, their removal has not impeded patronage politics: electoral democracy is not a sufficient condition for an inclusive state. Nor is it necessary: the most promising approach for Malawians seeking change is to ignite a bottom-up process analogous to the Bangladesh Youth Policy Forum.*

Becoming Denmark

In none of these very different situations has the state the competences that the Nordics have built. The predatory states and Malawi, though in most respects wildly different, share the common problem that at senior levels state officials are obstacles to change because they benefit from plunder. Parts of the state are a menace and need to be shrunk. Pouring public money into such states only

---

* As I was finalizing *Left Behind* in late 2023, increasingly insistent requests began to come in from the donor community in Malawi that, yet again, I re-engage. Readers may come to learn whether once again hope triumphs over judgement.

deepens the problem: there is more for these narrow interests to capture.

The Nordic states now undertake a vast range of functions, but that has not always been the case: Denmark has not always had inclusive governance: in the mid-nineteenth century an impoverished society was ruled by a brutal and self-serving aristocracy. A predatory elite lived in luxury, while poor farmers were killed, strung up on trees, and left as carrion to discourage protest. The passage from that to modern Denmark was fraught. Danes themselves have largely forgotten it: when Danish aid agencies advise Malawi or Peru, they do not talk of their own late-nineteenth-century transition. Nor should they: it would not be pertinent, because the world of the left behind in the twenty-first century is radically different from that of the nineteenth-century Nordic states.

DANIDA, the Danish aid agency, inevitably benchmarks its advice against the triumphs of the modern Danish state. But that has the potential to be very misleading. Although seductively attractive, most of the functions well performed by a thick state guided by inclusive governance would be badly performed in the very different conditions of Malawi. The transitions from Russia and Malawi to an inclusive thick state would be complex and of course differ radically, but a common feature is that neither can learn much from contemporary Denmark. Even the government of Somaliland, trying to build an effective state from scratch, will learn more from a similar place a decade or two ahead of them, where the scaffolding of state-building has not yet been taken down.

The goal of inclusive prosperity is now technically feasible: the miracles are no longer mysteries. But the political and social capacities that a country needs in order to implement them will take decades to put in place. Just as it took decades for Denmark to transform into a prosperous and inclusive society, instant leaps are fanciful: international pressure to take them is at best naive.

I now drill down into the practicalities of these transformations. I start with the politics and gadgets of the most common and socially disruptive change facing poor societies: urbanization. No country in the world has ever become productive without it. But not all countries which urbanize have become productive. And no poor country beginning a programme of urbanization should attempt to replicate Copenhagen: it is a fine city, but it works only because so many other features of a prosperous and inclusive society are already in place.

8.

Urbanization: Haven or Death Trap?

Most people in high-income countries live in well-functioning cities. We take them for granted, grouse about their downsides and sometimes dream of rural bliss. But our cities are testimony that urbanization has repeatedly been done successfully. Most of the countries now left behind are still predominantly rural, but they are rapidly urbanizing. By 2050, almost regardless of government policies, Africa and Central Asia, the world's two poorest regions, will have urbanized: Africa's urban population is projected to triple. From an economic perspective this is a vital structural transformation and so very good news: small, isolated communities are doomed to poverty and successful urbanization is entirely feasible.

Done well, rapid urbanization will boost people's productivity: it provides the easy connectivity that facilitates scale and specialization. No society has ever raised the productivity of its population to a comfortable level without it. The world's least urbanized country, Papua New Guinea, is 'extremely deprived'.* Rapid urbanization is not a sideshow for a few policy wonks, it is existentially important for many millions of people left behind by global growth. The choice is whether it is a rocket to inclusive prosperity or a cul-de-sac to frustrated lives. Urbanization can also strengthen social capital, bringing together the multiplicity of local identities of a country, such as clans or tribes. The different communities of Papua New Guinea are so badly connected that it is fragmented into over a thousand different languages and has a long history of intercommunal violence.

* As classified by the World Bank on 2022 data.

One of Lee Kuan Yew's triumphs was to master the cognitive gadgets and acts of inclusive governance that make a city productive and liveable, in the process quadrupling Singapore's population to 6 million. But although there are many examples of successful cities, some have grown extremely rapidly without becoming either productive or liveable. Dar es Salaam has grown even faster than Singapore, now having a population of over 7 million, but most of its people are shack-dwellers living in poverty. Effective urbanization is entirely feasible, but the transition from a rural society is not straightforward. Like other aspects of spiralling up, it poses huge problems of coordination that markets alone cannot manage.

Among other problems, there is a very clear market failure which propels urban growth towards congestion. If people flock to a city, it can soon become congested unless transport infrastructure keeps pace with it. As the congestion worsens, most of the costs are borne by the existing residents, not the newcomers who are causing it. Yet as long as the city provides better opportunities than the rural areas, people will keep coming. The potential nightmare is that they drag productivity back down to rural levels. Among the most dysfunctional cities with which I am familiar is Freetown, the capital of Sierra Leone. Its infrastructure is still adequate only for its tiny pre-Independence population of 35,000, but this grew to a million during a civil war when neither national nor local government could instal infrastructure. Sierra Leone is a peaceful democracy, and the government faces the enormous challenge of retrofitting the infrastructure for a vastly more populous city which has only a few tiny roads.* Retrofitting has been blocked owing to both political and financial obstacles. The Minister of Transport spelled out the political problem: a coalition of the powerful blocking change. Highly influential people have built houses where roads are now needed: it is impossible to demolish them. I knew

---

* As I was finishing this book, some army officers attempted a coup in Sierra Leone. The coup was swiftly quelled, but the event is indicative of the increasing fragility across West Africa and the Sahel discussed at more length in Chapter 10.

the financial obstacle: the cost of retrofitting infrastructure is on average triple that of installing it on a clear site.

Market forces can also warp the national pattern of urbanization towards the prime city: other cities fall behind. This happened in Colombia: the most promising city in which to make irreversible private investments always looks to be the capital, Bogotá. It is already the largest city, and rapidly growing. In 2023 I had an opportunity to discuss the future of Bogotá with the mayor. She was worried that unless national policy was redesigned to help other cities, Bogotá would become unmanageable. Those fears were already a reality in Mexico City, home to more than 30 million people. Tokyo also has over 30 million people, and is still growing, despite overall decline in the population of Japan. But Japan became rich before Tokyo became enormous: it could finance the huge infrastructure costs of expanding the city in such a way that even when its population reached 30 million it was still reasonably functional, albeit with long commutes and crowded living conditions. In contrast, Mexico City became big before the country could afford to make it manageable: it now faces an intractably costly problem of retrofitting.*

While market forces have evident limitations, so does central planning by a national ministry of urbanization: there are far too many tasks for government-knows-best. Even in central Moscow, where the urban planners are based, traffic flow is irreversibly dysfunctional. Beyond the capital, such a ministry is too distant from cities around the country to know the local context. The Moscow-planned cities of Siberia are now tragedies. Getting urbanization right is not automatic or even obvious. A city is both a place to work and a place to live. It should enable workers to be productive without sacrificing liveability.

---

* Japanese governments acknowledge that by draining workers from other cities, the continuing growth of Tokyo has bequeathed an acute problem of left-behind regions which should have been avoided.

Making cities productive and liveable

A productive city must offer its workforce the benefits of easy connectivity. Workers need to get to their jobs; firms need to get their
products to consumers; and since firms need to specialize, they
need to connect with each other. A liveable city must offer its
residents the benefits of decent and affordable housing. The technologies of connectivity and housing can be ranked in hierarchies
of sophistication: while marching up those hierarchies, the two
need to keep in step.

At the bottom of the technology for connectivity is travel by
foot, for which the only necessary infrastructure is footpaths. When
urbanization goes wrong, as it did in Nairobi, that became the most
common way for workers to get to work. It is the cheapest means
of transport, but it wastes many hours each day. Faced with long
journeys on foot, many people sacrifice liveability in order to
shorten the distance to work: they crowd into homes near the city
centre. How crowded those homes become depends in turn on the
technology for housing. The cheapest housing technology is the
shack: being only one-storey high, it needs no foundations. But a
single-storey building near a city centre is a hugely extravagant use
of land: if people need to buy the land in order to get a plot, shacks
will be wildly expensive for the small space they offer. Whether the
land has to be bought takes us back to the issue of whether the
rights of ownership of land have been sorted out: in the Rwandan
city of Kigali all the plots have been registered, but in the neighbouring cities of Dar es Salaam and Nairobi they have not. If land
rights are confused, then the cheapest way of acquiring land is to
squat on it and hope not to be evicted.

In the heart of Nairobi sits the enormous Kibera slum. Although
covering only one square mile, it is often claimed to be Africa's most
populous slum, the best guess being that about a quarter of a million
people live there. Being in the inner city, it could become part of the
central business district, which would enhance its contribution to

the economy. By one serious estimate, by maintaining its current low-value use the economy is losing future value of around $2 billion. Yet policies are gridlocked because the land ownership is contested. The legal owners of the land in Kibera are a small group of very well-connected people: generals, top civil servants and politicians. But they do not live there, and their claims to ownership are recent, coming from their privileged position on a government registry. The families who do live there are squatters, many of whom have occupied the same plot for several generations. An attempt by the well-connected people whose names are on the registry to evict them would, quite understandably, result in city-centre riots. Presidents are fearful of riots close to their seat of government, and so mass eviction has become inconceivable. The result is a stalemate in which land use cannot change. The residents pay a modest dribble of such rent as they can afford to the registered owners. There is no market mechanism for realizing that $2 billion of value, and the political process of negotiating a mutually beneficial deal requires acts of inclusive governance that have long been lacking.

The obvious solution to squatting is to give the people occupying the land the rights to it, as was done in Kigali. But if the process is done badly, it creates a classic problem of moral hazard in which squatting becomes opportunistic. For Kampala, Uganda's main city, a vital aspect of improving connectivity became widening the long, narrow road to the national airport at Entebbe, which had become completely choked. To ease financing of the road project the government submitted a loan request to the World Bank: infrastructure was indeed the prime purpose for which the World Bank had been founded. But as news of the request spread, well-connected but unscrupulous wealthy people bought up blocks of the land needed for widening. Once alerted, many poorer people also behaved opportunistically, flocking to squat on the land adjoining the road. At this point, well-meaning international NGOs cast themselves as warriors for human rights, arguing that the rights of squatters should be fully protected. The wealthy new owners hired lawyers and demanded absurdly high compensation for loss of the land they had just bought. Intimidated by the NGOs, the World Bank conceded. The road has been improved, but per mile, it became the most expensive road in the world.[1]

A key implication of these stories is that it is vital for the legal and physical infrastructure of settlement to get ahead of the inflow of people. The affordable technology that enables a city to keep ahead of settlement – the gadget – concentrates local government activity on providing sites and services: recent research has shown that it is effective.

The forgotten gadget: sites and services

Once the city's government plans ahead, it can buy farmland cheaply beyond the city's current economic footprint. It can then divide the land into small plots and enter each of them on the land register. The city authorities can then sell these rights to those arriving in the city, and to those living in slums who would like to be rehoused. A road grid can be laid out, beneath which the electricity, water pipes and sewers needed for fully liveable homes can be installed. If plot sizes are kept small, the cost of a plot is around $3,000. Many migrant households and slum-dwellers can raise such a modest sum using their family network. On it, they can gradually build a decent home as their savings accumulate. In the 1980s the World Bank experimented with this approach in a few cities such as Lusaka, the capital city of Zambia. But under political pressure to meet the needs of current residents, the Bank then switched from this preventive approach to the reactive remedy of retrofitting infrastructure into existing slums. The long-term legacies of these alternative strategies have recently been studied. Though the sites-and-services approach had been dropped, it turned out to have worked. Decades later, these serviced areas in Lusaka were providing good-quality homes, financed improvement by improvement by families as they gradually upgraded their housing. The road grid laid out through providing sites and services was still there, and the original infrastructure was still being used. In contrast, the slum-upgraded areas, though more recent, had already reverted to being indistinguishable from adjoining slums which had never been upgraded. Upgrading had turned out to be a failed strategy.

Once people have bought the legal title to their plot, enabled by the sites-and-services approach, they have an incentive to use their land efficiently, gradually building a structure of two or three storeys. This reconciles higher density of occupancy of the land with less crowded living conditions. At this density of occupation, a higher rung on the ladder of transport technology becomes economically viable.

Bus-rapid-transit (BRT) is a useful gadget for a large, low-income city: a low-cost version of an urban rail system with buses instead of trains and roads or bus lanes replacing the rail track. It needs higher density than shack-land, because for speed the buses cannot keep stopping everywhere: they need a few designated stations with sufficient people living nearby.

The last-mile problem

Walking long distances to work, as in Nairobi, is clearly incompatible with good liveability. Buses in bus lanes or the dedicated roads of BRT get people swiftly from the centre to the suburbs, where land is more abundant, but then commuters face the last-mile problem: how do they reach home? A low-cost but effective blend of technologies overcomes this problem. The buses can drive swiftly to district hubs, where minibuses and moped taxis complete the journey. A scheduled service matters because, as with many markets, an unregulated bus service doesn't work well. The incentive for a bus owner is to linger in the centre until the bus is full. Bus lanes are needed to prevent cars slowing the buses to a crawl. But although technologically this is a good get-started policy for a poor city, it is often blocked politically.

When Lagos, Nigeria, became completely choked by traffic jams the governor reduced congestion at a stroke by restricting car use according to the first letter on the numberplate: A to K cars could use roads only on Mondays, Wednesdays and Fridays; L to Z on the other days. The effect was to wipe out half of the city's investment in cars: it would have been far cheaper not to have bought them in the first place. Yet it was the preferred solution politically, because of the pattern of winners and losers: bus travellers gained, car owners lost, *but not all of them*. The wealthy simply bought two cars: since the roads were clearer, they gained too. The governor had spotted this coincidence of interest between the two groups that most mattered for him, voters and the wealthy elite: he had forged a winning coalition for change, but one which wasted the country's money. It was better than no change at all but left room to do better.*

Bus lanes do not have the same political attraction. Ordinary voters gain more, but *all* car owners lose, so powerful elites often block them. Social habits may also be an impediment. For bus lanes to work, car drivers must keep out of them; for bus schedules to work, bus owners must stick to them. Compliance collapses without enforcement, and this depends upon a chain of city government functions all working.† Valuable gadgets like bus lanes and bus

---

* This is a trivial instance of an important insight. Politics is 'the art of the possible' – building coalitions of interests which buy off or crush those groups with sufficient power to block nationally valuable changes that hurt their interests. The leaders discussed in Chapter 5 all built such coalitions. The key exponent of this approach to economic policy is my colleague Stefan Dercon; see *Gambling on Development: Why Some Countries Win and Others Lose* (2022).

† On the importance of enforcement see the experimental game reported in Chapter 2. The chain of enforcement is as follows. If a police officer stops a car for using the bus lane, she faces a choice. She can report the infraction to the city authorities or negotiate a bribe with the driver. If she reports it, the authorities must be able to link it to a reliable register of car ownership and an address. If a penalty notice is sent, the courts must provide a fast and effective way of enforcing payment. Introducing bus schedules faces a similar problem. The bus owner wants to wait in the central bus station until the bus is full. If there is a rule against it, will he try to bribe the official enforcing it? Will that official refuse the bribe? Collectively the drivers will lobby publicly against the scheduling policy, perhaps using 'fake news' to claim that it would raise costs and fares.

schedules get blocked unless the arts of governance build winning coalitions with the incentive to adopt them. New gadgets might help – many of the stages in enforcement can be automated using e-technologies which curtail the scope for corruption. Ordinary citizens can be encouraged to participate in enforcement: a brilliant Kenyan gadget was a sign inside minibuses asking passengers 'Is the driver driving safely?': it gave a site for texting an answer and once drivers realized that their passengers had this power, it reduced fatal minibus accidents by 85 per cent at a trivial cost.[2]

Alluring cul-de-sacs

The technologies of connectivity and liveability are interdependent and need to be upgraded in step. A fancy transport technology such as an urban rail network will fail in a city in which people are living in shacks. Some of the technologies that presidents, ministers and mayors of low-income cities can see working in high-income cities are alluring cul-de-sacs which tempt them into costly and unsustainable approaches.

The Los Angeles model

Los Angeles is a highly productive city: it evidently achieves high connectivity for those able to afford a car. The transport technology it uses is multilane highways matched to a liveability technology of family houses with surrounding lawns, spread over a huge, low-density area. There is virtually no central business district: Los Angeles is a city of suburbs, each with its own centre, all connected by the highways. It works for many of its residents because their high incomes enable them to buy the cars and houses on which their liveability depends.* But it is not a model for a low-income

---

* As noted earlier, it is also an astonishingly unequal city: its poor sacrifice liveability, either through overcrowding or dependence on an inadequate bus service.

country because the capital cost of the highways, houses and cars is prohibitive. Ghana, the first African country to gain Independence in 1957, spent its gold reserves building multilane highways, but the investment was far too early for the number of car owners in the country: the highways sat empty and there was no money left to implement changes that were more urgent.

The New York model

The antithesis of the low-density, high-income city of Los Angeles is the high-rise, high-density city of New York. Density is sufficiently high for a metro underground rail system to be financially viable. Presidents of poor countries see this model each time they go to New York to attend the United Nations General Assembly. Unlike the Los Angeles model, New York has been replicated in a country which started poor, namely China. Wuhan is the most spectacular instance of it: it is the closest to an instant, high-density city that urbanization has ever achieved. Presidents might conclude that if China can leapfrog into modernity, why not them? Unfortunately, China was exceptional in three respects, each of which helped to make the leapfrog strategy feasible. That people were willing to accept an astonishingly high rate of forced savings for an entire generation I have already noted. But this was only the start of exceptionalism. China had the largest population in the world, so the high per capita savings rate was multiplied by a billion: the state had enormous financial power. Nor did it create cities like Wuhan everywhere: many Chinese cities are dull, functional places lacking its glitzy glamour. The Chinese state had the practical authority to prioritize Wuhan and a few other urban showcases without arousing unmanageable resentments elsewhere. Not only was the state's financial power to invest in the New York model exceptionally strong, but the pace at which the rural population was moving to cities was exceptionally slow. Population growth had been arrested by the draconian 'one child' policy. Moreover, other draconian policies curbed the incentive to migrate; households already resident in cities were given access to rapidly improving public services, but those who moved to them were permanently denied rights of use. New arrivals were required to sleep in dormitories adjoining the factory in which they worked.[3] In combination, the state was able to build enough high-rise housing to keep abreast of the population inflow, avoiding a penumbra of shack squatter settlements. No other poor country meets these extraordinary conditions: the New York model is another tantalizing cul-de-sac.

Fusing the worst of both models in Angola

Most Angolans live in deep poverty and, despite a valuable offshore oil industry, per capita income is modest. The political system has been highly centralized and electoral manipulation exceptionally easy, perpetuating rule by one party. Oil enables the state to be big, but other than enabling its rulers to maintain their power, it is ineffective, analogous to the worst aspects of Nigeria. In consequence, incomes and life chances are highly unequal. The politically powerful use the revenues from oil to benefit their children, not those of the millions left behind. When those elite children wanted high-quality accommodation a Chinese business consortium offered to build it in return for oil. The consortium's construction company was familiar with Wuhan's glitzy apartments. The site chosen by the government was Kilamba, a new greenfield site around 25 miles from Luanda. Even with cheap land, the building costs of high-rise construction are staggering, and so the cost of each apartment was around $150,000, completely out of reach of the typical Angolan, but feasible for the offspring of the powerful. Wuhan is a well-functioning showcase city, not only with high-rise apartments but also with productive firms in which to work. Kilamba is not: the Angolan government had only asked for apartments, and so that is what they got, a high-rise satellite suburb. The well-paying jobs which the powerful ensured went to their children were 25 miles away in Luanda, and no thought had been given to the transport between the two places. Angola had none of the public services conducive to business that the Chinese state had put in place before it invested in Wuhan. So Angola ended up with an absurd blend of New York high-rise, Los Angeles long-distance driving and Sierra Leone-style inadequate roads. Around Kilamba, land was abundant, so high-rise had been entirely unnecessary: better and cheaper housing could have been built there using the low-density suburb model of Los Angeles. Given the need for a long commute, the appropriate transport technology would have been BRT. Instead, commuters had to buy cars and then found themselves on clogged roads. Alluring cul-de-sacs can become spectacularly costly mistakes.

Cities of consumption: from Washington DC, through Brasilia, to Abuja

Since government is a big employer, the major cities of a country vie for the role of being the national capital. Sometimes, rival cities agree on a location that cannot threaten any of them. Washington DC reflected a stand-off between Boston and Philadelphia; Canberra was a compromise between Sydney and Melbourne; Brasilia one between Rio and São Paulo. Such capitals are single-activity centres of politicians and bureaucrats. They can easily become cities of consumption in which the two conspire to abuse their power, favouring their city over others which are focused on production. In the US, this also sometimes happens at the state level: Albany, Hartford, Tallahassee.[4]

Abuja, the capital of Nigeria, is such a place: the result of a deal between the three politically salient regional capitals: the northern city of Kano, the south-western city of Lagos and the south-eastern city of Enugu. It has become a city in which much of the oil revenues are spent and so patronage has become its lifeblood. Within it, the few activities that are productive, such as restaurants and hotels, are merely servicing the consumption of those with power. Abuja has scale, but its purposes are predominantly parasitic and the powerful are greedy. Electricity is vital for productivity but, despite abundant oil, Nigerian governments have not delivered reliable electricity anywhere in the country. As the seat of government, Abuja was the place directly responsible for that failing. But the powerful people of Abuja addressed the city's electricity shortage at the expense of other cities. Public money was invested in a transmission line that diverted electricity from Lagos. When switched on, a tenth of the nation's power was sucked out of the country's most productive city, Lagos, so that the city of consumption would not suffer the consequences of its failings.

Harnessing the potential of urbanization

The liveability of a city contributes to its productivity. Workers are more willing to come to a liveable city than an unliveable one, and with good living conditions workers will be healthier and cheaper to recruit. By addressing liveability, urban authorities thereby make it easier for their city to become competitive in export markets. Because global markets are enormous, it ignites explosive growth if the city can enter those markets. Although there are many such cities in high-income countries, cities in left-behind regions and countries have yet to provide such transformative opportunities to their residents. Mayors and ministers have not mastered the pertinent gadgets and have not used the arts of governance to build the winning coalitions to implement them.

The sites-and-services approach is an instance of a valuable gadget that is little known and even less widely adopted. It could reduce the costs of making cities productive and liveable, but the process needs big public investment. Currently, many city governments are dependent on transfers from an overwhelmed Ministry of Finance. To finance investment at an appropriate scale, mayors need to raise revenues locally. But they are wary: if they raised local taxes, would it be electoral suicide?

Using the arts of governance to support city tax revenues

Lagos, Nigeria's largest city, is an example of how revenues can be increased once tax-collecting powers are granted. Lagos is fortunate that many tax-raising powers are assigned by the constitution to Nigeria's thirty-six state governors, and the city of Lagos sits within the larger entity of Lagos State. Since Nigeria returned to democracy in 1998, successive governors have innovated with gadgets that were within their powers, some of which succeeded in increasing local revenues very substantially. One gadget that worked in the local context came from the tiresome fact that the waiting room to see the governor was always packed with local CEOs wanting to lobby for a favour. These people were rich but were very likely evading the state's taxes: the pertinent missing cognitive gadget was scrutiny, as it had been in getting Nairobi's minibus drivers to drive more safely. The governor decided that in this case he personally should provide the scrutiny. But to do so he would need to see a tax return, if the CEO had bothered even to complete one. For this, he turned to one of the other instruments of governance: he announced a new *enforceable rule*. He would see a CEO wanting to lobby him only if they brought their completed tax return with them and presented him with evidence of payment. No receipt, no audience. Because it was a public rule, it had a valuable effect beyond the CEOs of big companies. It signalled to other businesses that the richest were now changing their behaviour: smaller firms lost their favourite excuse for not doing so themselves, and even tax payments by smaller businesses began to increase.*

Raising tax revenues became electorally popular: successive governors increased their majorities. The key step was to break an orthodox economic principle which says that you should not publicly assign in advance tax revenues to specific costs. Instead, governors linked specific increases in taxes to specific plans for

---

* That governor, Bola Tinubu, is now President of Nigeria. His early actions have shown the same astute and pragmatic political focus as he displayed in Lagos.

improvements in infrastructure and services that would be visible and popular. As voters saw that these plans were implemented, the governors gradually built trust in their competence, so the taxes-for-improvements strategy became a vote-winner.*

The governors in Lagos State show what is possible, but they had an important advantage over many mayors: the territory they controlled was larger than the city and so they could formulate a strategy for the city's expansion. In contrast, the physical expansion of Dar es Salaam has grown far beyond its original legal domain. Although presidents of Tanzania could have used the authorizing environment to expand Dar's boundaries, they neglected to do so. The economic footprint of the city now spans five mayoralties. The five mayors vie with each other for the favours of central government and do not trust each other sufficiently to collaborate on the integrated improvements in connectivity the local economy needs.

Tanzania at last has a president and finance minister aligned in their intention to transform the country's economy and pragmatic enough to listen to recent research. They have an opportunity to use their command of the nation's authorizing environment to unify Dar es Salaam under a chief mayor analogous to the governors of Lagos and give that person tax-raising powers. Once they are raising local taxes, mayors have a stronger incentive to grow the city's economy, since they capture some of that growth as extra revenue. This also enhances the president and finance minister electorally: mayors can no longer blame deficiencies in local services as being due to inadequate finance from central government.

Land taxes

A source of tax revenues which economists recognize as both efficient and fair is a tax on the appreciation in land values. As the city grows and infrastructure is installed, productivity rises. In turn, this drives up land values. Often this benefits only the landowner, but

---

* The practice is known as hypothecated taxation.

who *should* benefit? Unlike those working in the city, landowners have not necessarily contributed anything to the rising productivity. That is why land taxes make such good ethical sense in the context of rapid urbanization. Yet few cities have adopted them: they sense that it would be political suicide as wealthy landowners would finance damaging campaigns to discredit the policy and the leadership.[5]

One model exception is Singapore under Lee Kuan Yew. By 1973 his economic policies were driving up productivity and land prices and he decided to capture that appreciation for the government. His sociopolitical strategy was ingenious. He announced a new policy *rule*: the price that the state would pay henceforth for the compulsory purchase of land would be frozen at the 1973 level. Initially, the new rule did not provoke much opposition because there were *no immediate losers*: the few landowners forced to sell their land to the government received its current commercial value. Over the next couple of years, land values rose, so those landowners forced to sell at prices a little below the market value must have complained, but there were few of them. Besides, their land was still worth much more than it had been before Lee Kuan Yew became prime minister. He had created a creeping land tax in disguise. Having bought the land at far below market prices, he later sold it to developers at the much higher rates. With the profit he improved economic infrastructure and built social housing. Like the governors of Lagos, he breached economic principles and linked social housing, which became a huge programme, to land policy. There were far more beneficiaries of the social housing than there were losers. Lee had built a voter base which outgunned that of belatedly alert landowners. By 2020, some two thirds of the entire city had been purchased by the government at 1973 prices and either sold at market prices to developers or used as sites for social housing.*

---

* The low-tax lobby in Britain's Conservative Party that advocates 'Singapore on the Thames' appears not to have understood how Lee Kuan Yew actually developed the country.

In China, the political economy was similar. Although most forms of private ownership of property were respected by the state, it retained the ownership of land. The initial rights of ownership to urban land were devolved to city authorities. Under-used land could be seized by the city authorities and sold to developers who thereupon gained full rights to own and sell it. As in Singapore, the revenues financed social housing that anchored political support, and infrastructure that enabled the cities to avoid the syndrome of congestion.

But although land taxes are efficient and equitable, they are often successfully resisted. The Rwandan government, so effective in other aspects of transformation, has yet to introduce effective land taxes. The president and finance minister took the trouble to understand the gadget of giving city governments the power to tax land appreciation.* They found it politically attractive for the reasons set out above: it would provide more finance for economic development while making mayors responsible for the new tax. Yet they were blocked in parliament by a coalition resistant to a land tax. The approval of members of parliament was needed for a new law to authorize the tax, and, as in Nairobi, the USA and many other parts

---

*I know that President Kagame understood land taxation as a cognitive gadget: in 2016 he became sufficiently concerned about urbanization in East Africa to read the Cities that Work analysis and invited me to discuss it. I was grilled on its implications and appointed pro bono to chair a committee of international architects, predominantly African, to advise the mayor of Kigali. Our overarching instruction was to avoid the mistakes manifest in the other major cities of the region. Kigali had already become a beautiful and safe city with little congestion. But part of the price for the success of high-end tourism had been an alienating international architecture of High Modernism. Learning fast from each other, our committee united around recommending greater use of local design, local materials, local skills and the organic growth pioneered by Jane Jacobs. Three years later, a new minister expanded our brief from Kigali to include all Rwanda's cities: we had become a small input into Rwanda's authorizing environment for urbanization. Our instruction was to spread economic opportunities more widely: Kigali should not become too dominant. Our new role might be summarized as pre-empting the emergence of left-behind places in Rwanda.

of the world, the wealthy had helped many members of parliament to be elected. The wealthy are also disproportionate owners of the land.

Using the arts of governance to support the sites-and-services approach

Through Cities that Work, several mayors and ministers have become familiar with the sites-and-services gadget by which plots of land are prepared for settlement. But despite the research evidence of its value, it has met considerable political resistance. Even in Zambia, where the most convincing research originates, the government is wary. The obstacle is again political economy. Urban residents prioritize the cul-de-sac policy of upgrading the infrastructure where they are living – the costly process of piecemeal retrofitted improvements which are soon eroded. Ethiopian governments have found ways by which urban residents become supportive of a package that links the sites-and-services approach to the taxation of land appreciation.

The Ethiopian government began by understanding the economic value of a range of gadgets that might be pertinent: not only sites and services but the taxation of land appreciation, light urban rail systems that could reduce congestion and multistorey apartment blocks that could increase the density of land use.* The government then found fruitful innovations that combined aspects of each gadget which could work in the local context.

The government drew a distinction between the right to own private property and the right to own land: urban land was deemed to belong to the state. It used its power to introduce an invisible land tax. Addis Ababa had experienced growth in such a haphazard manner that to find public land on which apartment blocks could be

---

* Four-to-six-storey apartment blocks are often an efficient housing solution for a country at Ethiopia's level of income because they save land owing to their height, but the building costs are kept low because they are not high enough to require the considerable expense of elevators.

built it was not necessary to use land on the periphery: there were pockets of empty land well within the city's boundaries as well as shack-land slums like Kibera. To upgrade shack-land while avoiding the high costs of retrofitting, new infrastructure would need to be installed only once the whole area had been bulldozed, so that rebuilding could be done at scale on a greenfield site. The political economy challenge was to persuade an entire neighbourhood community to move out so that a site could be cleared. The solution recognized that the government lacked sufficient citizen trust for any promises of future benefits to be credible, so it devised a sequence in which trust was not needed. First, the government used its limited revenues to build simple apartment blocks on those pockets of empty land close to the expanding urban light-rail system: it used this public investment in rail to anchor expectations that the value of the new housing would appreciate. The construction cost was kept as low as possible: the apartments were basic, with scope for improvement in subsequent years, and standardization enabled the scale that lowered costs to an average of only around $20,000 a unit. Since the land had cost the government nothing, it decided to pass this cost saving on to potential purchasers: they were getting the land free of charge. It then selected a neighbourhood, chosen because the social indicators suggested that its residents were particularly ill housed. Within the neighbourhood it ran a lottery which determined the sequence by which households would receive an invitation to purchase one of the new apartments at the attractive price of only $20,000. The offer was time-bound; after a specified date, if not taken up, it would lapse and transfer to another household. This was a *new rule* combined with good communication. This was a clever marketing technique which addressed the question of why now? It transpired that even in a very poor society like Ethiopia most households could use family networks to raise the money. People moved to the new apartments and their previous home districts were cleared for further development. Mistakes were made along the way, but the strategy enabled the city to become more liveable and more productive.

Building standards

Building standards matter – they depend on a rule to set the standard and an institution to enforce it. The countries that gained Independence from Britain after 1947 inherited standards of building inappropriate for their conditions. Just as they inherited administrative boundaries of cities that were inappropriately small, the building standards were too high. The culprit, the 1947 Town and Country Planning Act, was paved with good intentions. That did not prevent it doing terrible damage when it was imposed on places about which British legislators in London knew nothing. Building standards and minimum sizes of plots were set at such lavish levels that even in Britain they were far too high relative to income levels and were still too high thirty years later. So they were stratospheric for newly independent emerging economies where building housing to standards that met the new regulations was unaffordable for all but a tiny minority. Unless the burgeoning urban population was to sleep in the streets, almost all homes had to be built outside the formal approval process. This had two damaging consequences: directly, it meant that almost all homes were constructed without the scrutiny of any enforced building regulations whatsoever.* More subtly, it meant that ignoring government rules rapidly became normalized.

The Tanzanian government took the trouble to use *Cities that Work* to understand the pertinent cognitive gadget of appropriate building standards. But despite the research evidence, it decided not to lower building standards and the minimum size of plots. Psychologically, to do so was regarded as a step 'backwards'. Instead, a minimum size of plot that was already absurdly high was actually *raised*.

Once such powers are devolved to localities the political economy becomes easier. In India, those local governments which have

---

* In areas prone to earthquakes, hurricanes and floods, enforcing *appropriate* building standards is a matter of life and death.

built a degree of trust have been able to find a variant of the Ethiopian process of community resettlement. The entire community is offered permanent relocation back to the neighbourhood where it is currently living if people will move temporarily while the site is cleared and infrastructure installed. In return for a free new house with improved infrastructure, the household's plot will be reduced to 40 per cent of its current area. To avoid the potential problem that by refusing to move a single obstinate person might prevent the site clearance and scupper the deal, a referendum is held on whether to give the local government the right to evict such blockers (or stressors), if at least 80 per cent want to move. The deal proceeds only if the community grants this right. After rebuilding, 60 per cent of the land accrues to the local authority. Some is used to install a proper road grid which improves connectivity, and the rest is sold to new residents at market prices. These sales make the package self-financing despite the free housing given to existing residents.

Embracing urbanization

Effective urbanization, such as that achieved in Singapore and those Indian slum communities successfully rehoused, devolves agency to the lowest level at which an objective can be achieved. At that level it encourages firms, government and civil society to find common interests: this is the German model. In our interconnected world, we all have a role. Most notably, by embracing the principles of effective urbanization, diasporas that help their relatives finance rehousing and upgrading, and NGOs that pioneer new approaches, can be significant forces for good. Resisting the steps needed to implement urbanization effectively would not stop people coming to cities but would condemn their inhabitants to unproductive and unliveable lives.

There is one further dynamic at play in the fates of left-behind countries that, like urbanization, can have two wildly differing outcomes. And it is much more powerful than urbanization: some countries have been supercharged while others have plunged into catastrophe. It is contentious and morally contested: welcome to the casino of natural resource extraction.

9.

The Gilded Cage

For millennia, the oil, gas and minerals we currently use lay undiscovered beneath the ground. In many countries of the left behind, they lie hidden still, and so the process of managing natural resources begins with discovering them. Once found, profits will accrue to the businesses selling them, so if citizens are to benefit, these businesses must be taxed. While businesses gain, inhabitants living around the messy process of extraction are liable to lose as it despoils their land. Some public process needs to give them a voice and protect their interests. Finally, tax revenues need to be used for the public good. This is often the most fraught stage in the long chain of actions by which resources once hidden beneath the ground end up transforming people's lives.

To perform this wide range of functions adequately, the state needs distinctive new competences which need to be built and then work together. As will become apparent, at an early stage in the discovery process the society is likely to need a competent military to maintain security. Local governments will need to be sufficiently empowered and effective to deliver key public services. A new public agency will need to collate and share geological knowledge; the tax administration will need a specialist unit; and a financial team will be needed to manage a portfolio of foreign assets.

This is demanding: it has often been done, but it is not a walk in the park because of powerful counter-pressures. This makes a natural resource discovery a two-edged sword. At its best it provides finance that is substantial, secure and unconditional: with it, a government can transform opportunities for everyone. That is what happened in Botswana and many other societies. But equally there is exceptional potential for disaster. The process of extraction may despoil the land of a marginalized community while attracting criminal gangs which take control of its resources. At its worst, the finance accruing to government may ignite a violent contest in corruption for control of the state. Diamonds transformed Botswana, but they devasted Sierra Leone. The murderous Revolutionary United Front plunged Sierra Leone to the global bottom of the UN's measure of well-being.*

Discovering your resources

People imagine that Africa is resource rich. Yet before the year 2000, most countries had discovered little resource wealth. Per square mile, the continent had found only around a fifth as many natural resources as North America and Europe combined. The elementary statistical law of large numbers tells us that a random geological process such as the resource endowment of a country, when averaged out over two sufficiently large areas such as continents, will converge towards the same number. Africa and North America-plus-Europe are huge areas of about the same size, so what is actually under the ground should be very similar. So much less had been discovered in Africa only because there had been far less investment in exploration. With comparable exploration, Africa *could increase its resource wealth fivefold* and, during the resource scramble of 2003–13, this began to happen. The passage from prospecting to

---

* As I became increasingly aware of the gulf between the transformational potential of resource extraction and often squalid reality, I built a course, 'Managing Natural Resources for National Development'. Launched in 2012, it is aimed at senior government officials, senior executives of companies, and movers and shakers in civil society. Held at Oxford University's Blavatnik School of Government, it is a partnership with the Natural Resource Governance Institute, an NGO. An international cast of academics and practitioners join me in teaching on it, largely pro bono. Cumulatively, hundreds of people from around the world have taken it: in the process I have learned a lot, distilled into this chapter.

commercial extraction is a slow process, so by 2023 many poor societies were at last on the threshold of potential transformation. Should they cross that threshold, or should the resources stay in the ground?

Extinction Rebellion and other climate activists are rightly concerned that if all the carbon-based fuels already discovered were to be burnt, our planet would be in trouble. Carbon emissions would far exceed levels consistent with environmental sustainability. But from that undeniable fact, there is an immediate leap to impassioned advocacy for a policy that is deeply unethical: that all unexploited fuel should be left in the ground. This might sound quite sensible at first, but in fact it would be grotesquely unfair. The carbon fuels yet to be extracted belong mainly to poor countries; those already in process of extraction belong mainly to rich ones. Leaving unexploited natural resources untapped inflicts the largest burden of losses on those least able to bear them. The question that climate activists should be asking is *whose* carbon fuels like oil and coal should be left in the ground? Should it be those of the rich, or those of the poor? Once posed, the question virtually answers itself: the list should be headed by the richest carbon-emitters like America's oil, Germany's coal and the gas of Qatar. To the extent that oil and gas still need to be used, they should come from those poorer, resource-rich countries that are able to use them well.

Paradoxically, the most politically sensitive form of carbon fuel is the least valuable: coal. For economists, the case for closing coal first, then oil and only finally gas, is self-evident.[1] But closing it would hit some left-behind communities very hard. The mining jobs provide well-paid work in places where such jobs are scarce. To reap the environmental benefits of closing coal mines without wrecking these disadvantaged communities, new well-paid jobs are needed to replace them. Generating those jobs is feasible, but costly. One option is to raise taxes, as Chancellor Kohl did, but our politicians lack the courage to persuade voters. Another option is that environmentalists accept more gas production in return for the big environmental benefits from closing down the coal industry, while gas producers pay for the new jobs in return for being allowed to produce the extra gas. Dogmatic environmentalists and greedy producers of coal and gas frustrate that way forward, each preferring a high-noon shoot-out.

Left-behind countries in Africa with valuable but unexploited carbon fuels face a similar blockage. The fact that Africa had before 2000 discovered so little of its natural resource wealth has a further implication for public policies. *There must have been major weaknesses in the discovery process.* One of them is a conundrum termed the time–consistency problem.

Suppose that the president of an African government is desperate for revenues. He invites Mega-Oil to prospect the country's virgin territory: it is geologically terra incognita. The chances of finding anything sufficiently valuable to justify the huge costs of search and extraction are consequently negligible. Even with the best geological information money can buy, the chances of a commercially viable strike are only one in nine; in unknown territory they are far lower. Suppose that Mega-Oil's best guesstimate is that there is a one-in-a-hundred chance of finding a field worth $1 billion. Now suppose, less plausibly, that Mega-Oil makes a mathematically fair offer of $10 million for the rights to this potential bonanza. The CEO of Mega-Oil should be dismissed by his board because he is dangerously naive.

To bring the problem out as clearly as possible, I have imagined only two possible outcomes: one is that Mega-Oil finds nothing, in which case the CEO has lost not only $10 million but the much larger costs of the search. The other outcome is that the company strikes it lucky: it finds oil worth $1 billion. What might then happen? The president is now revealed as having parted with $1 billion of this impoverished country's assets for a payment of only $10 million. In that case, someone is going to cry foul. If neither the president nor Mega-Oil are widely trusted, the suspicion will circulate that Mega-Oil knew in advance it would find something and bribed the president to sign the deal. To defend himself against the smear, the president accuses Mega-Oil of deceit. Recriminations abound and the contract that was so misconceived becomes impossible to honour. Quite properly, what is happening here is that sociopolitical notions of justice and fairness make any market for such high-risk investment in discovery unviable.

The problem can readily be addressed by pertinent government action. The president should spend some money gathering geological information. As evidence of the country's valuable but hidden resources builds up, the prices offered by companies will rise considerably, so contracts can become fairer and therefore viable. This is what the government of Nova Scotia did: by spending just $15 million on a modern geological survey, it unleashed commercial investments in prospecting. They revealed huge fields of oil and gas which have substantially enhanced people's incomes and opportunities.*

Another common weakness in the discovery process is missing regulation. Suppose the country gets enough promising though rudimentary geological information that Mega-Oil, Global Petroleum and Oil-is-Us each buy a prospect. The new CEO of Mega-Oil is wily. The prospecting rights have been cheap because the geology is still only sketchy. But he proposes that the company waits before spending the much bigger bucks required for drilling a well. Global Petroleum and Oil-is-Us have bought the other plots. If either of them sinks a well and finds something, Mega-Oil should also drill: if neither company finds anything, Mega-Oil should not waste its money. But the new CEO is not as smart as he thinks: Global Petroleum and Oil-is-Us reach the same conclusion, so no drilling happens. The loser is the country: inadvertently, by selling these rights it has frozen the search process.

Again, the problem can readily be addressed by government: companies acquiring prospecting rights need to be regulated. They

---

* In 2011, I persuaded the World Bank to lend money cheaply to African governments wanting to finance a geological survey. Given the current passions and influence of the major Western governments, it is now inconceivable that the Bank would finance such surveys.

should be required to drill to an agreed timetable, and to share the resulting new geological information with the government. But the poor record of regulation makes clear its limitations: governments with little regulatory capacity should reserve it for essentials like this one.

Auctions are another potent gadget in the hands of a government. The companies specializing in resource extraction know far more about the true value of a prospect than the government. By pitting them against each other, an auction reveals to the government their estimate of its worth. Auctions can also be tweaked to phase the process of prospecting, first to sell off just a few plots to properly regulated pioneer prospectors. As the geological evidence from their exploration builds up, the prices bid in subsequent rounds will rise.

Taxing the economic rents

If Mega-Oil has found oil through a well-regulated auction, so far so good. But from now on, the benefits for anyone other than Mega-Oil depend upon effective taxation. Taxation is in the government's hands, but it faces three hurdles: designing the tax rates; getting enough information from the companies; and guarding against corruption.

How Norway beat Britain*

The importance and difficulties of tax design are dramatically illustrated by comparing Britain and Norway. The two countries share the rights to oil and gas in the North Sea and, by chance, the quantities extracted have been almost identical. Yet the tax revenues collected per barrel have averaged $33 for Norway but only $11 for

---

* British readers at risk from high blood pressure are advised to skip this section.

Britain.* My inclination was to draw a veil over this astounding incompetence, but my incredulous editors have insisted that I set out the embarrassing detail. It takes us back to the three defining characteristics of Britain's Treasury: its obsessive short-termism; its reliance upon inexperienced juniors straight from university; and its hermetic paranoia against expertise. Desperate each year to find more revenue, senior officials order juniors to increase tax on the oil companies, and so the tax regime is ostensibly tightened. On average, over fifty years it has been changed every two years, making it one of the least stable in the world. Confronted by these fidgety changes, the oil companies counter with armies of specialist tax lawyers who easily sidestep the ill-informed efforts of the young Treasury amateurs. In contrast, Norway has a dedicated, stable and highly specialist team of forty professionals. Further, unlike Britain, it established a national oil company in competition with the oil majors, using the experience gained from it to understand the industry from the inside.

For poor societies with a valuable natural resource this should be very encouraging. Like them, until the twentieth century, Norway was a colony. It is a small country and until the discovery of oil it was quite poor. In comparison with Britain's Treasury, its Ministry of Finance was a minnow. Every country with natural resources can afford to build a team of forty civil servants who learn about the resource they are aiming to tax.

Slippery accounting

The lack of industry knowledge exemplified by Britain's Treasury is a small instance of the larger problem of unequal information. At its root is the fact that the pertinent economic concept – the surplus of value over cost generated by natural resource extraction – is not a concept recognized by accountants. The details of accounting are tricky. Confusion arises because of the difference between this

* The data I use run from 1971 through to 2017.

surplus, known as *resource rent*, and a profit. Once oil has been discovered, it can be extracted for about $2 per barrel. But for an oil company to remain viable, it must also recover the costs of discovery, including raising the risk-bearing finance to cover the eight dry wells it typically needs to sink for each strike that is commercially viable – even with the best geological information. Once the oil is in the company's hands it can sell it on the market, the price in late 2023 being around $90 a barrel. Since $2 is the operating cost of extraction and $20 covers the true costs of discovery, this leaves $68 as the *resource rent*. But accountants writing their annual report on the company's finances will show the operating cost as $2, revenues as $90, and profit as $88. The two different concepts befuddle ideas about who should get what. The resource rent should belong to the government, on behalf of its citizens. The proper return to the company should be the $22 that is enough to attract it to discover and extract the oil. Instead, companies negotiate over sharing the $88 'fairly', as if $44 each would be the reasonable benchmark. They genuinely think it fair to keep twice as much as they should really be getting.

Bad as that is, it gets worse because competition drives many companies into being greedy: profit turns out to be surprisingly elastic when stretched by company accountants. Further clouding the picture to the advantage of the resource companies, the company registered for tax purposes will be a local subsidiary, such as Mega-Oil-Chad. That subsidiary will sell its crude oil either to the parent company, or to another subsidiary such as Mega-Oil-Antilles. Mega-Oil-Antilles will pay Mega-Oil-Chad an internally agreed 'transfer price'. The lower the transfer price, the more profit can be shifted from Chad to Antilles. Similarly, Mega-Oil-Chad will, quite legitimately, buy services and borrow finance from its parent, or from another subsidiary, and again these will be priced.* The upshot is that profits can be shifted from high-tax

---

* International companies specializing in resource extraction are not intrinsically evil. On the contrary, they are intrinsically valuable: they develop sophisticated

countries to low-tax ones: the companies end up with even more than $44 per barrel. Since the profits from resource extraction include that resource rent, they need to be taxed much more heavily than the profits of other types of company. Chad will need to impose high profits taxes, but this incentivizes profit-shifting, and oil companies are very good at that. For example, Chevron, a US oil major, kept its vast profits from its Angolan subsidiary parked in a tax-haven for years, waiting for a president who would let them bring the money to America tax free: President Trump fulfilled its dream.*

To combat this, the capacity to observe what is taxed can be strengthened: an effective way of building the capacity to observe is to learn from success. The OECD already has a useful programme called Tax Inspectors without Borders. It seconds tax inspectors from OECD countries to work in the tax departments of poor countries. An improvement would be to make the arrangement reciprocal and apply it to *teams* of inspectors instead of just individuals. Ghanaian staff dealing with oil taxation could periodically exchange roles with their Norwegian counterparts.

---

specialist capabilities useful in places that lack them. The large ones have diversified activities that enable them to finance the huge upfront costs of extraction cheaply, despite high risks. They have the potential to bring massive benefits to poor societies and many of the people working in them are highly motivated to do so. But the companies face big temptations, and sometimes succumb to them.
* Profit-shifting is not confined to resource extraction. Here is a chilling story from the world's favourite coffee company. For ten years, Starbucks sold billions of cups of coffee in Britain, yet it never made any taxable profits. It appeared to be run as a charity, providing coffee at cost to a grateful public. Gratitude would have been misplaced: Starbucks (UK) had shifted all its profits to Starbucks (Netherlands Antilles). As the company indignantly said when this was revealed, it had paid all taxes due in the Netherlands Antilles. Somehow, it forgot to mention that the corporate tax rate there was zero. Such profit-shifting is entirely avoidable by effective government action.

Corruption and how to counter it

Some large resource companies are all too willing to sink into corruption. Beny Steinmetz, the owner of a huge mining company and a tax exile from Israel living in Switzerland, was sentenced to three years in jail, having been convicted by a Swiss court. His company had bribed the wife of an African president who had induced her dying husband to sign an indefensible contract days before his death giving Steinmetz's companies valuable rights to mine iron ore. In return for a few million dollars in bribes, Steinmetz gained 'the deal of the century', as an astonished press dubbed it. He appealed his conviction, which was upheld, and has appealed that verdict too.

Once politicians control how resource revenues are spent their patronage becomes more valuable: crooked businesses will offer bribes. Worse, once crooks realize how profitable political office has become, they use their resources to get elected, undermining the electoral process.[2] Additionally, the large revenues from taxing resource extraction tempt politicians to reduce taxes on voters, who then have less incentive to scrutinize how government spends its money. In this way, resource revenues menace good governance twice over. But the menace can readily be overcome; although Norway is an oil-rich democracy, voters have accepted taxes that are among the highest in the world. This, in turn, has underpinned intense scrutiny of how all public money is used. Public acceptance has been built through intelligent communication by government.

The key task has been to persuade voters that since oil extraction is inherently unsustainable, it is wise to accumulate much of the revenues in a national fund. The fund was launched in 1990 but initially provoked popular pressure to spend revenues more quickly. The government realized that it needed to communicate more effectively and spotted an effective analogy. The long-term savings decision with which the typical voter is most familiar is contributing to a pension. Once the government started referring to the accumulated oil money as the national pension fund, people soon grasped why saving was wise.

Norway's oil fund, like Botswana's diamonds fund, was built on the bedrock of effective communication combined with rules and institutions. The rules tell public officials how revenues should normally be handled. The institutions are specialist teams of officials empowered by a mandate and motivated by an important public purpose. Between them they have provided effective checks and balances against corruption. Since natural resources increase the pressures to be corrupt, such checks and balances are vitally important. Inevitably, if public officials are corrupted, they push back against checks and balances. In Norway and Botswana, the checks and balances were put in place sufficiently soon after the resource discoveries that officials were not corrupted. But looking at all the countries in which resources have been discovered since 1970, in the thirty following years it is more typical to see checks and balances undermined.[3] Effective governance is a struggle that needs to be won, society by society. Without it, natural resource wealth actually *reduces* long-term growth.[4]

Dealing fairly with the locals

The process of resource extraction is unlikely to bring many direct benefits to local communities. But it is likely to inflict costs. The most vulnerable affected communities are geographically peripheral. The subsoil natural resources in a country could be anywhere, and most are remote from big cities. Consequently, oil and mining companies have learnt to run self-sufficient operations that do not interact with the locality – *enclaves*. Oil and gas extraction have never generated many jobs, and with new technologies neither does mining. The work is skilled, and local people are not equipped to do it.

Nevertheless, there are plenty of ways to create mutual benefits for local communities, governments, citizens and companies.

Especially in remote places, the company will need to generate electricity for its own operations. By building more generating capacity than it needs, a company can run a local grid, selling the electricity to the local community at a price that covers the small extra cost incurred. This can dramatically change local business opportunities and improve well-being – a practical example is that households, clinics and local firms find themselves able to run fridges: cool stores can transform opportunities for local farmers to get fresh food to market. Similarly, the resource company will need road and perhaps rail connections. By designing them so they also serve the local community, further opportunities are opened for local people. Local government can benefit from new tax revenues from the company, and the growth of the local economy. At the national level, there is scope for benefits beyond just the extra tax revenues. There may be opportunities for skilling up local companies so that they can be suppliers. In Nigeria, a global oil company worked with a local firm for years, helping it to manufacture pipes that met international standards. Now the firm not only supplies the oil company but exports its pipes internationally. Sometimes it is possible to add value to the resource being extracted before it is shipped out. In Indonesia, the government succeeded in diversifying the economy: it pump-primed a major plywood industry by requiring the logging companies to sell their wood locally.

Local damage and how to avoid it

Such benefits are vital because both locally and nationally there are costs. At the local level, extraction is a messy process: oil pipes leak, mines create waste, and trucking fleets bring disturbance and diseases spread through sex workers. Local people are often not in a position to do much about this damage other than suffer it.

In April 2010, the oil rig Deepwater Horizon exploded, spewing oil into the Gulf of Mexico. BP, the company responsible, spent $500 million to commission independent studies on who had suffered and by how much. It realized that the best outcome BP could possibly hope for in American law courts was to accept liability for the true cost of the damage. They feared that otherwise American lawyers would have an incentive to exaggerate the damage, incentivized by no-win-no-fee claims in which they received half of any award. Across the Atlantic Ocean in the Gulf of Guinea there have been repeated major spills, but the companies responded rather differently. For many years, one of the major oil companies managed the consequences of spills through its public relations department. Instead of seeking to reduce spillages, it tried to manipulate how news was reported in the press. It took decades of mounting local anger before that line of management responsibility was changed.* Understandably, in the absence of redress, anger had turned into vengeance. Local gangs had formed, kidnapping oil workers and ransoming them. The gangs became predatory and wreaked huge damage, blowing up pipelines and corrupting local politicians. The companies ended up paying heavily for their negligence. This could have been averted if they had shown the same ethical decency of which nearly all of us are capable in our ordinary lives. For managers to devote some resources to reducing damaging oil spillages should not depend on the menace of lawsuits. Nor should establishing an effective way of compensating people for the inevitable accidents. Local communities suffering oil spills in the Gulf of Guinea had lacked legitimate means of protecting their interests. They were failed both by the companies and by their governments.†

Since the local community is not the only group in society with legitimate interests in resource extraction, there needs to be some government-provided forum. Local communities in which resources are found have strong claims to compensation for any damage, and for participation in the benefits. But there is no fixed formula. Successful resource extraction depends upon a prior

---

* I was fortunate to get information of this quality, but the price paid for it is confidentiality regarding my authoritative source.

† I do not regard the American legal system as a solution because it is hugely costly and introduces many perverse incentives.

process of bringing communities together with some sense of shared purpose. But even in more united societies, local communities can become greedy. In 2012 Tanzania discovered offshore gas, and the government invited me in for advice. I warned of these dangers, but my hosts reminded me of Julius Nyerere's most valuable legacy. 'Nyerere taught us to think of ourselves as Tanzanians; since it's offshore, it's obvious that the gas belongs to all of us.' Yet within six months, in the region closest to the find, youths were rioting and chanting, 'It's Mtwara's gas.' Four of them died as police struggled to subdue the crowds. In Tanzania's peaceful society this was unprecedented. In retrospect, the head of the civil service viewed his failure to anticipate and manage this risk as the government's single biggest mistake.*

The pre-source curse

Places like Mtwara are now said to suffer from the *pre-source curse*. Once a discovery becomes known, popular expectations leap ahead of any immediately feasible benefits. The gas field discovered off the East African coast in 2012 extended to Kenyan waters. Shortly after Kenyans learned of it, I met their Minister of Finance. Far from looking hopeful, he was a very worried man: within weeks a euphoric civil service union had lodged a demand for a large wage increase. Many fields turn out not to be commercially viable: in those discovered by companies controlled by unscrupulous mavericks the

---

* British readers may recognize the parallels with North Sea oil, discovered in 1966. As in Tanzania, it was offshore, in a country called the United Kingdom: a 300-year-old union of Scotland with England and Wales. A tiny Scottish nationalist party adopted the clever slogan 'It's Scotland's oil' and over subsequent decades grew to become Scotland's dominant party. Recent statistical research has established a causal connection from changes in the world price of oil to changes in the SNP vote share. Since between 1966 and 2000 the oil price rose from $3 to more than $100, the fluctuations were around a strongly increasing trend. Nobody asked why, since Yorkshire's coal had been nationalized for the benefit of everyone in Britain, offshore oil should benefit only a tenth of the population.

potential is often exaggerated. A maverick's goal is to boost the price of shares, then quietly offload them. He makes a killing, the government gets a headache and, seeing no benefit, voters conclude that their government has embezzled the non-existent windfall. Most astonishing of all, the euphoria turns out to be shared by the IMF. In response to discoveries, it raises its forecasts of growth to unrealistic levels. Given its authority, the government and capital markets believe these forecasts – the markets offer loans more willingly and the government borrows commercially, only to find itself over-indebted.[5]

The little nation of São Tomé and Principe graphically illustrates the combination of local greed and the pre-source curse. It consists of two islands, with 96 per cent of the population living on São Tomé. In 1997 there were preliminary indications of offshore oil and gas, and the IMF was concerned about exchange-rate mismanagement.* No oil or gas has ever been found. But the prospect was enough to trigger community greed. Early indications were that the field would be offshore, but closer to Principe: its inhabitants claimed the expected oil for themselves. An outcome in which 4,000 citizens effortlessly became rich while 130,000 of their fellow citizens remained paupers would have been a travesty of justice, not a triumph of local rights. Next, the government sold prospecting rights, raising about $60 million. Since nothing has since been found, this one-off payment amounting to only $440 per citizen was the entirety of the windfall: hardly a future of effortless wealth. But the news that the government was getting the mesmerizing sum of $60 million, together with the tantalizing prospect of a discovery, was enough for local people to catch the pre-source curse in full measure. Voters expected big benefits but received only trivial ones. They told themselves that the discrepancy was due to government corruption. People were not entirely wrong – Pedro Vicente, a brilliant

---

* The IMF team generously invited me to join their mission. Once I researched the situation, I suggested that the risk of exchange-rate appreciation was peripheral to the issues that the government would face and so declined.

young researcher in my team, gathered clear evidence that public officials had themselves been infected by euphoria and the widespread presumption that other officials must be looting the public purse. Licensed to be bad by this imagined looting, many officials had indeed become more corrupt.[6]

Greed is not good

These dangers of violence and corruption due to local resentments and the pre-source curse are compounded by the stronger force of predatory greed. A remote region may have been peaceful because of its poverty. Once valuable resources are being extracted, the situation changes dramatically. Following discoveries, gangs form to prey on the economic activity by looting or extorting. They use part of the money they raise to buy guns and recruit fighters, even creating no-go areas in which the state can no longer provide security.[7] This can be averted, but again it requires action well ahead of any extraction.

In 2012 the government of Colombia devolved a share of oil revenues to the localities from which oil was extracted. Where local government was already weak, drugs gangs diversified into an extortion racket against the politicians. Those that did not become the pawns of the gangs were murdered and replaced by more compliant alternatives. Devolving big money to weak places proved disastrous.[8] In contrast, where local government was already effective, the new money was better used than when decisions had been taken in Bogotá: it was being spent by officials who were locally based, better informed and accountable to local voters.

Visiting Burma, I was invited to an intriguing lunch with a self-confessed former guerrilla leader who wanted to tell me how he had run his business. His gang controlled an area of forest. By felling trees and transporting them across the border to Thailand they earned dollars; with the dollars they bought Kalashnikovs to be able to control more forest. He told me the precise formula of tree acreage per hundred Kalashnikovs. To his great credit he quit, realizing that the violence and destruction his business inflicted had become the antithesis of its purported goals.

If a country is at risk of being endangered by resource extraction, delaying prospecting can buy the time needed to build effective defences. This was the wise policy of Meles Zenawi, who led the government of Ethiopia from 1991 up to his death in 2012. He recognized that Ethiopia was extremely fragile and prone to violent conflict and saw that a resource discovery was likely to be divisive. His strategy was gradually to build state capacity before prospecting: better to maintain a veil of ignorance over which regions had the resource endowments. Only when approaching his death in 2012 did he become interested in the potential of resource extraction as a source of revenue. By then he had embarked on an ambitious national programme of economic infrastructure to connect the country to world markets, so resource wealth would have attractive uses.

Using the revenues

Norway now wisely saves some of its resource revenues in foreign assets held in a sovereign wealth fund. But it waited two decades before doing so. During those first decades the revenues were ploughed into infrastructure and education that while sometimes profligate was transformative.* The government of Botswana also has a sovereign wealth fund, but it too used the first decades of revenues for infrastructure and education. That sequence of investing locally followed by saving abroad in a sovereign fund was sensible given the Norwegian and Botswanan contexts: they both reached the limits of how their large revenues could be used productively by their small workforces. In contrast, most resource discoveries in

---

* One unanticipated but valuable fruit of its lavish vocational training was the work of Karl-Ove Knausgaard, whose books, initially state subsidized, became a global publishing phenomenon.

poor and middle-income countries are modest relative to their large workforces and so best invested domestically.

For many years, the IMF favoured sovereign wealth funds even for small discoveries in poor countries with large workforces and vast needs. It justified saving the money abroad because poor countries had little 'absorptive capacity'. This was international-agency language for three capacities that were often missing. Government would be unable to manage an expanded public investment programme; the financial sector would be unable to manage an expanded private investment programme; and the corporate sector would be unable to manage rapid growth because of the paucity of firms professionally managed and legally registered. These concerns of the IMF are often reasonable, but the remedy should be to build the capacities.* Until a left-behind country (or region) does so, it cannot transform. Governments can learn how to manage public investment by experiment and by learning from others. Central banks, often the most capable part of the public sector, can learn how to strengthen the financial sector. Corporate capacity can be built by attracting foreign businesses from which local firms can learn.[9]

Although these capacities can be built, they cannot be created instantly. Until they are in place, the resource revenues should indeed be parked abroad, to be brought back once capacities are strong enough for the money to be well used. The IMF is belatedly building objective, publicly accessible measures of these capacities, to help governments and their citizens judge when they are in place. For resource-rich countries the decision is complicated by large short-term fluctuations in the price of their resource.

The finance minister needs to monitor three different time frames. As on a dashboard, she needs three clocks tracking

---

* Economic modellers also favoured this IMF strategy, invoking a separation theorem between the savings decision and the investment decision. This rests on the assumptions that a poor country can borrow and lend as much as it likes at 'the world interest rate', and that the risks to foreign investors are identical to the risks facing the government and private investors. Neither assumption is warranted.

different concerns. One tracks the price of the resource: the oil price, for example, is notoriously volatile: in recent years it has bounced between $10 and $140 per barrel, producing wild swings in revenues. If public spending in an oil-rich country mirrors fluctuations in revenue, it will be chaotic. Indeed, it can be worse than chaotic.

When revenues are high, the government might make spending commitments such as higher wages for civil servants (or employing more of them) that cannot swiftly be reversed when the oil price falls. Other spending must then be cut. Politicians will then look for the spending cuts that minimize protest, and those will be the investment programmes in economic infrastructure. So, as revenues bounce up and down, there is a ratchet effect in which public spending on civil servants rises, offset by plummeting infrastructure investment. At one stage, Nigeria found that this ratchet had left its public sector wage bill so high that it used up the entirety of its revenues. That is by no means atypical. Astonishingly, on average in resource-rich countries, public investment ends up lower than in countries without natural resources.[10]

The world leader in managing such wild swings in resource revenues is Chile. Andrés Velasco, the finance minister who pioneered the new approach, and Eric Parrado, who built the sovereign fund, which was the key new institution, were its architects. The core idea is simple: if resource prices are volatile, then estimate a long-term average. In Chile, the key resource is copper, so when copper prices are above the long-term average all the revenues above that price are saved abroad in a stabilization fund and brought back to be spent in Chile when the price of copper falls and revenues with it. Since it is not possible to bring back assets until you own some, Velasco, then finance minister, realized that the plan had to be launched when copper prices were atypically high. The short-term political consequences for him were cataclysmic: he was depicted as heartless and brutal. Why, when there were acute social needs, was money from the bonanza of high copper prices being placed abroad? He was denounced by opponents, there were mass demonstrations, and he had to explain to his young children why he was being burnt in effigy in the streets.

Meanwhile, Parrado set up the fund, buying only assets that would hold their value when copper prices collapsed. Whether Velasco would have survived his critics we will never know, because suddenly world copper prices crashed, and almost overnight he became a national hero. He was able to explain to parliament that spending plans could continue to be fully implemented because the assets held abroad were now going to be sold. So, managing volatility is feasible, but it takes political courage and good fortune. Ngozi Okonjo-Iweala, currently the head of the World Trade Organization, twice served as Nigeria's finance minister. When first appointed, in 2003, she immediately prioritized overcoming the volatility problem and adopted a variant of Velasco's approach: she suffered the same outbursts of angry denunciation. A brilliant communicator, she used the analogy of 'saving for a rainy day'. It was appropriate for the Nigerian context, and the best that her political opponents could muster against it was 'It's raining now!' In the battle for persuasion, she was able to face them down.

In her second period as finance minister Okonjo-Iweala prioritized a longer timeframe of depletion and obsolescence. Depletion is inevitable for resources like oil: at some point a well runs dry. For the boost to living standards to be sustainable, much of these unsustainable revenues should be invested in assets. Ngozi inherited a budget in which this was not happening: the revenues were being spent on subsidizing petrol. Opposing her, groups that should never have been allies came together to prevent the price being raised. Subsidized petrol had been a gift for those looting the nation's resources. Small crooks bought subsidized petrol and smuggled it out of the country; mega-crooks made big money from fictional trades. Had Nigerians understood what was going on, they would have accepted the removal of the modest benefits they were getting from subsidized petrol in return for larger benefits in a form less susceptible to being looted by crooks. There was an acute shortage of productive jobs for young Nigerians because public investment had been squeezed out by the petrol subsidies. Eliminating them should not have provoked protests, but even though Okonjo-Iweala personally had earned the citizens' trust, the government had not. The mega-crooks and their allies in the government pre-empted the possibility of a political package in which most people would have gained more than they lost. The price increase was announced, but not by Okonjo-Iweala. While she was out of the country, her opponents within the government announced the end of subsidies without any compensating measures. In a campaign likely pre-planned, agitators brought disaffected young people onto the streets. The president ordered a retreat, and she lost the battle.

But it was a battle that had to be won. In his inaugural speech to the nation in May 2023 the newly elected president of Nigeria, Bola Tinubu, bit the bullet once again and announced the removal of petrol subsidies. As one of the successful former governors of Lagos, he had understood that freeing up revenues for public investment was vital. The media were astonished and critical that he told the nation about the immediate withdrawal of the petrol subsidy only by departing from his written text, as if it had been a last-minute whim. I suspect the president knew that if he had circulated the written text in advance, it would have been leaked, and those who gained from the continued subsidy would have organized protests to block it, as had happened before. The best time to commit to a better future strategy is at the very beginning of newly acquired presidential authority.

In Zambia the battle to invest the revenues from copper mining had been fought and lost in the 1970s. Instead, the government had subsidized urban consumers: Lusaka had become a city of consumption. A Zambian friend reflected: 'When the copper is gone, what will our children say about us?'

The need to invest to offset depletion is reinforced by obsolescence. In Chile listening to the views of others is seen as normal, so in 2015 I was invited to advise on natural resource management. Since in my view Chile already had world-class policies for volatility, I focused on the long term. Depletion looked to be a non-issue: Chile was sitting on vast amounts of copper, so I focused on obsolescence. Global demand for copper depended upon one thing: copper wires conducting electricity. I suggested that it was unlikely that in a century our cars and computers would still need copper wires: if so, copper would become obsolescent. When this would happen could not be forecast, but once it did, copper would permanently lose much of its value. In consequence, Chile needed to convert some of its copper revenues into productive assets.[11] My co-presenter illustrated my argument with examples from Chilean history. In the late nineteenth century, Chile had been the world leader in guano, a natural nitrate, so much so that half of all government revenues came from taxes on nitrate exports. But in 1920 a German chemist discovered how to synthesize nitrates and the world price collapsed, never to recover: Chilean finances were devasted. The message was: 'We should not have forgotten our own history. We need to take this advice.' Depletion and obsolescence warn us to invest resource revenues; and there is a policy rule that could reconcile political feasibility with ethical behaviour: start modestly, but gradually increase the share of revenues invested. 'God make me good, but not yet' is overcome by 'God make me a little better each day': an ethical policy of which voters may approve.*

The final timeframe over which the minister should be tracking progress is whether the capacities to invest are being strengthened: the process of investing in investing. It enables a left-behind society that is resource-rich like Nigeria to reverse its downward spiral. Once these capacities are objectively measured, both minister and civil society can benchmark subsequent progress against backsliding, making it easier to improve. By standardizing the

---

* The policy of gradually increasing the share of revenues invested is doubly ethical. Using more of the revenues for consumption now is justifiable partly because the next generation is likely to be better off than the present one: it will benefit from the rocket of resource wealth. Further, as the absorptive capacities to use the revenue for investment get stronger, it makes sense to use a smaller share of the revenues for current consumption.

measure internationally, each society can also compare itself to its neighbours and sometimes learn from them. That is why the recent Public Investment Management Assessment of the IMF is a valuable contribution. It measures four different aspects of the capacity to manage public investment and needs to become better known.*

Many countries that are now rich launched their historic ascent out of poverty by managing some sort of resource extraction successfully. An early phase of resource-fuelled growth was followed by diversification into a modern multisector economy, so that many have now forgotten the origins of their prosperity. Modern Britain was launched by the extraction of coal and iron, modern California and Australia by the extraction of gold and modern New York by the capture of the resource rents on oil.

The complexities of resource extraction are real enough, but they are worth mastering because the prize is so spectacular. Just as Botswana used diamonds to become the world's fastest-growing economy, many left-behind places blessed with hidden resource wealth could catch up with the rest of mankind in a single generation. New geological information on the minerals needed for batteries suggest that Tanzania and Malawi possess unrealized treasure troves. Uganda has oil that although costly to extract is still well worth it at prevailing world prices. South Sudan has abundant oil and Mauritania has both oil and minerals. All these societies are currently mired in poverty, yet their untapped resources could be transformative if managed well.

There are many potentially useful distinctive technocratic gadgets such as building institutions that collate geological survey data, tax resource extraction and manage sovereign funds. But only if

---

* The Public Investment Management Assessment (PIMA) rates the capacities for design, selection, implementation and evaluation of public projects. It was pioneered by an African American with expertise in Africa. The capacities of West African governments differ so much that although all are weak overall, if each learned from the best for each capacity they would be among the best in the world.

they are complemented by equally distinctive social and political gadgets do they work. The geological institution depends on being financed and enforced; the taxation depends on being staffed with motivated specialists; the sovereign funds depend on being protected from plunder by a subsequent government. In turn, each depends to some extent on the support and patience of citizens. With limited capacities it is not possible to build all these gadgets at once. Nor is it necessary, since what matters changes over time: that is why the three clocks are useful.

In resource-rich poor countries, the state is usually familiar with neither the technocratic nor the complementary social and political gadgets. Some of the technocratic gadgets are brought by the two powerful external influences that arrive hard on the heels of natural resource discoveries – the IMF and the companies. The staff of the IMF are economists trained in the complexities of macro-economic modelling. The staff of the corporations are predominantly geologists. But neither is trained in the complementary social and political gadgets without which the technocratic ones often fizzle out.

So, if the value of a country's resources is to be unlocked, the opening priority is to identify the sequence in which missing vital capacities of the state will be needed. That sequence needs to be appropriate for the ambitions and context of the society and so has to be chosen by it. Having identified the sequence, the capacities then need to be catalysed. We have arrived at the Sinews of the State. Building them is the agenda for the people of any poor but resource-rich country: the president and her team, the civil servants, the business community and the organizations of civil society.

Building the Sinews of the State

No society can prosper without a state. There is an irreducible core of functions to be done by government – both at the national level for entire countries that have been left behind, and at the local level for left-behind regions – without which no society can thrive.*

At the start of spiralling up, the capacities for governing that will be needed may have atrophied or never existed. So, the first steps should be undemanding – not requiring those capacities that are lacking. Yet they should be liberating, and begin to strengthen those capacities that are urgently needed. The priority is to build those functions that can *only* be done by the state: they can neither be imported nor provided by the private sector or NGOs. The importance of identifying the few capacities that fit those criteria – what will be the sinews of the state – has been overlooked.† I will focus on two of these sinews that, as they are built, commonly accelerate spiralling up. The foundational capacity is taxation: until a government is raising its own revenues, it lacks agency: money from all other sources comes with strings. The admirably inclusive government of Somaliland would not have been permitted to spend half its budget on security had it been dependent on donors.

---

* This was why, in the story of the Las Vegas billionaires told in Chapter 2, their escape visions were aptly called *fantasies*. In the event of global disorder, there is no contract by which a yacht-bound billionaire can incentivize the security staff to protect him rather than seize the yacht for themselves.
† Readers familiar with critical path analysis can think of the problem as a shrunken version of CPA modified for radical uncertainty. The critical path is not planned through to the end but only for the first few steps. Transitions are too uncertain to warrant grand plans for thirty years.

Yet to meet its immediate needs, a national security force was vital, and this is indeed usually the second of the sinews, and a precondition for accessing the potential wealth of natural resources.

Taxation and security: these I think of as the bedrock of the state. Without taxation the state is impotent; that it should protect its citizens through 'a monopoly of violence' has long been recognized as crucial. There are many other functions of the state that are desirable, and some can be built in parallel. But many left-behind countries and regions are not yet even providing these two essentials. Examples of similar places that are already succeeding can inspire societies to embark on renewal and demonstrate how they might go about it.

The capacity to tax

In Uganda in 1986 the state revenues from tax were a mere 6 per cent of national income, a level at which no functioning state was viable. Yoweri Museveni had just seized power through a well-organized rebel movement, but he initially lacked broad-based popular legitimacy. Many people in Kampala identified more closely with the pre-colonial kingdom of Buganda, whose king, the Kabaka, had been exiled by Idi Amin. To heal rifts, President Museveni wisely allowed the king to return. To provide an income for his position, the Kabaka sent his own, unauthorized, tax collectors into the street markets, in competition with the official tax collectors of President Museveni's new government. Traders willingly paid the Kabaka, but they hid their incomes from the official tax collectors.

Recent research on taxation illuminates why the Kabaka was able to raise taxes without having recourse to any legal enforcement mechanism: an explanation with powerful implications. Leander Heldring, now working at Northwestern University with Jim Robinson of the University of Chicago, has kindly summarized their recent joint research on Rwanda: it bears closely on the analogous deep historical roots of the Kabaka's practical legitimacy.* The formal capacity of the Rwandan state was not as important as had been expected. What mattered was whether people had learnt to cooperate with other people for common purposes, and from that had been able to take the further step to cooperate with purposes promoted by governments. Historically, the Rwandan state had gradually expanded from a core. Leander discovered a strong correlation between big public voluntary efforts – manifestations of willing compliance – and how long a locality had been within the authority of the state. People living in the original core of the pre-colonial state were most compliant with government agendas, while in other areas compliance steadily declined as the duration of their state membership shortened. Robinson and Heldring also attribute a successful agricultural transformation of rapidly rising food yields in Rwanda to the voluntary efforts made largely in those parts of the country that were already part of Rwanda prior to colonialism. That same willing compliance with government purposes had been used by the Hutu extremists who had briefly controlled the state to mobilize people into genocide.[1]

So, traders may well have been willing to pay tax to the Kabaka because, like people in the core of the Rwandan state, history had slowly built habits of willing compliance. If our futures are determined by our past – or by our memories of it, perhaps 're-imagine your history' is the implication for left-behind places: it has sometimes been done. But that conclusion would be premature: can left-behind places develop habits of willing compliance more rapidly?

How Uganda increased tax revenues

In Uganda in the 1980s President Museveni evidently lacked practical legitimacy. He was also over-confident in his abilities beyond military command, ordering his officials to arrest inflation by

* I have also repeatedly learned from discussions with Jim Robinson, most recently in Oxford in late 2023.

revaluing the exchange rate. Emmanuel Tumusiimi-Mutebile, the technocrat told to implement this instruction, despite knowing that it was an elementary economic blunder, obeyed, but added, 'Permit me, Mr President, when you have to reverse this policy, to remind you that I advised against it.'* The president indeed had to reverse it, and similar mistakes continued for six years before he recognized that Tumusiimi-Mutebile, rather than his own cronies, had to be the authority over finance and planning. Once empowered, Tumusiimi-Mutebile established a new revenue authority and built a loyal team of staff there who modelled themselves on his own moral and workaholic standards.

By 2010, President Museveni wanted a further large increase in revenues, predominantly from Kampala, the booming capital city. Parliament created a new agency, the Kampala Capital City Authority, shifting power from the mayor, a patronage politician, to Jennifer Musisi, the KCCA's executive director. A protégé of Tumusiimi-Mutebile, strongly motivated and with deep technical experience, she began by sending dismissal notices to all the city's tax collectors: overall, their performance had been unimpressive. Instead, she created an independent Directorate of Revenue Collection within the KCCA, rehiring those collectors with relatively respectable reputations for competence and integrity. She saw that staff expectations of working practices had to be reset and so changed all the job descriptions – nobody went back to their previous job. About a hundred people work there, all becoming specialists with skills enhanced by monthly on-the-job training. The culture was transformed as people became proud to be working to a purpose. These organizational changes were complemented by a mass-education campaign in the city promoting tax payment as a mutual duty: a moral dimension pitched to Kampala's residents by linking it to a credible, forward-looking common purpose: paying your taxes

---

* I was a close friend of Governor Tumusiimi-Mutebile for thirty years and this is a personal story. He died in January 2022, while still in office. My obituary of him was published in the *Financial Times*, 5 January 2022.

builds a better city for all of us. Tax receipts in Kampala swiftly doubled.

What works in the early stages of tax capacity

We now know from recent research why tax increased so rapidly in Uganda. Partly it was that these astute practitioners had hit on some cognitive gadgets that are likely to work. In essence, Tumusiimi-Mutebile built a small but dedicated team of hard-working, mission-driven people, analogous to what Father José did in the Basque region. There, it had taken fourteen years to build a fully trained and committed team of five; after eighteen years, Tumusiimi-Mutebile had a somewhat larger group, and drew Jennifer Musisi from it to seed the new tax unit in the KCCA. Strongly motivated teams innovate until they find ways of achieving their goals. Ingenious recent research in the neighbouring Democratic Republic of the Congo demonstrates rigorously that key innovations of retaining only the best performers and concentrating them in a high-tax-payer unit worked there, as they had in the KCCA. Matching good tax collectors with each other introduces team-based norms of how to win respect and induces everyone to strive harder [2]

The Democratic Republic of the Congo offers another example of why devolving decisions to those with local knowledge is valuable. It compared the efficacy of using government-appointed officials to collect taxes with shifting the task to local chiefs, who were better plugged into gossip and similar sources of information. The chiefs increased revenue by over 40 per cent. They did so not by possessing greater legitimacy – as had enabled the Kabaka to raise tax – but by redirecting the tax collectors to those willing to pay, and timing the visits when they were most likely to have some money.[3] The core implication of this study is that there are some cognitive gadgets appropriate in a low-income society taking the first steps in building tax capacity that are utterly different from those applicable in well-functioning tax administrations. Another such gadget from the same team concerned tax rates levied on property owners.

Compliance was abysmally low: less than 6 per cent of the property owners receiving a tax demand actually paid it. By lowering the tax rate, the payment rate increased sufficiently that revenues rose. The lower rate made it more likely that the cash-on-hand of the property owner would be sufficient to pay the collector; essentially, clever research confirmed the adage: don't try to get blood out of a stone.*

New e-technologies can also help to raise revenues in the early stages of building capacity simply by linking GPS data to property ownership. A study in Ghana found that it enabled tax collectors to find out where the high-paying property owners lived and concentrated their efforts accordingly.† A technique that certainly would not be used in developed economies is paying collectors a bonus linked to the amount they raise. But at least in the short term it has proved effective in Pakistan.[4] We also know that tax evasion by firms can be reduced by improving scrutiny through third-party reporting of transactions.[5] None of these gadgets is transformative, but they all help raise money that is vital in states that would otherwise be terminally left behind.

The Democratic Republic of the Congo provides evidence of what being induced to pay some property tax to the city council does to the attitudes of those who pay. A tax campaign simply registered property owners and asked them to pay tax. Prior to the registration, only one in a thousand owners were paying tax: the registration campaign raised it to 116, still very low, though a dramatic increase for little effort. But the indirect effects of the campaign were more important and encouraging. Suddenly, these new taxpayers became interested in what their council was doing with their money. They took practical steps to find out and were far

---

* A. Bergeron, G. Tourek and J. L. Weigel, *The State Capacity Ceiling on Tax Rates: Evidence from randomi us tax abatements in the DRC*, NBER Working Paper 31685, September 2023.

† The research, supported by the International Growth Centre, is by L. Dzansi, A. Jensen, D. Lagakos and H. Telli, *Technology and Local State Capacity: Evidence from Ghana*, NBER Working Paper 29923, January 2022.

more likely to participate in town hall meetings and fill in evaluations of council performance. These were costly actions of political participation that *Homo Economicus* would not do: instead, the Congolese taxpayers were starting to behave as *citizens*. The effects were surprisingly large, increasing political participation by a third. Not only did people engage more with the local government, they became more positive towards it. The very fact that it was reaching out to them was seen as indicative of its competence. They also urged the government to improve its performance: there were early signs that people wanted a political deal – more tax in return for better services, as had been built in Lagos.[6]

This has three encouraging implications. One is that attitudes can be changed swiftly in the direction of increased compliance in paying taxes. A second is that the political effects are benign for local politicians, so that not only do they get more revenue, they go up in voters' assessment of their performance. A third is that although the revenue gains from the cognitive gadgets are modest, focusing on those that increase the proportion of people paying tax, its *incidence*, rather than just on extra revenue, can substantially accelerate early progress to inclusive governance.

There is also a more fundamental benign interaction between tax capacity and inclusive prosperity which continues throughout economic transformation, from the earliest steps in thin-state societies like the crashed Uganda of 1986, through unequal middle-income countries like Colombia, to the thick-state inclusive prosperity of Denmark. As the economy develops, its structure changes in ways that make tax collection easier. To reap the gains of scale and specialization, firms become larger and more formal. The workforce shifts from self-employment and microenterprises to wage employment in these formal firms. The records of these wage payments are far easier to tax than the unrecorded cash payments of the informal sector. The Uganda of 1986 struggled to increase taxes from 6 per cent of national income. It would have been impossible, regardless of tax capacity, to raise it to the 53 per cent of modern Denmark because the Ugandan economy of the time was almost entirely informal. This is the deadly combination of the thin state and a stag-nant economy from which Ugandans began to escape from the 1990s.[7] Willing compliance has a common feature which was appar-ent in the mundane issue of enforcing bus lanes. If most people comply, the cost of enforcement on the recalcitrant minority is low and manageable. If most people break the rules, as they would have done in the Uganda of 1986, the cost of enforcement is prohibitive.

Recent research suggests some valuable gadgets that are appro-priate for the early stages of spiralling up. It also suggests that there is a virtuous circle that links increased tax compliance to increased tax effort. Both can enhance political participation in the state. Inclusive governance, tax compliance and tax effort can all spiral up together from initially very low levels: they reinforce each other. None of the gadgets individually has spectacular effects. But in combination, by raising revenues, they can inspire a virtuous circle. In the context of left-behind places, tax design encourages econo-mists to think beyond narrow technicalities, integrating culture, politics and team-building into advice and analysis.

Security: how states build security capacity

The physical security of a country's citizens cannot safely be con-tracted out to a commercial provider.[8] Yet in some poor countries the state is currently too weak to protect people, despite massive international support. Other poor countries have managed it des-pite the challenges. There is much that leaders in weak states struggling to protect themselves, and those in high-income coun-tries trying to support them, can learn from such failures and successes.

Learning from success: restoring security in northern Mozambique

By 2021, the security situation in northern Mozambique had been deteriorating for four years, following the discovery of an offshore gas field. The field extended into the coastal waters of southern Tanzania, where it had triggered the Mtwara riots, as we saw in Chapter 9.* But in northern Mozambique the situation was far worse: the area had long supported the political opposition, RENAMO, and as punishment the government had starved the region of public spending. This discriminatory policy had made it fertile ground for trouble, a situation aggravated by the gas discovery. The terrorist organization ISIL, an offshoot of Al Qaeda, seized the opportunity to build a network of support, rapidly taking control of the territory, where it perpetrated grotesque outrages in which thousands were killed and 800,000 people displaced. As violence escalated, the company with the rights to develop the field, TOTAL, halted its $20 billion offshore investment programme. With such big money at stake, the government instructed the national army to regain control of the region.

The army completely failed. Not only did it lose control of the countryside, but ISIL was able to seize the key coastal town of Mocímboa da Praia and establish its headquarters there. The president swallowed his pride and requested his regional neighbour President Kagame to send troops to assist him. Kagame agreed to provide a force of 1,000 from the Rwandan army and, to make clear that this was motivated by solidarity, refused any payment. Within the African Union he had long advocated for African solutions to African problems. He was confident that Rwanda had succeeded in building an effective army and might also have value had an opportunity to demonstrate it. To widespread astonishment, this small Rwandan force was so effective that within three months the ISIL fighters had not just been beaten, they had surrendered. How had this been achieved?[9]

We have valuable information from a rare journalist on the spot, who was able to interview one of the ISIL fighters who had given themselves up. He surrendered because, 'We couldn't contain the

* This was despite Nyerere's successful nation-building: evidently, the sensational nature of a valuable resource discovery powerfully erodes previous loyalties.

confrontation, they have better weaponry, we couldn't do anything.' Rwandan soldiers were indeed equipped with modern light arms, superior to those of the ISIL fighters, much of whose equipment had been looted from Mozambique's well-financed but ill-equipped army. Yet this superior weaponry was not because the Rwandan army had a large budget. On the contrary, Rwanda spent only 1.4 per cent of its national income on the military. Having been emblematically insecure during the genocide, such spending was remarkably low: the damage done by civil war is so high that if military spending is effective, it is well worth the money.[10] NATO members commit to spending 2 per cent of national income, and the allied forces in Afghanistan thought fit to spend the vast sum of $3 trillion – two hundred times Afghanistan's national income.

The fighter further explained: 'We were overwhelmed by their number; they were also extremely fierce.' Since the Rwandan force was only a thousand soldiers, the comment suggests that the far larger Mozambique army had been reluctant to engage ISIL sufficiently closely to 'overwhelm' them. But what might the description 'extremely fierce' imply? Were Rwandan soldiers going berserk? Fortunately, we again have unusually high-quality information, this time from Louisa Lombard, a Yale anthropologist researching Rwanda's peacekeepers. She described Rwandan soldiers as being among the most disciplined and least corrupt of all African missions. How did the Rwandan army instil such discipline? Paul Kagame's foundational skill was the practicalities of building an accountable military hierarchy.* Across the hierarchy every layer of command understood that it was responsible for the moment-by-moment conduct

---

* I have direct experience of President Kagame's process of hierarchical accountability, since he extended it from the army itself to all the key public institutions. Each year he summoned their top 200 public officials to an army camp for three days, at which each person had to stand up and account for their performance against an agreed benchmark. As his guest, I was impressed that we all ate the same army food and slept in the same army tents: Kagame had visibly earned the right to say 'we' to his troops.

of the troops directly under its command. Each private would know that the sergeant leading the platoon would punish not just cowardice but mistreatment of civilians. He knew because that sergeant in turn would be punished by his lieutenant if civilians for whom he was responsible were hurt.

In gaining the confidence of local people, a further valuable restraint was that the Rwandans did not use airpower. In practice, airpower is not able to discriminate between civilians and rebel forces, most obviously with bombing. As bombs fall on them, people inevitably cease to regard the military responsible as a protector. But even discipline and the absence of bombing are not enough; local people need to be confident that the protectors will be effective in *permanently* routing the terrorists. This is why the mission of the Rwandan army was to wipe out the Al Qaeda nest, not merely to drive them away. Al Qaeda fighters proved to be cowards. Like many bullies, they had been sufficiently motivated to terrorize and slaughter defenceless locals, but not to fight those prepared to confront them. Once cornered, they surrendered, and the group rapidly imploded. The great value of winning the confidence of local people is that they are then willing to give soldiers what they most need when fighting an irregular force: intelligence.

Mozambique may stay trapped in patronage politics that precludes that cascade of military accountability. But clearly, success in the country is feasible should a leader or social movement choose to pursue it.

Learning from success: building an effective air force

Rwanda demonstrated that in many contexts an air force is an unnecessarily expensive luxury. I include the following example only because it illustrates two principles applicable to any military: motivation and devolution.

The Israeli air force is widely recognized as the most formidable in the world, plane for plane. Its effectiveness has been achieved partly by exceptional motivation through its high status as the ultimate guarantor of Israeli security. This status means that selection for the air force is analogous to Deng Xiaoping's recruitment of provincial governors: all teenage Israeli school-children specializing in mathematics and related sciences are tested for their aptitude. Conscious of its high status, many of the most able apply.

Exceptional devolution is reflected in a highly distinctive operational rule. Like all militaries, the Israeli air force is hierarchical: in all patrols a squadron of Israeli planes will be commanded by a wing commander. But once an enemy patrol has been encountered and combat looks to be likely, command passes to whichever pilot is in the best position to see the strategic situation. All pilots are therefore trained not just to fly their plane, but to claim and take strategic command based on their judgement that they are best positioned to view the situation.

Lessons from failures

We can learn from surprising failures almost as much as from surprising success. There has been no shortage of them.

The manifest failure to build an effective domestic security force in Afghanistan raises two questions. One is why Afghan governments, like those of Mozambique, failed to build an effective military despite ample time, finance and motivation to do so. The other is why the US-led allies failed to build any capacity in the Afghan military despite vast resources, twenty years and strong political incentives. Even more astonishing is the fact they did not even realize they had failed to build that capacity.[11]

The Afghan governments were vastly better resourced than the Taliban and, being democratically elected, should have been more aligned with what their citizens wanted. But the foreign money that provided the resources undermined citizen trust in the elected governments: they were seen as corrupt puppets of the allies. In this, the Afghani people were largely correct. The allied money corrupted politicians and officials at all levels: the state was being looted by those elected to serve its citizens, periodically revealed in scandals of grotesque proportion. Nor did Afghanistan's governments have much incentive to serve their citizens. Their vast revenues from western donors absolved them of the need to tax their citizens. The continuing presence of a huge foreign military force gave them an excuse to postpone building an effective Afghan military. Their primary interest became to deceive the allies into continuing both the financial inflows and the military presence that they assumed would guarantee their own security. In that complex purpose of deception, they were entirely successful. Meanwhile, they argued among themselves. Throughout his term of government, President Ghani was at loggerheads with his vice-president and failed to convince his citizens that he was prepared to sacrifice his own interest for the public good. Their suspicions were graphically confirmed in 2022 by his flight to safety while his troops were expected to fight and die for their country.

The deception of the allies was made far easier because they connived at their own deception. The truth of what was happening would have been so painfully inconvenient to the allied governments that cognitive dissonance hid reality. It was embarrassingly like the later Russian military failures in Ukraine that were hidden from President Putin. In Afghanistan, putting a rosy gloss on bad news infused allied militaries at all levels. The junior officers on the frontline of the fighting would tend to present failures as 'not yet working', while excessively trumpeting the few successes. The senior officers collating this information would showcase the successes and argue that the failures indicated the need to scale up the existing efforts. The yet more senior officers reporting to the chiefs of staff would amplify this misinterpretation, and they, in turn, would mislead the key politicians whom they briefed.[12] The politicians desperately wanted to hear any reassurance because they were accountable to the voters and their party. Voters with soldiers in the family wanted fewer casualties. Those in the political parties of allied governments wanted their ideologies respected: that typically included greater accountability for the money being spent, and

Afghan adherence to the moral norms that enthused party members. Hence, to the extent that Afghan politicians were accountable to anyone, it was to the voters and ideologies of allied democracies, not to their own citizens.*

The crucial but awkward lessons from this are that the governments of countries being supported by external resources must have clear operational responsibility over them. Consequently, their president and key ministers must get deep personal experience of the front line.

This overarching failure was overlaid by operational ones. If foreign troops are initially welcomed by the local population, the welcome soon fades. As a rule of thumb, seven years is the limit.[13] During that window, the capacity of the Afghan military had to be built. In turn, that depended upon a public American commitment to leave, which would have disabused Afghan politicians of their belief in permanent American-provided security: it didn't happen. Over-reliance on bombing alienated local populations. The doomed British strategy revealingly termed by mid-level officers 'mowing the grass' contrasted with the Rwandan strategy in Mozambique. A brigade would be posted to a locality for a gruelling six-month tour of service during which they would drive Taliban fighters out of the area. But once the brigade had left, the Taliban would return. This rapidly came to be understood by local inhabitants, so those who might otherwise have helped the soldiers with information could not risk doing so. The Rwandan strategy of sticking around until the forces surrendered, giving locals the confidence to share information, is a final valuable lesson.

All in all, the failure of the allies in Afghanistan, though profound, is not mysterious.

---

* The attempt to impose profound changes in moral norms breached the hard-won wisdom of the United Nations 'Brahimi Report', which had recommended that military forces under its control should leave 'a light footprint'. The next chapter develops a more general critique of this arrogant detachment of politicians in left-behind places from their voters.

How security collapsed in Mali

Mali is an impoverished left-behind country in the middle of the Sahel, the vast sweep of desert running from Mauritania in the west to Somalia in the east. As concerns about fragility mounted, international agencies developed three distinct lists of countries in which the state was judged to be fragile. In 2010, Mali was not on any of them: it was regarded as a peaceful democracy, although in many respects it was a cleverly disguised predatory state; its small army was emmeshed in looting the donor-financed budget, and not designed to fight. To Mali's north in Libya, Muammar Gaddafi, the tyrannical ruler of oil-rich Libya, was coming under domestic and international pressure. He responded by buying a vast arsenal of armaments and paying mercenaries from the Sahel handsomely to protect him. Mercenaries seldom have much motivation to fight – as Gaddafi's regime collapsed, they looted his arsenal and in January 2012 headed back to the Sahel. Suddenly, Mali was confronted by large, well-armed predatory gangs. When Mali's ill-equipped army tried to impede them, they were swiftly slaughtered: a third of the entire army reputedly died in a single day. In desperation, the government asked the French, the former colonial power, for protection. The French air force swept in, bombed the gangs and established a large air and army presence of 5,000 troops. But as French casualties mounted, French public opinion turned against the operation: in 2021 President Macron halved the force. By then, as in Afghanistan, this foreign force had become unpopular with local people. Following two military coups in quick succession, the unrecognized military government whipped up anti-French sentiment and ordered their forces to leave the country, along with newly arrived British and Danish support. In desperation, Mali's new rulers turned to the Russians for protection, specifically Yevgeny Prigozhin's Wagner mercenary company, and swiftly became his satraps.

Alongside this manifest collapse of the domestic provision of security, Mali continues to have a large United Nations peacekeeping force, MIMUSMA. Like the allies in Afghanistan, having been there since 2013, it has likely overstayed its welcome. Manifestly, it has become ineffective. Yet it is extraordinarily expensive, its annual cost having mounted to $1.3 billion. This vast and growing expenditure of over $10 billion has failed to suppress gang violence, but it could have made a decisive impact. Mali is a quintessentially left-behind country in which a fast-increasing youth population desperately need job opportunities. In their absence, the many disaffected communities-of-distress around the country, such as the Berbers in the north, are an easy recruitment pool for the gangs. The underlying failure here is siloed thinking by the governments of high-income countries. The objective of physical security in countries deemed fragile is typically delegated to a Ministry of Defence with a large budget and a narrow purpose; the objective of economic development in the same countries is typically under a ministry responsible for aid, with a small budget and scattered purposes.

Explaining the international failures

Taxation and security are core tasks of every state. Demonstrably, they are feasible: on both, there are inspiring examples of success and gadgets that might be useful in some contexts and phases. Yet despite massive international efforts, and sometimes inadvertently because of them, tax and security capacity are still far from universal. When advising or insisting to the left behind, the governments of high-income countries have contrived to be too prescriptive on some matters and too lax on others.

They are too prescriptive in insisting on tax increases even in times of crisis when it is politically too damaging to be accepted by voters. On security, they have been too prescriptive in insisting that governments receiving help should conform to the moral norms of the donor countries, which may be impossible, inappropriate or regarded by local people as an impertinent attempt to coerce them into breaching their own moral norms. As a result of these demands, left-behind governments sometimes cease to be accountable to the values of their own citizens.

Western donor nations have been too lax in failing to prevent their financial support being looted by politicians and civil servants. They have been too lax when they failed to commit to an early withdrawal of their military forces. That would have made clear to the governments of left-behind nations that they had to plan for when they must take over that responsibility. As a result of donors being weak-kneed, some governments have not faced up to the task of becoming trusted by their own citizens.

At the heart of these failures are moral confusions. Donor governments have perceived themselves as behaving well while repeatedly breaching core rules of moral conduct. It is time to unravel that confusion.

The Morality of Common Purpose

Morality matters: when it becomes confused and contested, once-cohesive societies fracture.

In the summer of 2023, domestic crises engulfed the USA, the UK, France and the Netherlands. The US Supreme Court ruled that diversity can no longer be used to justify favouring black applicants to university. Presidents Obama and Biden immediately gave televised speeches condemning the decision.* In Britain, new international evidence on longevity revealed that life expectancy was eight years longer in communities-of-success than in communities-of-distress. Despite the National Health Service ostensibly giving equal access to care, this gap was far wider in the UK than anywhere else in Europe. In response, Prime Minister Rishi Sunak gave a televised speech announcing new fifteen-year targets for treatment times. In France, following the shooting of a young man of Arab origin by the police, cities erupted into escalating riots. President Macron curtailed a European summit in Brussels and cancelled a state visit to Germany, returning to Paris to condemn both the shooting and the disorder. In the Netherlands, a coalition government collapsed, triggering a national election owing to a disagreement between two parties, the

---

* President Biden's recent speeches are consistent with his State of the Union address repudiating past decades of policies which had negligently caused the emergence of hereditary disadvantage. See his speech on 'Bidenomics' in Chicago on 3 July 2023, which repudiated '40 years of trickle-down economics'. Note that the forty years since 1983 includes the Clinton and Obama presidencies. See also the rather clearer articulation of the same argument by his National Security Advisor.

VVD and D66, on the morality of curbing the increase in asylum seekers. Both lost to an anti-Islam party.

The common underlying condition that provoked these events was the emergence of entire communities facing hereditary disadvantage: African Americans; English children growing up with less educated parents in left-behind places; French teenagers who are ethnic Arab; and culturally detached asylum-immigrants in the Netherlands who do not feel part of a highly integrated majority society. Such communities emerged over decades – or centuries in respect of African Americans – because of policies that had satisfied a majority of voters as fair.

What has been revealed by these crises is a profound rupture between what angry members of disadvantaged communities regard as morally right, and what most other voters continue to regard as morally right.

The evolution in moral philosophy: from Rawls to Sandel

The first decades of the post-war era saw major practical advances in moral behaviour, among both leaders and individuals, but they were driven by pragmatism rather than any new moral understanding.* Eleanor Roosevelt, as First Lady of the United States, launched a Declaration of Human Rights at the new United Nations. Official delegates treated it as a piece of theatre, with unanimous applause, rather than as a serious commitment by their government. Otherwise, Stalin's Russia, apartheid South Africa and Papa Doc's Haiti would not have been clapping. Overall, it was not a genuine political commitment to a moral advance. It was indeed de-linked from any mechanism by which the newly itemized human rights would be achieved, and from any foundations in moral philosophy. At its best, it functioned as Eleanor Roosevelt intended, inspiring neglected

---

* See Chapter 2 on the cohort of modest wartime leaders who rose to the severe challenges of the times but were leaving public office by the 1970s.

communities like African Americans to campaign for better treatment. At its worst, it opened the door to empty gestures: governments realized the political benefits of making grandiose commitments to lofty objectives that were unlikely ever to be implemented. By lulling their citizens into the illusion that action was being taken, they could look decisive without the need to finance the consequences of genuine action.

A major philosophical advance came in 1970 when John Rawls published *A Theory of Justice*. It proposed that to be *just* a public policy should benefit the living standard of the least well-off community to the maximum feasible: the policy of maximizing the minimum. Inequalities were permissible only if they enabled the living standard of the poorest group to increase.* It was intended as a moral constitution to constrain the majoritarian process in a democracy. The implicit assumptions about motivation were that, unconstrained, democracy would accommodate the self-interest of the majority, whereas for justice, they ought to behave altruistically towards the most vulnerable. Although intellectually influential, it had negligible impact on public policy since it failed to convince either political leaders or members of political parties *quite why* the constraining principles should be adopted.† Rawls regarded his

---

* For instance, if incentives to CEOs induced them to work harder, that would be justified if indirectly it benefited deprived communities.
† See Jonathan Wolff in the *Times Literary Supplement*, 6268, 19 May 2023, and subsequent correspondence. The tensions with political democracy arose since there was no reason to expect either that a majority of voters would be so risk averse as to want to maximize the minimum, nor that they would accept a constitution requiring the limitations on majority preferences that Rawls proposed. According to Professor Christopher Hookway – a former president of the pragmatist school of thinking followed in the Pierce Society – Rawls never intended his norms as a global moral code, but as something that would be determined contextually through dialogue within each society according to its own norms. Consistent with this, the context which influenced *A Theory of Justice* was highly unusual: the brief window of technological optimism of the British Labour Party in the mid-1960s, as Professor Wolff convincingly argues.

principles of constrained democracy as the only alternative to Utilitarianism. Since his principles gained no traction, the major effect of Rawls's ideas was inadvertently to rehabilitate the Utilitarianism he was trying to move beyond. This appealed to economists: it left *Homo Economicus* as the inhabitant of their models – fundamentally amoral and incapable of anything beyond self-interest. The models then predicted this ugly human's responses to public policies such as tax changes. Finally, Utilitarianism swept in to add up the costs and benefits of the policy. Although modern economics became vastly more sophisticated than this simplistic picture, it never decisively replaced that bedrock conceptual framework.

Meanwhile, moral philosophers moved on from Rawls and embraced the Utilitarianism that he had wisely feared. The most celebrated among them was Derek Parfit, who spent a lifetime at All Souls, Oxford, agonizing over questions such as 'Should I be prepared to kill three people today if I thereby save the lives of four people somewhere else on the planet in the twenty-fifth century?' Such absurd ratiocination took moral philosophy into tangled and fruitless dimensions of hypothetical future selves that were nothing to do with the practical moral choices in people's daily lives.*

---

* I introduced the work of Derek Parfit in Chapter 6, in a footnote. He was the atheist son of missionaries. While rejecting his parents' faith, he wanted to derive the most extreme variant of Christian morality from axioms of moral necessity. Specifically, we should care for all future people born anywhere just as much as for our own children. He did so by dismantling the concept of individual agency: each of us is merely an infinite succession of moments, each with its own interests – me now! Only if we care for every moment of every possible future person's life can there be any basis for morality. In effect, his account of Utilitarianism was equivalent to an instruction for a benign central planner of human behaviour – an all-knowing, benign autocrat replaced the God of his parents. Individual moral agency evaporated. Only thus could absurd questions like 'should I kill three people now to save four in the future?' become planning dilemmas, since the most striking point of the question – that I, Paul Collier, and you reading this are expected to use our agency to murder innocent people – is not included as part of the dilemma. Once highly influential in restoring Utilitarian morality, by the end of his life he recognized that, like Rawls, he had failed. See 'A

The Morality of Common Purpose

Michael Sandel and Contributive Justice

Moral philosophy was rescued from this scene of disarray by Michael Sandel's concept of Contributive Justice, which returned the subject to the question of how I should use my agency.[1] The idea was introduced right back in Chapter 2 as one of the recent intellectual revolutions, but before putting it to work here a refresher might be in order. Contributive Justice proposes moral norms which are fully compatible with what we know from the recent advances in human evolutionary biology, social psychology and anthropology. Unlike Rawls and the Utilitarians, Contributive Justice does not demand that we behave altruistically, but it does argue that we have a duty to contribute to our community as long as others are willing to do so.

Recent advances in human evolutionary biology tell us that although we have not evolved to be altruistic, sacrificing our lives for others unconnected with ourselves, we are an unusually pro-social mammal. There were strong evolutionary pressures on humans to contribute to common benefit: we cooperated in order to survive in competition with animals that were faster, stronger and better defended – but less cooperative. Individuals within a group learned to behave well towards others in it if others did the same. In those human groups in which more than 3 per cent refused, cooperation by the rest was not sustainable and so they all suffered extinction. We probably have a genetic predisposition to cooperate with others, and we learn from cooperative behaviour in others that looks to be successful. This is why *homo sapiens* is the most pro-social of all mammals.[2] Although we can be selfish, our nature urges us to rise to our better selves as angels of mutual care within our community. This new evidence from evolutionary biology is also

philosopher's philosopher', by Sarah Richmond, *Times Literary Supplement*, 6266, (2023) and the powerful critique of 'small world' reductionism by Nancy Cartwright, *A Philosopher Looks at Science*, (2023). Other notable Utilitarian philosophers are Peter Singer and Joshua Greene. The philosophy's *reductio ad absurdum* was Sam Bankman-Fried.

consistent with earlier evidence from social psychology and anthropology that we are strongly inclined to belong to a group, thrive through belonging, and die early if we are isolated.[3] We have also evolved so that as we repeat an action, the attitude behind it becomes habitual. If we are exposed in our work to humiliation, and in our neighbourhood to indifference or worse, lacking opportunities to behave well, we tend to become more selfish. If instead we are repeatedly exposed to mutuality so that opportunities for our own generosity abound, we tend to become more inclined to contribute to common goals.

Not only is Contributive Justice consistent with the evidence from evolutionary biology and social psychology, it also chimes with the practical politics of spiralling up. It tells us why, unless there are good moral reasons to the contrary, we should join others in striving for a better future for our community and society. As the Cambridge economist and public policy expert Diane Coyle expressed it, people need a 'shared sense of direction and optimism'. That shared sense comes from the power of shared *agency*, the benefits of mutuality being the key intellectual advance.

Agency and disadvantage

A fundamental difference between Distributive and Contributive Justice is who has agency. Distributive Justice imposes conditions on the actions of powerful people *but leaves agency with them*. It tells them they can consider themselves virtuous only if they help the weakest. In contrast, Contributive Justice forces the powerful to share agency with the weak and applies a checklist to test whether this has really happened. Have the weak equality of voice in determining the common purposes for which their society should strive? Have they equality of respect in that discussion of goals? Do they earn enough to be able to contribute meaningfully to the common purposes?

In applying that checklist, a useful gadget is a humble device from political science called *process tracing*, something that is unknown in economics and business schools. It is simple but effective and highly apposite to a crucial aspect of reversing the spiral down in left-behind places. Reversing a downward spiral requires that some actions must change – some people must behave differently. Process-tracing searches back through the key decisions that initiated an attempted change and the key people who authorized and implemented it. It asks why and how they did it. As such, it is methodologically mundane but drags economists out of their comfort zone of *forces* such as economies of scale to recognize the importance of *people*, their strategies and their motivations.*

Process-tracing can be applied to answer two vital questions about agency. Who has been doing what to whom? Who has been accountable to whom? We can apply that question to left-behind places everywhere, whether Sheffield, Barranquilla or Zambia. We can ask it of economic issues like job growth and political issues such as influence. But given the three crises with which I opened this chapter, I will apply it to one highly specific aspect of moral dispute: opportunities for education, both at elite universities like Harvard, Oxford and Sciences Po in Paris and to schooling at earlier ages. What do the criteria of Contributive Justice reveal to us about these policies?

During the centuries of slavery, Black Americans suffered extreme lack of voice, lack of respect and inability to contribute to common purposes. These deep-rooted impediments are still far from rectified, as reflected in their very low representation as students in private schools, as students in the top-rated universities and in the higher-paying workplaces of business and the professions. Compensating selection criteria at top US universities would have been a very small gesture towards rectifying these inequalities in the life chances of Black Americans, but it would have been fully justified. Yet instead, US universities offered the selection advantage largely not to Black Americans but to the most advantaged of the pool of a billion black *people* worldwide.

* In that it complements a key benefit of RCTs: both force economists into fieldwork on local contexts – an important benefit that Nobel laureate Michael Kremer noted for RCTs.

Worldwide, there are now thousands of black teenagers who are clever, privileged and well schooled. Some are children of African politicians, some of successful entrepreneurs. They could gain places at elite universities without the additional privilege of favoured entry. Faced with the perceived need to fill a quota of black students, America's top universities often select these privileged black students in preference to clever Black Americans who, burdened by centuries of prejudice and discrimination, indeed warrant preferential entry. Had eligibility for the quotas been restricted to Black *Americans*, the contrived argument used by the Supreme Court to declare affirmative action unconstitutional would not have been an option, since it would not have been based on race but on demonstrable and enduring disadvantage. Other than the minority of privileged teenagers, most of the world's non-American black people have indeed suffered historic disadvantage. But in contrast to Black Americans this has not been due to entrenched American misgovernance. The culprits were the past European colonial powers. Elite American colleges are relying on the reverberations from that abusive European history to avoid their current obligations to their fellow Americans.

The marginalized communities in Bradford and Sheffield, Glasgow and the Welsh Valleys have not suffered centuries of disadvantage comparable to Black Americans, but they too have faced growing educational disadvantage. In recent decades their chance of gaining entry to elite British universities has fallen sharply, relative to more fortunate children.[4] To be just, public policies need to change, but nothing effective has been done about it. Britain's political right tends to pin responsibility for low aspiration on the parents, along with the idea that excessive welfare benefits have enabled multigenerational cultures of life without work to persist. On the left, the need to change attitudes has been accepted, but with the difference that education will be the remedy. Keir Starmer, the leader of the Labour Party, has taken up this theme in speeches prioritizing 'education, education, education', echoing his political mentor, Tony Blair. His objective is to encourage able students from poor communities to gain entry to university: the opposite of what happened even under Blair's period in government. But inadvertently, he has conflated two distinct problems: unequal opportunities and unequal respect. His exclusive emphasis on opportunities has the unfortunate consequence of judging the half of the population who do not go to university as failures, including a large majority of those suffering from hereditary disadvantage. The implicit message is that everyone should aim to go to university, which is untrue and disheartening. The agenda for equalizing respect needs equivalent emphasis to that of equalizing opportunities. In practical terms, both depend on equalizing life chances, starting with pre-schooling, continuing through schooling, and then into employment and earnings. Currently, neither respect nor life chances have been addressed by the ideologies of Britain's right or left.

In France, citizens of Arab descent face similar disadvantages at all stages in their lives, from pre-school through schooling and university to employment. They also have far less voice in shaping common purposes, the little scope for voice that they have is less respected, and their capacity to contribute to such common purposes as they agree with is modest in the extreme. However, there is far less quantitative evidence on these disadvantages because it is illegal in France to gather information on people's ethnicity or religion. The motivation for this stems from the distinctive constitutional commitment to a secular state, implying that citizenship should be blind to ethnicity and religion. But as with the US Supreme Court ruling on positive discrimination, and the importance of university education in Britain, insisting on the principle *when it is belied by reality* does a disservice to disadvantaged communities.

Contributive Justice combines the agenda of equalizing life chances with the more fundamental one of breaking the link between respect and success. It also points to specific practical changes that would provide the preconditions under which left-behind places can catch up. It demands parity of voice in place of exclusion, respect in place of disdain and enhancement of earning power so that the left behind acquire the capacity to contribute. It demonstrates that all three of these are currently grossly unequal, and it homes in on how they can best be met. To make further progress, two complementary ideas are useful: *scaffolding* and *boundedness*.

The moral implications of scaffolding

Left-behind communities can learn more from those that are a little ahead of them than from societies that have completed the transition to inclusive prosperity. Analogous to scaffolding, once the transition has been completed, the techniques used in the ascent are often discarded and forgotten. This has subtle implications for the moral standards which the communities-of-success may legitimately use when judging the actions of those currently in transition. Evidently, the menu of techniques useful for the left behind in reversing a downward spiral potentially includes all those which have been used by communities-of-success in their own transitions. That principle has implications for entry to America's elite universities.

Incredibly, until recently, Harvard and most other private universities had an explicit practice of favouring the relatives of donors. At Harvard, their chances of admission were seven times higher than equivalent applicants. Only in 2023 did the US Department of Education open a formal probe into this egregious practice.[5] Having exploited this unjustifiable opportunity for privileged entry for decades, neither donors nor their favoured children could credibly object to preferential entry routes for those from left-behind communities like American Blacks. *Having legitimized the technique for an unworthy purpose, they could hardly object were it to be used for a purpose that is worthwhile.*

Historically, recognition of this principle was the moral basis for the GI Bill of 1944, which historians recognize as transformational for post-war American society. It gave those who had been on active service in the US military privileged access to free education for the next twelve years. President Roosevelt had been persuaded by the compelling evidence of Anna Rosenberg: she had given serving soldiers voice through hundreds of interviews. She found that those whose education had been disrupted feared being left behind by younger upcoming applicants for places whose lives had not been diverted into fighting a war. The GIs had contributed to a vital common purpose, their views were heard, and society reciprocated with targeted benefits: *the GI Bill was Contributive Justice in action.* During those twelve years of the Bill, this scaffolding of successfully equalizing the life chances of Americans was kept in place. As an inspiring model, it lived on for a further decade, being applied by Martin Luther King to the inclusion of Black Americans and President Johnson to the Great Society. The consequences of its impact on Harvard were captured by scholars who tracked that cohort of GI entrants. Their finding that a Harvard education could transform the life chances of those from left-behind backgrounds makes the subsequent bias in entry yet more indefensible.*

The moral implications of boundedness

Elinor Ostrom was an anthropologist who won the Nobel Prize in Economics for her discovery that indigenous communities commonly protect their natural environment by overcoming the problem of free-riders – the selfish people who cut down more than their fair share of firewood. The communities succeed by coming together in a self-enforcing mesh of mutual obligations precisely corresponding to Contributive Justice. Ostrom's key contribution was to show *how* mutuality was built by adhering to the principles of *boundedness*. Membership of the community-of-mutuality had to be well defined: everyone had to know who else was a member and who was not. All those who chose to be members had to commit to contribute to the whole, and only by contributing were they entitled to the benefits generated by it. Using the criterion of *boundedness*,

* See G. E. Valliant, *Triumphs of Experience: The Men of the Harvard Grant Study* (2012).

the remedy of preferential access should be limited to those citizens whose life chances had been blighted by the legacy of slavery because they were Americans descended from a slave and not simply because they were non-White.

One of Elinor Ostrom's principles for building mutuality was that those who accepted mutual obligations must have the right to control both the composition of and the pace of entry to the group. In this instance, the group is American citizens, and this principle would confer an important right upon those descended from slaves. As citizens for whom opportunities are still woefully inadequate, it would empower them to delay widening preferential university entry to non-citizens until their own chances of entry had caught up with other citizens.

Bringing Contributive Justice and Elinor Ostrom's principles together illuminates an issue often seen as a dilemma. Many successful people from left-behind places want to fund scholarships at medical schools for those from their homeland. Their purpose is partly to give a bright kid from their homeland a helping hand and partly to provide their homeland with a well-trained doctor. But once graduated from a top medical school, high-paid jobs in glamorous places beckon. Has the donor the right to make returning home a condition of the scholarship or is it an unreasonable restriction on freedom? I think that had Ostrom and Sandel discussed this, they would have concluded that the condition was fair. Those beckoning job offers are temptations to freeride: grabbing a scholarship intended for those who want to help their homeland. As long as applicants are made aware of the condition, those not prepared to accept it are free to apply through other routes.

The original GI Bill was timebound: the returning GIs had twelve years to use their privilege of free education. The deadline of 1956 was doubly valuable. Directly, it gave the veterans agency over their lives, but their futures would improve only if they got themselves trained. Indirectly it affirmed a key principle. It was timebound because the purpose of the privilege was to equalize their life chances with those of younger non-combatants. The aim was to erase the disadvantage, not to compensate for it over their entire lifetime. This is a general principle of Contributive Justice. In circumstances where the hereditary disadvantage of an entire community has become entrenched, as with Black Americans, it may take two or three generations to overcome it, but that is the legitimate objective of public policy. Affirmative action does not get its justification as a token apologetic compensation for past wrongs. It applies with equal force to groups of citizens who have fallen into hereditary disadvantage simply through the ill luck of living in the wrong place. Which takes us back to the main theme of this book: the places left behind because of a shock outside their control.[6]

The moral implications of left-behind places

The process of catching up takes time. During those first steps on the cusp of spiralling up the capacity for change is at its nadir. This has both moral and technical implications. Morally, the actions needed for those first steps cannot be judged by the same norms that apply in established high-income democracies. In all of them, these norms were breached while they became high income. That was quite possibly because in most of their initial circumstances there was no feasible route upwards that was compatible with their current norms. Even the basics of raising tax revenue, suppressing predatory gangs, managing natural resources and building functioning cities posed formidable problems to the now wealthy democracies, and still do. The most shameless departure from current norms was the exploitation of other societies through colonialism, Belgium being the most gruesome of a lurid cast of European empires. Across Europe, much of the imperial wealth was captured by the politically powerful. Fortunately, since they squandered much of that wealth on lives of idle luxury, spiralling up is feasible without trampling on the lives of other societies as they did.

Not only was the journey difficult, but even today, in all three of the high-income democracies of the USA, Britain and France, communities suffering hereditary failure persist. So, all three should get off their moral high horse: they have repeatedly breached their own professed standards of meritocracy and so are in no position to condemn those struggling to escape entrenched disadvantage.

What we now know about catching up

We know that the first steps are the hardest because places that have been left behind, whether countries or regions, have little capacity for change. So, if only a few actions can be taken effectively, what should be done first? We know that in predominantly rural countries like Ethiopia, many people will need to leave their homes and move to cities for better jobs. In contrast, in already urbanized regions like fly-over America, moving out accentuates decline: the jobs should move to them – evidently, the priorities should vary depending on the context. However, there is a simple technique for determining priorities that works regardless of context: critical path analysis. It was pioneered in the 1960s to manage large undertakings dependent on hundreds of distinct actions.* Take the challenge facing France of countering Islamic extremism. CPA can help to organize the potential ways of tackling it into an effective sequence. Moreover, when integrated with more recent advances, it can be made less daunting and even more effective.

In France, a majority of voters want a secular state and faith-blind identification of citizens. But currently, one community-of-hereditary-disadvantage, French Muslims, uses religion as a criterion for membership. Tackling Islamic extremism depends upon transforming the life chances of this community. That, in turn, depends upon complementary actions by the state and civil society. The state can do things such as provide preferential access to vocational training and jobs, like the GI Bill. Social movements can ask Muslim families about goals that could become common purposes, similar to how Anna Rosenberg discovered overlooked priorities. They might find that

---

* Readers alert to footnotes will have already spotted it in Chapter 10.

many Muslim parents are worried about the lack of job opportunities and social facilities for their teenagers and the attendant risks of getting into trouble. What can CPA tell us about which of these problems should be tackled first? It will point out that before anything else can happen, the members of the community must be identifiable. For that, the prohibitions imposed by secularism that prevent the collection of data on religious identity will need to be suspended until the objective of equalizing life chances is achieved. This echoes the value of timebound privilege built into the GI Bill. It reaffirms that the secular state is a distinctive core value of French society, while enabling hereditary disadvantage to be rectified.

CPA tells us that asking Muslim families about their goals should come next, so that those that are common with many other communities can be identified and become a cross-communities undertaking. From that point CPA needs to recognize radical uncertainty: instead of attempting a master plan for a generation, the plan should not look too far into the future. Beyond a horizon of around ten years many uncertainties increase explosively. Commitments that purport to extend far into the future, such as the fashionable government pledges to achieve 'Net Zero by 2050', are dangerously close to being theatrical deceptions: decisive action appears to have been taken, but it has not. No French, British or American government can commit its successors to actions beyond the end of their own term of office. And everybody – businesses, lobbyists, the public and politicians themselves – knows it. Promises far into the future are a virtuous-sounding version of kicking the can down the road.

That implication of radical uncertainty protects us from such deceptions, but it also has a more energizing message: if the French don't know how to integrate disaffected Muslims, then they must find out. Both the state and social movements need to learn. They can learn from variation: are some French cities doing better than others? They can learn from other societies which have done better. In Singapore, Lee Kuan Yew successfully inculcated a spirit of Contributive Justice in a society that lacked it. As elsewhere in the world,

Singapore's Muslim community broadcast the call to prayer five times a day from its mosques. But as people from many different identity groups benefited from mixed social housing, they learned to listen to each other. The many non-Muslim people living near the mosques gently objected that they and their children were being woken very early each morning. Had Singapore been a society in which disputes went straight to court, it might have erupted into bitterly contested antagonisms. Instead, the communities met and the Muslims agreed to turn the speakers to face inward, towards those assembled in mosques. The call to prayer was heard by those who had chosen to go to the mosques. It was theologically sound, but not so loud that non-Muslims couldn't sleep.

The timeframes for catching up

I introduced the image of a dashboard for tracking timeframes in the context of managing natural resources, but it applies equally well to our current topic: the challenge of fully integrating disadvantaged French Muslims. In the short term it tracks immediate action: some decisions need to change within French society. Process-tracing can identify the decisions and the people with power to change them. A likely reason why they have not yet happened is that they would have conflicted with the interests of the powerful. Highlighting that is the rationale for monitoring: it tracks 'what decisions and implementing actions are going to change this year'. It rolls forward each year, insisting on tracking annual progress. On a longer horizon it tracks the strategy, asking 'what will be different in 5–10 years as a result of our actions?' A strategy worthy of the name should expect to make measurable progress. By setting this out, government, society and Muslims can each assess the plan as it is implemented and at its end. It, too, insists on a reality check: if nothing is working, the strategy of integration will need radical revision; if it has worked but not as well as expected, perhaps it needs to be scaled up. A final timeframe tracks the growing capacity of the state and social movements to tackle the problem: if that capacity is genuinely being strengthened, successes should be becoming more common. Between them, the three timeframes tracked on the dashboard protect everyone from self-delusion. Given the widespread and persistent failures to tackle the inclusion of left-behind communities in France, Britain and America, they are manifestly needed.

Looking at ourselves in the mirror

We make moral choices not only in public policy but in our daily lives. The concept of contributive justice liberates us from unattainable standards and replaces them with graspable actions needed for societies capable of integrating communities-of-distress.

At the core of contributive justice is the notion that although our personal freedom is valuable, our social relations create obligations. Contributive justice implies that to consider ourselves as morally responsible, we are not free simply to please ourselves.

Getting up in a morning

Can we ever get up in a morning for some purpose beyond our self-interest? Can we feel obliged to get up in order to help others? Evidently, we can – many grandparents do it routinely when they care for grandchildren. Their action is not in their narrow self-interest – they know the grandchildren will outlive them, and a more purely selfish act would be to insist that since their own time left to live is shorter, they should not have to spend it looking after infants. Yet we are not wired to think that way. Beyond relatives, many people make small, caring self-sacrifices. If I were to acknowledge the many such kindnesses towards our own teenagers it would be a lengthy list, including teachers in their previous schools still helping them and their dentist, who is attentive to the minds behind their teeth – and all these people have showered us with their kindness willingly, as do many others in society in their daily lives as they interact with those in their community.

Such myriad small acts of kindness are inexplicable and ignored in the models peopled by that greedy, selfish individual *Homo Economicus*. He behaves like a sociopath; thankfully culled by our evolutionary need to cooperate, he has shrunk to around 3 per cent of humanity. Unfortunately, in America and Britain post-1980 these characteristics became favoured for CEO appointments, so they have had a disproportionate influence on work-based habits. The other 97 per cent of us have evolved to overcome short-sighted behaviour, unless we are dragged down by ill fortune. But that ill fortune is precisely what has happened in many communities-of-distress: self-respect has been shattered by repeated failures, producing self-fulfilling despair. Despite this ill fortune, those in left-behind places working for change can be encouraged by understanding that these attitudes are unnatural: we are capable of better, and our self-respect can be rebuilt, step by step. What is the moral responsibility of those whose lives are more successful? At a minimum, it is to challenge ourselves to assess whether aspects of our behaviour have contributed to such damaging attitudes.

Contributing to our communities-of-place and -work

There are circumstances in which we should *not* contribute to the purposes agreed by our community, but they are exceptional. Contributive justice and evolution argue that our default setting should not be to pursue our own self-interest regardless of what our community is trying to achieve. Usually, I should match the contributions of other people in my community according to my abilities to do so. I have a responsibility to take part in reciprocated generosity: it is the moral code Father José introduced that transformed the Basque region in Spain and that Toyota introduced into the assembly line. If I am of fighting age in Kyiv, I have a moral duty to join or support my local militia and defend my city.

What are the exceptions? Fighting might contravene my moral code: suppose I am a pacifist. In that case I become a conscientious objector and serve my community in some other capacity. Or I might choose to wash my hands of being Ukrainian: I can join some other society and live by its moral standards. What I am not free to do is to leave for a more comfortable country while continuing to think of myself as a full member of my community back in Ukraine. But while defending a common home is a compelling purpose, attacking the homes of others is not: if I am a Russian, I do not have an obligation to conquer Ukraine. There are other important caveats to my obligation to contribute to common purposes: I should be treated by my community with equality of respect and be given equality of voice.

For most of us, evolution has equipped us for these moral choices to come naturally. Since most of our decisions are taken not by our individual brains but by the collective mind of our communities-of-work and -place, this is the level at which we most readily get our moral choices right.[7] Within our community we form habits. The Muslims of Singapore were already habituated to cooperating with others in their city, as were Danes when COVID-19 became a common challenge. As a community spirals down, such habits can be weakened. If the daily experience at work at Amazon or in a call centre is to be at the bottom of a hierarchy of humiliation, it may shatter the community into mutual recrimination. Yet this is far from inevitable: shared adversity can bring out the best in people: to invert the words of President Bush, 'The *have little* support the *have less.*' Contributive justice invites the communities-of-success to celebrate these heroes of the communities-of-distress.

Contributing to diverse nations and workplaces

At the larger level of human interaction, the moral criteria of contributive justice are less likely to be apposite: the caveats are more likely to matter. In a diverse nation I am less likely to have equality of voice and respect and less likely to find myself in a position to be able to contribute. More viciously, the successful members of my polity may actively peel off from shared identity with those who are left behind, rejecting any obligation to mutuality. The Brexit vote divided Britain into successful people who mostly voted Remain and people in left-behind communities who mostly voted Leave. A celebrated journalist described the sentiment in prosperous London, which unlike all other English regions had voted heavily for Remain, as like being 'shackled to a corpse'. The disdainful phrase was devoid of empathy.[8] Moreover, decisions taken at national level in a multicommunity entity are more distant from the context in which many of these communities live and work and so less knowledgeable about them.

Compounding the difficulties of multicommunity decision-taking, evolutionary instincts do not come strongly to our assistance at this level. Our experience of living in multicultural communities is probably too recent or too shallow. This is compounded by experimental evidence which shows that we are naturally 'groupy'. We have evolved to form into rival groups even if the differences between them are trivial. This augurs ill for taking many decisions at a high level where such differences abound. But even here, there is some hopeful contrary evidence such as cooperation for long-distance trade since prehistoric times: it implies that different tribes have long been able to cooperate for mutual interests. Further, it is possible that the new generation of youth, familiar with networking across former boundaries of identity, could alter this situation for the better. But the evidence that social media has led to tribal hardening, atomization and isolation suggests the contrary.

Contributing to international alliances

At the 2023 G7 meeting in Japan, the closing communiqué included many moral commitments that most people in high-income democracies found appealing. The members of the G7, mostly former colonial powers representing seven high-income countries, are probably the highest level of international cooperation sufficiently cohesive to be able to function together. One finance minister told me that confidences were exchanged among them that if leaked would sometimes force resignations. This level of mutual trust had become possible because habits of mutuality had been built over many years.

The moral judgements of that G7 meeting were so wide-ranging as to read like an assertion of governance for the world. Yet its composition is so wildly unrepresentative of the global population that any claim to legitimacy will be viewed by nations outside the G7 as an outrage.[9] Even though most citizens in the G7 countries will approve of the moral values promoted by that G7 they should not approve of its attempt to usurp world governance. The leaders were guilty of *moral imperialism*. Robing values in the ennobling language of human rights and planetary survival does not rectify this lack of global legitimacy. Equal voice, respect and empowerment – the conditions for contributive justice – are all spectacularly breached by the G7. While on a few issues the G7 can legitimately forge a common purpose among its members, it cannot legitimately project those purposes on to others. It is not entitled to impose its views on societies which have had scarcely any agency in the process by which the G7 formed its opinions. Indeed, preaching and threats by powerful societies impede the struggles and debates by which other societies revise their moral norms. Their norms will evolve nation by nation by the same internal processes by which the norms of the G7 societies have evolved. Threats are counterproductive: our instinct to preserve agency is so strong that it induces us to do the opposite of what is being demanded – psychologists call it *reactance*.

In September 2023, during the Indian-chaired G20, a dispute flared up between the G7 and the rest of the G20 on support for Ukraine. Faced with a choice between embarrassing India and climbing down, the G7 minority accepted that to forge any common purpose in a bitterly divided world they could no longer insist on their own priorities. Like most other citizens of G7 countries, on the specific issue of Ukraine I agreed with the G7 minority view, but on the larger issue of decisively rejecting the instinct of the G7 to moral imperialism, I applaud India's leadership.

Moral imperialism was evident in the debate about gay rights in

Ghana. Survey evidence showed that Ghanaians were changing their attitudes in much the same way as they have changed in Britain, albeit with a lag of a few decades. By the early twenty-first century, most people were comfortable with gay partnerships: the prevailing norms became non-judgemental acceptance of difference. But then, foreign-funded NGOs arrived, most notably the American evangelical churches, which wanted the Ghanaian government to enact legislation banning gay marriage. Under pressure from the evangelical churches, which have become a powerful group, the Ghanaian government introduced a law to this effect. Foreign pressure did not end there.

As a result of borrowing during the poly-crisis, by 2023 the government was heavily indebted and in need of a loan from the IMF. Whereupon the American government, which has the most powerful voice on the board of the IMF, imposed the condition that unless the Ghanaian government dropped that law and introduced one granting gay rights it would block the loan. The effect of this opportunistic external intervention was so nakedly imperialistic that Ghanaian public opinion turned against gay rights: an instance of reactance to re-establish agency. Between them, these two foreign interventions had frustrated the natural process by which the values of a society evolve.

As I was about to send *Left Behind* off to my publisher, a similar infringement of gay rights induced US Secretary of State Antony Blinken to throw Uganda out of the Africa Growth and Opportunity scheme. I have marched on gay rights parades, but such moral imperialism is shameful, counterproductive and damaging to America's reputation. Shameful, because the scheme gave preferential market access to Ugandan and other African goods: the decision hit the jobs, skills and firms of a poor society at a time when, like much of Africa, its economy is precarious. Counterproductive, because as in Ghana it is likely to set the cause of gay rights back. Reputationally damaging, because in the context of a rapid erosion of African support for the West, it signals that the US is an unreliable ally even towards a long-standing friend.

The world of success can contribute a lot to the world of the left behind, but moral imperialism is not the way to do it. We need to start with the modesty to recognize that in the process of catching up, agency rests with the left behind, as does the knowledge of context without which even well-intentioned support risks blundering into making things worse. In partnership with governments, social movements or local businesses, we need to forge strategies of support: Chapter 12 shows how much scope there is to do this better.

12.

Supporters, not Saviours

There is a role for outsiders – most evidently, through support rather than punishment. But those who offer support must guard against the delusion of being saviours. Left-behind countries and communities cannot be saved by the interventions of the wealthy. Introducing dependency on the wealthy provider compromises and undermines agency. Often, those who offer support compound this by being unreliable, increasing fragility. Saviours have a habit of assuming they are morally superior even if they are simply more fortunate or the beneficiaries of historically contemptible smash and grab. Only if distressed communities are encouraged to have the agency to save themselves can parity of respect be achieved.

The legitimate role for outsiders begins with the modesty to recognize how limited it is: *we* cannot save *them*, nor should we aspire to do so. By usurping the agency the distressed need, or denigrating their efforts to make progress, we impede transformation. At best, we should listen to what they want, then provide support that follows their lead – do what we can to help it happen.

Each year, the world's central bankers meet at Jackson Hole in Wyoming in the USA to discuss the implications of current financial events. In 2009 I was invited to address them and noticed that no African countries had been invited to the meeting. That was a typical instance of how the powerful breach the conditions for parity of voice and respect. African Central Bank governors now gather annually in Oxford as a substitute; they meet with the global finance experts of their choice and share their experiences.

By the summer of 2023, many of Africa's Central Bank governors were facing crises of popular discontent as their governments hit the buffers because of closed capital markets, declining export prices and the rising cost of debt service. They realized that with so many young people unproductive, social peace depended upon rapid growth of jobs. Some felt that their country was being pushed dangerously close to the extreme edge of fragility beyond which lay the unknown territory of collapse.

Although high-income societies now struggle to appreciate these fears, their experience of situations even more extreme has only recently receded from their collective memory. The choices facing many Germans in the late 1940s were so stark that, as you may recall, Cardinal Fringen proposed a distinctive moral code for the thousands of people who were starving. Recognizing the dangers of desperation, the Allied powers had enabled German policymakers to design and implement their own economic strategy. They recognized that 'starving people needed jobs; jobs depended upon local firms hiring workers; and to do so the firms needed to borrow from local banks'.* The African central bankers came up with something similar: job growth could come only from firms, but their countries were desperately short of them. They could try to induce established foreign firms to come into the countries through some form of financial incentive. Or they could accelerate the growth of local firms through more risk-bearing finance for the best to expand. Since their governments had no money, how might either of these options be financed?

How help goes wrong

The problem of a lack of finance in left-behind places for private sector job growth has long been recognized. In 1960 the World Bank, the international community's premier development agency, established a sister agency to meet the need: the International Finance Corporation. Governments provided some initial risk

* See Chapter 6.

capital and guaranteed the money the IFC borrowed on international capital markets, enabling it to borrow at risk-free rates and lend on to businesses in developing countries at a small premium. That became the model for many nationally owned public agencies which were collectively known as development finance institutions (DFIs). Without them, firms in countries and regions perceived as risky would have faced ruinously high borrowing costs. They enabled those firms which they judged to be well run to finance investment at moderate rates. In 1990 Chancellor Kohl successfully repurposed West Germany's DFI to catalyse a private sector in the East. By 2020 there were around forty DFIs but, as in the Germany of 1990, they should have been repurposed.* They were no longer needed to finance private-sector job growth in many of the rising middle-income countries: since the New Normal of 2014, international capital markets had expanded into the role. But there was an acute unmet need in Africa. With rapid job growth, African societies will stabilize politically and move forward. Without it, they are at risk of being destabilized, as those African central bankers feared. In mid-2023 their fears were proved right when Niger, a well-led Sahelian democracy, fell to a coup. The antecedents to that coup began with Friedman's corrosion of business schools and end with why you need to understand this section.

Why the DFIs are trapped into ineffectiveness

If the somewhat purposeless DFIs were to pool their cheap money, they could meet a crucial unmet purpose – supporting the private sector job growth Africa needs. They could do it in two ways. One would provide seed money for enterprising young Africans to put their ideas into practice and then put risk capital into the most

---

* Most donor governments have a DFI – the Americans have recently expanded and rebranded theirs as the Centre for Development Finance with $60 billion. Britain has the oldest of them, also rebranded, as British International Investment.

promising for some to become the gazelles propelling job growth. The other would provide financial inducements for established foreign firms to bring jobs to the country. To date they have fumbled both opportunities. This is the story of those missed opportunities and why change depends upon voters in high-income countries. We do not escape our obligations by covering our ears.

In parallel with the meeting of central bank governors, the DFIs now also meet annually in Oxford. They gather there because there is no official forum where they all convene.* That is a symptom of a deeper problem.

Since their job is to invest in firms, the DFIs are staffed by recruits from business schools: people with MBAs. As this book has already lamented, too many business schools since the 1970s have drummed into their students the morally undemanding dogma that the only duty of a business is to generate profits. A good MBA graduate is the one who gets the deal ahead of rivals.† That is why there is no official forum where DFIs meet: the DFIs see their situation as a zero-sum game against each other. This is a very limited view of the world and brings almost no intellectual suppleness to assist in helping solve the challenges of the left behind. Inadvertently, it undermines the only way in which they could accomplish their challenging common purpose – by working together.

Moreover, the DFIs are each beholden to their only shareholder, a government minister responsible for aid. For example, among prominent British ministers, Baroness Amos and Justine Greening, and in the US Hillary Clinton and Antony Blinken. As a politician, this government minister naturally wants to please voters, many of whom have covered their ears to the needs of people seemingly distant from themselves. It comes about because the minister faces a

---

* The meetings began in 2019 at the request of the IFC and have continued since, the most recent being in April 2023, with about thirty of the DFIs participating.
† See Chapter 7 and also Rebecca Henderson, *Reimagining Capitalism in a World on Fire* (2020).

dilemma: DFIs are liked by neither the right nor the left. The right is instinctively suspicious of aid, seeing it as a waste. The left is pro-aid but hostile to using it for the private sector. While it won't win votes, the DFI could easily lose them if it provokes the hostility of the major aid-supporting NGOs including Oxfam and World Vision, or if there is pushback from the investment banks about 'unfair' competition for their pricey services. So, the minister confines the DFI towards minimal, risk-free intervention.

She requires its projects to carry no risk of reputational damage or provoke a major lobby group. So, they must be corruption free; they must be green, gender sensitive and respect human rights; they must be profitable. Each of these conditions is desirable, but applied to the countries of the Sahel, it is hard to find many profitable projects with all these other characteristics. Perhaps there are none. That frustrating reality is what the DFIs meeting at Oxford call 'the pipeline problem'. They face this problem partly because they have not pooled their resources to undertake the costly and slow work of nurturing enterprising young people in the Sahel looking for jobs. But behind that failure lurks the straitjacket imposed by risk-averse politicians.

Suppose that, encouraged by its central bank governor, a government in the Sahel such as that of Niger were to choose the route of fast growth of local firms. For that, it would need to ask the DFIs to risk their money in launching a rudimentary venture capital industry for start-ups in the country. This form of venture capital works by investing in a portfolio of promising start-ups: by funding a hundred of them in a country like Niger, twenty may survive. Of those, five might make the money that offsets losses on the others, and one of them might be sufficiently successful to generate nationally significant job growth. Done at scale over decades, this DFI strategy might have been the best means of stabilizing Niger. But for a Western politician being grilled about a loss-making investment that emits some carbon, it has offered an unattractive return.

Now suppose that the government were to choose the route of

attracting foreign firms – again, it asks the DFIs to assist.* They face a different problem – no firm wants to go in because they know that viable businesses depend on clustering. If five foreign firms in the same niche might be viable in Niger, the DFIs would need a strategy to find them, meet some of the initial costs of pioneering and coordinate their entry. Again, if the DFIs pooled their resources and were given permission by their ministers to adopt the strategy, it might complement venture capital, transform job opportunities and stabilize the country. But within the DFIs the zero-sum mindset of competition has blocked cooperation. Were the politicians to want it, they could require the DFIs to change, but the politicians don't want it either: it would expose them to criticism from both the left and the right.

By 2023, those DFIs meeting in Oxford were sufficiently aware of these problems that they had decided to add a closing session with their ministers to the event. Since no DFI could risk speaking truth to their minister, I was put up to set out the need for a change of approach. Whether owing to my own ineptitude or cognitive dissonance, the session was not a success: the politicians explicitly insisted that all projects indeed had to respect each of the conditions enumerated above. That gruesome experience convinced me that only by making enough of their voters aware of the problem could change be achieved. Hence, the addition of this section to *Left Behind*. This inertia describes the situation across Sahelian Africa for decades – the neglect of an entire swathe of left-behind countries such as Niger.

Until the nineteenth century, the Sahel had been a crossroads between North Africa oriented on the Mediterranean and the fertile lands to the south. At its heart, Mali's goldmines had financed a powerful and sophisticated kingdom until the entire region was overrun by colonial expansion. As that receded following Independence, recovery was patchy and precarious, complicated by reactive

---

* On the potential benefits of foreign investment see Chapter 9, 'using the revenues'.

Western crisis-driven interventions which repeatedly left the situation worse, as they had in Mali.*

Ultimately, Western politicians needed to wake up to three aspects of reality. They had to begin with recognizing their own failure: their style of intervention had made things worse. Next, they had to recognize their common purpose: the Sahel needed to provide hopeful futures for its burgeoning youth. Finally, they had to recognize their own limitations: progress would have to be led from within the Sahelian societies. Given these realities, the role of their DFIs was to support those local initiatives that enhanced youth opportunities so they could be scaled up. Some of the initiatives would be from Sahelian governments, others from local communities.

Countdown to collapse in the Sahel

I begin the countdown to collapse with the first significant opportunity the DFIs and their political masters had to face these realities. In 2016 there was a radical change in the leadership of the premier DFI – the World Bank's IFC. At last, a rainmaker had arrived. His leadership offered a new beginning. Had it been matched by support from Western politicians it might have been able to stabilize the Sahel. But time was running out: as events unfolded, within a decade those politicians were paying a high price for their failure to seize it.

Philippe Le Houérou, the rainmaker, realized that fundamental change was necessary: the IFC's role should be to catalyse opportunities in places like the Sahel. To get started, he needed to change the mentality of his staff so that their ambition became to 'transform an economy'. In doing so, he faced severe obstacles.

Some were entirely due to the World Bank's own rules. The IFC would need to work with governments such as those in the Sahel on a common strategy. But advising governments was done by a completely different part of the World Bank Group. Until Philippe's

---

* See Chapter 10, 'How security collapsed in Mali'.

arrival, the prevailing mentality was that since the group's private-sector agency, IFC, was trying to make a profit on its investments, there was a potential conflict of interest between the advice given to government by the staff of the World Bank and the IFC's deal-chasers. Fearful of criticism, barriers had been created to prevent such conflicts of interest. Philippe recognized that this was ridiculous: the World Bank Group had a common purpose: to help poor countries escape from mass poverty; as long as both IFC staff and World Bank staff were pursuing it, no conflict of interest should arise. Gradually, the culture changed. Staff started to work together.

There was also scope for collaboration between the IFC and the other agencies in hunting the firms needed to seed the new cluster: the German agency could try to find a German firm and the British could do the same with their companies, both supplementing those that IFC itself managed to find.

Philippe also realized that his agency needed some money that did not depend on its ability to borrow cheaply: it needed some donor aid. The World Bank Group was receiving over $20 billion of aid for the poorest countries from the governments of high-income countries each year. It was negotiated in three-year tranches and flowed into a pot called IDA. But although the governments of low-income countries could spend the money, the IFC could not use it to support a firm trying to pioneer a business in one of these countries. If jobs were to be generated, IFC would need to use money from the IDA pot. Yet the internal rule of the World Bank Group was precisely the opposite: any profits the agency made were transferred back to the IDA pot. It made investing any profits impossible because the IDA scooped them up.

The task of persuading the high-income Western governments who contributed to the pot was won by what diplomats term a 'constructive ambiguity', more commonly called 'a fudge'. It resulted in 3 per cent of IDA being used on a pilot basis for a 'private sector window' that the agency could use in very poor countries.

Meanwhile, IFC and the other DFIs were still being urged by the politicians to become 'more efficient'. What they meant was lend more money with fewer staff. This would drive the DFIs out of places like the Sahel, where deals were small and took time and effort. The high costs of keeping a team of agency staff in a left-behind country to hunt out pioneering opportunities should be seen as a necessary overhead. It should be financed by the IDA pot. Similarly, unavoidable pioneering costs such as training a workforce in new skills should be subsidized by aid, not added to the already daunting risks facing a start-up in a left-behind economy.

With the IFC at last well led and refocused, the aid ministers in charge of the DFIs had a newly effective institution as a model. They had the good fortune to be in pole position at a pivotal moment: by seizing it, they could reset the course of history.

They didn't seize it. The aid ministers feared their voters: voters on the left didn't like using aid to help businesses; those on the right didn't like publicly funded DFIs competing with the international banks. The Sahel continued to spiral down as governments collapsed and local communities were intimidated by gangs backed by ISIS and Al Qaeda. But five years later, Western politicians were given a second chance.

The year 2021 began with a major opportunity for international support. In the Eastern end of the Sahel, the Sudan had long been a predatory state, using oil income to reward a militarized elite which used brutality to retain power. In consequence, it had long been a centre of humanitarian tragedies. More recently, it had also become a pariah state, driven by suspicions that it was harbouring terrorists. Through an astonishing combination of courage and shrewdness, from within civil society a social movement emerged with the power to block central Khartoum with instant protest. The predictably gruesome military response was that many were slaughtered. But the regime was not as united as it looked. The suspicions of terrorism had led to international sanctions on travel and finance. The habitual slaughter was no longer happening in remote areas unseen by global media: it was there in the streets of Khartoum and became world news. Because Western voters saw it, their politicians no longer had reason to be fearful: they rose to the occasion and sharply tightened the sanctions. This seriously inconvenienced the military elite. Within it, one faction realized that the old tyrant had become a liability: only with a more credible national leader might the sanctions be eased and some of their own privileges salvaged. They switched from protecting the tyrant to protecting the street.

This new alliance between that part of civil society not committed to vengeance against the entire army and that part of the army willing to switch sides was a marriage of convenience. It was effective in breaking the coalition-of-the-powerful who had blocked change. To function, it needed a leader each side could trust to protect its core aims. The two sides were fortunate to find someone on whom they could agree: Abdalla Hamdok, a career civil servant. He rose to the moment, recognizing that his role was to improve the condition of his fellow citizens. Since the alliance was fragile, he would need to get tangible results as soon as possible. He decided to seek advice on opportunities while building teams which could implement them. He reached out to the International Growth Centre to second our staff to his office, which is how I came to know him. As we worked together, I came to regard him highly: he had the makings of a transformational leader. By building on the opportunity they had helped to create, Western politicians could reset the prospects for the largest Sahelian society.

They didn't build on the opportunity. This time, it was distraction, not fear of voters. With Khartoum's streets no longer full of protestors being slaughtered, the international news reverted to the war in Ukraine and climate change. The politicians followed them. Sanctions were just left in place; no money flowed in from the DFIs. A year later, Abdalla Hamdok had nothing to show for his efforts: on each side, patience started to wear thin. Protestors returned to the streets, heavily influenced by two naive but noisy Western narratives: all societies needed democratic elections; there was no role for the military in government. As events soon proved, neither of these was true in the circumstances of the Sudan. Instead of withdrawing from government, the army launched a coup and took it over. Hamdok, briefly reappointed but with diminished authority, soon resigned in despair. By 2023, the Sudan was back on the front pages of the media: two factions of the military were fighting each other, slaughtering people as never before as they intimidated them into submission. The only winner was Putin's Wagner group. Western politicians were busy wringing their hands in dismay.

The year 2023 was not a good one for the people of the Sahel. The coup that had toppled the government of Mali two years earlier was repeated in Niger and Gabon, the leaders turning to Russia's Wagner Group for the effective security the West had failed to provide. In the same week, the president of the Central African Republic won a referendum to give him a third term, overriding the constitution. As with Mali, Niger and Gabon, the CAR resorted to the Wagner Group for security. Timbuktu, the ancient city in northern Mali, was overrun and terrorized by affiliates of ISIS.

In 2021 the world had been waiting thirty years for a tyrant to be overthrown in Sudan. With a new tyranny installed there, how long it will take for another opportunity is unknowable. But when it comes, a critical mass of Western voters need to be ready – sufficiently up to speed that their politicians do not fear to seize it.

How help goes right

We now know enough to understand why the DFIs and similar outsider interventions have been failing. They breached basic principles of contributive justice: there was too much 'donor knows best'; too much of the moral imperialism that arouses reactance; too much of the saviour mentality. But we are also learning how we can redesign them to work better.

Morals at work in Somalia

Black Hawk Down, a Hollywood production released in 2002, is a gripping account of a disastrous attempt by the US military to restore peace to Somalia after the collapse of the state. In the wake of the film, many Americans concluded that Somalia should simply be avoided, but Marcel Arnault and his family, good-hearted philanthropists from Santa Fe in New Mexico, viewed it differently: this was a society that needed help. From that preamble you may anticipate another illustration of the damage done by well-motivated naivety, but it is not. Marcel Arnault was an astute businessman who combined a kind heart with a shrewd head. This is an exceptionally unlikely success by someone nobody in Washington, London or Paris has ever heard of, achieved in the most extreme conditions. It shames those responsible for the repeated failures.

Somalia is the nearest the world has come to the libertarian dream of a stateless society, but libertarian billionaires prefer New Zealand. Implicitly, they choose a country where the state protects them from predatory violence to one where the state is threadbare. Yet in the right conditions, as Elinor Ostrom established, communities can enforce pro-social behaviour even without the state. East African communities can meet these conditions, as demonstrated by the success of determining land rights by communities in Kigali contrasted with the failure of using courts in Dar es Salaam. In Somalia the state has been too weak for court rulings to have had much credibility, so community enforcement is the only option.

Modern economies have come to depend on a vast web of court-enforceable claims: for most people in the West, the most familiar would be the struggle to buy a home by getting a mortgage. For Marcel Arnault, the key insight came when he thought about his parents' struggle to buy the home of his youth. He asked himself what had motivated them to keep up the monthly payments. He immediately realized that, given their character, it was *not* fear of a court order; it was the guilt and humiliation that would follow if they were unable to repay the debt. The same applies to business loans. Banks need courts only because they cannot accurately judge character. Marcel wondered whether people in Mogadishu were so different. Loans for business expansion might work if you could learn enough about potential borrowers to judge their characters. He realized he couldn't do it, nor could any American. He would need local Somalis, and they, in turn, would need to buy into the purpose of the venture. He set about it rather like Father José: first, he slowly assembled a dedicated team. Working in Mogadishu is not a walk in the park, but using its diaspora in the US to provide introductions he built a team of twenty-one Somalis and taught them how to assess creditworthiness. His foundation capitalized the enterprise, but he explained to them that they were jointly running a business, not a charity. If they succeeded, they could each take personal pride in having become a credit professional and collective pride in restoring a socially valuable financial activity for the growth of small firms. Without their knowing about each other, Marcel Arnault had pioneered the model for business expansion subsequently adopted by Philippe Le Houérou at IFC, albeit with very different enforcement methods. Marcel stressed that while he was pump-priming the operation it would become a business, not a charity. It would charge an interest rate, aim to preserve the capital and pay their wages: every default would eat into their job security. Within ten years it was viable – honest businesses with good opportunities for expansion were able to get a loan to finance it.

Not all Somalis are sufficiently secure to be trusted with a large loan, any more than are people in Santa Fe. But assuming that everyone is an amoral *Homo Economicus* is false, dispiriting and would have condemned Somalis to giving up on loans. This help succeeded not only by recognizing the potential of Somalis but by giving them new agency: Somalis were helping Somalis, the foreign help simply pump-primed it.

Marcel Arnault is an exceptionally innovative philanthropist: such people will always be scarce. But there are large agencies within civil society that work day by day in fragile and violent situations and also try new approaches to bottom-up peace-building. In December 2023, frustrated with the impasse we had encountered with the DFIs, a team from the International Growth Centre invited a civil society group to find a way forward. At their best, these organizations are quietly impressive. The Red Cross, Save the

Children, MercyCorp, Oxfam and similar humanitarian charities have developed deep contextual knowledge, in the process accepting danger as routine. Save the Children has realized that in places beset by violence, children need mothers, and mothers need to earn a living. They are finding how to enable women-run small businesses to form and prosper despite the violence, and how such enterprises gradually become a voice for peace. By such steps, the needs of desperate people have driven these humanitarian charities into the same business as the DFIs: both organizations are non-profit and both operate at scale: Save the Children's annual budget is $2.3 billion. That role reflects the pragmatic, courageous humanitarian charities at their best.

But being an advocate of rapid learning, I chided them to show me any instance in which one of them had learned from another. They told me why it was inconceivable: they were competitors for the same pots of money, just as the DFIs are competing for the same few tick-all-boxes deals. Worse, they could not even scale up their own successes. Donors wanted to fund something new: they were condemned to generate clever boutique operations only to abandon them. Like the DFIs, they readily admitted that they were trapped in performing way below their potential.

Must we accept that these are two irresolvable problems, or can fresh ideas transform them into a single upward spiral? Part of the charities' budgets comes from small donations: they face outwards to millions of people who participate through little acts of kindness. By facing outwards, the charities have the voter appeal the DFIs so conspicuously lack. For their part, the DFIs are potentially the missing ideal donors for the charities: they are striving for the same purpose, understand the importance of building stable work opportunities in dangerous situations, and themselves have stable funding. Is there scope for partnerships, albeit built step by step, place by place? Under the common banner of facing fragility, can the new community of DFIs begin to fuse with the new community of charities? We are trying to be marriage brokers between agencies, our only advantage being that we are no threat to any of them. It is easy to mock such aspirations as naive, or worse. But cynicism does not resolve these human tragedies.

Building a jobs strategy in Djibouti

Adjoining Somalia is Djibouti, a small, politically stable middle-income democracy which finds itself at the centre of a violent region. Although small with a synonymous capital, with 200 miles of coastline it is not a city-state and has four immediate neighbours: Somalia, Eritrea and Ethiopia are adjoining, and Yemen faces it 16 miles across the Red Sea. All four are mired in violence. Eritrea has been ruled by President Afwerki ever since Independence. He has clung to power by using a permanent state of warfare to justify keeping his restive youth conscripted in the army. Ethiopia, though much better governed, stumbled into ethnic cleansing in 2016 followed by civil war, ended only in 2022 by an African-brokered peace. Yemen has had recurrent civil wars for decades and by 2023 it had escalated into a full-blown humanitarian disaster. So much for the neighbourhood. Within four hours of flying time, the yet more grievous violence of Central Asia can be reached: Afghanistan, Iraq, Syria, Pakistan and Iran.

As a stable democracy in a sea of escalating violence, Djibouti had long been strategically attractive as a military base for major international powers. By 2023 they were all there: the USA, China, France, Japan and others with an appetite to strut the international stage. The presence of the bases guaranteed peace, which addressed the evident risk that the adjoining violence would be contagious. Yet while the benefits of external protection were unquestionable, economic opportunities from the bases delivered little. By 2023, Djibouti had joined the club of the left behind. Local incomes had been stagnant for many years and its youth faced a dismal choice. They could sit idle at home, where they became restive and disaffected. Or they could leave for places like Qatar and work as low-wage servants for the pampered life of luxury tourism. Not only did the bases deliver little; the government of Djibouti found itself in a straitjacket that closed off promising opportunities. Being familiar with my work, in 2023 they asked me for independent advice on whether that straitjacket could be loosened. Was there scope for the international powers and the government of Djibouti to agree on a common purpose that offers local people better prospects?

The first step turned out to be disentangling the contributions of the visiting navies and air forces. The city of Djibouti adjoins a fine deep-water port, but piracy has made the coastal waters dangerous. The navies are there to protect commercial shipping and the naval presence gives the captains of the commercial ships the confidence to use the port. Since the port is large enough to accommodate far more traffic than it receives, the military and civilian uses are complementary. The air forces are a different matter. Like the port, the airport adjoins the city of Djibouti and military traffic cohabits with commercial airlines. But in contrast to shipping, the air forces are not there to protect the airlines; they are in competition for the facilities. The port is big enough for everyone, but the airport isn't. The team managing it explained that the immediate constraint was not the runway but the much larger spaces needed for taxiways, parking and terminals. On every side, expansion of the airport was frustrated by space leased to the visiting air forces. There are also more subtle constraints. When a military emergency arises anywhere within that four-hour flying range, commercial flights are curtailed to free up space for military and humanitarian planes, so airlines have become wary of scheduling stopovers in Djibouti.

There is plenty of space elsewhere in the country to build another airport, so the military and commercial uses could be separated. Which should move: is it more important for the commercial airlines to be near Djibouti city, or for the air forces? Commercial airlines bring tourists who usually want hotels, restaurants, bars and the rich life of a city centre. Providing those facilities generates opportunities for entrepreneurship and a range of jobs, many of them skilled. In contrast, most air-force bases are designed to be self-sufficient with sleeping and eating facilities on site. Djibouti is a rare exception, with military personnel finding themselves in the anomalous luxury of five-star hotels. There is a compelling case for it being the air forces that should relocate.

A new airport costs around $1 billion, so who should pay for it? Ultimately, the people of Djibouti would benefit from untying the straitjacket, but they are currently in no position to pay for a new airport. With prosperity choked off by the bases, the Pentagon and its counterparts have not put them in a position to contribute – they have not met the criteria of contributive justice. A just settlement would therefore require the visiting military to pay for the airport. Recall that this would not be as recompense for the past but because bringing prosperity to the disaffected youth of Djibouti is in their own interest – the Pentagon will want an airbase in Djibouti for the foreseeable future. If disaffection from youth unemployment were to spread, the future of that airbase would be in jeopardy, as happened to France in the Sahel. Enabling Djibouti to catch up is in the Pentagon's own interest, just as enabling the Sahel to catch up would have been in the interest of the French Ministry of Defence.

The scale of France's failure in the region over which it has tried to retain a stifling influence is staggering. By 2023, over half of young Arabs in Francophone North Africa aspired to emigrate in search of better jobs abroad.[1] French politicians should have switched the vast resources spent on deploying their military in the region to supporting opportunities for better lives. That French political reluctance to divert funding from the military to such a purpose finds echoes within those high-income societies that now have neglected regions.

Political neglect of marginalized places is widespread

Decisions are constrained by the political interests of the powerful. In Britain, £10 billion was committed to building aircraft carriers on the Clyde, not because they were needed for security but to reduce the risks of Scottish secession from the UK. More recently, the same risk has been countered by the threat that a vote for secession would result in the submarine fleet being moved from its nearby base in Faslane. Yet neither deferring the decline of a doomed shipyard, nor retention of low-grade jobs at a naval base addresses what Glasgow needs. It is a big city of the left behind: as in North Africa and the Sahel, Glasgow's youth need investment in a better future. Although Glasgow has become one of the poorest cities in Western Europe, it was once a proud hub of enterprise, known as the Second City of the British Empire.

The US has equivalent stories. Many left-behind places are heavily dependent on military bases that have become politically unclosable. But the local job opportunities offered by the bases are dead-end work at the minimum wage. The US mountain division is based at Fort Drum, NY, in the north-western Adirondacks, a poor region in an area otherwise known for being a tourist destination for wealthy New Yorkers. Ironically, it got a commendation for service in Somalia in 1995. Directly, American politicians have been responsible for this double failure: a military base that has offered neither the Adirondacks nor Somalia a better future. But in all democracies, voters get the politicians that they elect. Leaders need to explain the crucial realities to citizens, and the citizens in turn have a responsibility to become adequately informed about those realities.

Glasgow is a left-behind city in the prosperous country of Scotland; the north-western Adirondacks are a left-behind area in the prosperous state of New York; Barranquilla is a left-behind city in fast-growing Colombia; Somalia is a left-behind country in a prosperous world. They have all fallen behind unnecessarily because of the same universally lethal combination. They have been stripped of local agency, neglected and subjected to ill-informed micro-management from elsewhere. That truth has been denied because facing it implies a fundamental critique of past policies. But once it is faced, it is liberating. The past cannot be changed, but the future can be.

Epilogue: Time Regained

Since 1980 we have lived under the tyranny of the complacent. Suddenly, in the third decade of the twenty-first century things have fallen apart. The media present a daily diet of wars, active and feared; new extremes of climate; disruptive technologies. It is easy to become despondent. Alongside these problems, which we face in common and about which we are constantly being reminded, the opening chapters of this book have revealed a further global problem that has been neglected. In every continent, communities of the left behind have been diverging from communities of success. Divergence was triggered by a conjunction of shocks and weaknesses, but it has persisted owing to a moral failure within the communities of success. Life in them has become so detached from life in the communities of the left behind that many of the successful are barely aware of how inequality between the two communities has widened. Such inattention is itself negligent. Within a country it is a failure to fulfil the duties of citizenship; at the international level it reveals misplaced complacency.

Sometimes inattention is tinged with a shrug of contempt – the left behind brought their difficulties on themselves. This travesty of the truth compounds the injury of neglect with insult. Unsurprisingly, it undermines the cooperation between communities needed to address the problems common to all of us. By ignoring the problem that most directly affects the left behind while vociferously lamenting the other problems, the communities-of-success seem to the left behind to be selfish and heartless. On the metric of morality used in this book, contributive justice, they get a resounding F. They breach the principle of mutual respect; they breach the principle that the poorest should be able to contribute to common purposes.

Justice demands that divergence be reversed, but doing so is also a practical imperative. Until justice has been done, that angry frustration of the left behind induces many of their voters to oppose the expressed priorities of the successful regardless of the consequences for themselves. They live in America's fly-over cities and England's northern regions yet behave akin to the rivalrous workers in that Kenyan flower-packing factory and the despairing voters in Colombia's Atlantic-Caribbean. They support 'my enemy's enemy' and refuse to cooperate with the communities-of-success – and their exasperation is understandable. Once a country becomes so bitterly divided that each side works to frustrate the other, even the problems they have in common continue to mount. Britain and America have reached that point.

The comfortable world of their communities-of-success has become unsustainable, socially and environmentally. The longer the successful continue to bask in complacency, the more drastic the consequences. In the 2020s, their complacent negligence risks tipping the electoral balance into disaster.

The despairing testimony of Stefan Zweig is the iconic account of that illusion of permanence among a successful community. He recounts the misplaced complacency of Viennese Jews before the First World War. In the late 1930s, time speeded up: as now, crises cascaded upon their world. By 1938, its grotesque consequences were already apparent as Zweig fled to Brazil, killing himself as despair deepened.* The world of which Stefan Zweig despaired was immeasurably more alarming than our current global worries. Yet our ancestors surmounted it. What did they do, and why should we care?

As to what they did, they got their priorities right: a war had to be won, and a peace built that forged unity within and between countries. In Britain, Churchill brought urgency to the war effort with 'Action this Day', while the radical changes in social policy needed for unity were set out in the Beveridge Report during the war and implemented by Attlee from 1945. Equivalent dramatic changes in the USA were Roosevelt's New Deal and Truman's 'The buck stops here'. As

---

* Stefan Zweig, *The World of Yesterday: Memoirs of a European* (1942).

to why we should care, though our present worries are less daunting, both Stefan Zweig and that wartime history are helpful if we learn from them. Their simple messages for us are to recognize the immediate priorities and act on them: procrastination is folly. The priority is to heal the divisions in our societies by bringing justice to the left behind. We already know enough about the actions that will reverse divergence to get started. We know thanks to the abundant mistakes that have been made and the evidence from success.

We know three essentials

We know that a sustainable world will need three essentials: communities, states and moral bounds. Around the planet there are many instances of each thriving in isolation, but far too few in which all three are found together. This book has shown that in combination they have the power to transform societies into being prosperous and inclusive, and that building them is within our collective power. Why do they matter?

Without communities, nothing much can work. All of us except a tiny minority of sociopaths have evolved to belong to communities. Depending on the context, much of our behaviour is shaped by our community-of-place and our community-of-work. Within them, we care about what other people think of us: that is the glue that induces us to behave well towards each other. That glue is essential to a sustainable society. A world without it – a world of disconnected people – would fall apart. It would be brutal and transactional because people's selfish instincts would be unrestrained. In recent decades, both in Britain and America we have brushed close enough to such a society to appreciate how ugly it would be. Only with that communal glue are we able to forge and sustain willing compliance in common purposes. Such communities are by no means enough for a sustainable world and in the absence of moral bounds can be predatory on other communities. But without the glue of community, our chances of a sustainable world are slim.

We also know that without a state nothing much can work. There are several countries in which the state is so thin as to be almost completely ineffective. The Central African Republic has become such a country, with negligible state presence further than a few miles from the capital. Rural CAR and other state-free areas closely approximate to that dream of some of the West Coast billionaires: their stateless society. But recall that no billionaires choose to live there: rich outsiders would be in peril. Small stateless communities have been able to enforce social rules, as Elinor Ostrom showed. But none of them reaped the scale economies for prosperity. Our distant ancestors lived in these stateless communities for millennia, but the global population they sustained was tiny. Our present world of more than 8 billion is only sustainable by reaping the scale economies that depend on states that are effective. Even if this technological problem could somehow be overcome by new technologies productive at small scale, a stateless community would face other problems. If environmental change pushed it into destitution, there would be no safety net of assistance from other communities. The libertarian dream would turn into a nightmare as we reverted to the world of prehistory in which many communities died out before they could adapt.

Since Elinor Ostrom's death in 2012, her colleague David Sloan Wilson has taken her work forward. If people all share the same identity and norms, the rules that enforce the glue of stateless communities can be scaled up from tiny populations to large ones. An implication is that the citizens of a state can also be a community. Yet Stefan Zweig was escaping from a country in which this fusion of community and state had just happened.

Finally, we know why such a fusion is perilous without the bounds of moral decency. In Zweig's Vienna of 1938, the merger of his native Austria with Hitler's Germany transformed the members of Austria's National Socialist Party into a community of success which used the power of the state to turn greedily on Viennese Jews. Although the intensity became paranoid, the pattern was normal, communities-of-success have routinely aimed to capture the state, and when successful use its scale for violence to subjugate stateless societies. Sometimes it was on the modest scale of the Zulu and Inca empires, sometimes driven by the grandiose pretensions of the nineteenth-century European ones. In the twentieth century Japan and Soviet Russia built replicas.

When a state fuses with a community, moral bounds are imperative. The academic depiction of the bounds of moral decency on which I have drawn in this book applies the work of Michael Sandel. I find it convincing, unlike the alternatives. It is also compatible with how evolution has equipped us to behave. Although his work is known by students around the world, it is as yet too recent to have influenced the older selectariat who set public policies. However, perhaps because we have evolved to be suited to it, there are approximations in some clusters of small countries in which state and community have fused. The most notable examples are the Nordics such as Denmark, the Baltic states such as Estonia, and a few in East Asia such as Singapore. Consistent with the value of moral bounds for the success of a society, these clusters are among the most successful in the world: their inhabitants have a very high standard of material well-being. Not only are they prosperous, they are politically stable and inclusive societies that are not a danger to the rest of us.

We need the glue of communities, but without states they are doomed. Communities and states can fuse, but without moral norms they are catastrophic. We need all three in combination because each contributes something to the whole.

Communities are there to bind people together with social glue. Place-based communities only fail in that role if forced into an extreme range of distress in which they spiral down. Their community can implode into self-blame; their communities-of-work can collapse, to be replaced by aggressive hierarchies of humiliation. Where that has happened, reversing divergence will take longer.

Moral norms are there not only to avert states from fascism but to curtail those spirals down within a community: contributive justice encourages communal adversity to be met by solidarity instead of blame. It judges the trash jobs brought in to take advantage of desperation as breaches of the duty to restore opportunities to contribute. Instead of these new hierarchies of humiliation, places spiralling down need the finance for their most innovative local firms to prosper.

States are there to deliver prosperity and equalize life chances. Many states fail to do either. Malawi, for instance, is controlled by a greedy selectariat that retains the few good life chances for itself. Those good life chances are so scarce because even if the selectariat wanted to grow the economy, the state is too thin for effective action. Outsiders can easily make this situation worse, but it is hard for them to make it better. Good intentions have paved the road to Malawi's current situation. The selectariat has sought to attract and misuse aid. Malawi needs official donors to have the patience to wait until there is a better government. After repeated misjudgements, the only reliable criterion is that a new government is demonstrably already succeeding in creating economic opportunities around the society. Meanwhile, Malawi can progress by means of its social entrepreneurs. It needs a Youth Policy Forum (YPF) and a Grameen Bank like Bangladesh, and a Mondragon like Basque Spain. But just as Malawi needs donors to be savvy about its government, it needs them to be so about its social entrepreneurs. To date, they have chased Western funding instead of building not-for-profit organizations that are self-financing like YPF and Grameen.

And then donors need to face reality. Creating inclusive opportunities for prosperity in places like Malawi is hard. It can be done – Botswana, Malaysia, Ethiopia, Singapore, Rwanda, Burma, Ghana and Senegal all succeeded (even if currently faltering). Where it is under way, we should not undermine it by moral imperialism. Foreign pressure is no more acceptable when it promotes Western norms of the twenty-first century than it was when promoting the norms of the nineteenth. Both subvert the agency that is fundamental to contributive justice. This does not mean that foreign support should be blind – but it always calls for informed judgement. Look at the record.

In Ghana, the rivalries between two American social movements, the evangelical churches and gay rights, manifestly subverted a domestic process of social change. In Ethiopia, a small American diaspora from rival tribes first ignited domestic hatred, leading to 3 million displaced people, and later threatened to abort an African-brokered peace deal that ended a civil war. In Burma, naive foreigners first elevated Aung San Suu Kyi into the status of a living saint and then smashed her down into damnation. I knew her: she was a politician struggling to help her country by manoeuvring to build domestic support for change in fluid situations that were highly constrained. In that, she was analogous to Abdalla Hamdok in Sudan. In both Burma and Sudan, ill-informed foreign pressure has left the situation immeasurably worse.

Learn from that record: it has a lot to answer for. Perfection was not on the menu of feasible options in any of these situations. Americans and Britons, more than most, should recognize that our own polities are far from perfect. Our appetite for rapping the knuckles of poorer societies for their deficiencies seems to have increased *pari passu* with our own deficiencies. As yet, we have been unable to put our own houses in order, and so should curb our enthusiasms for bringing enlightenment to societies in complex situations about which we know little. Having learned from failure, we can then act by reinforcing changes generated within the society that are already clearly under way.

We know some useful cognitive gadgets

Contributive justice is a crucial concept that is rapidly spreading among young people.* I have also drawn on two others, less widely known: the collective mind and cognitive gadgets. They help in the

---

* Michael Sandel's online course has been followed by tens of millions around the world, but awareness is highly segmented by age group and politicization. Those under thirty-five are accustomed to online learning and are far more aware than those over fifty. The latter have built the world we have; the former will rescue us from it. Politically, the passionate warriors of the left and right each want victory;

quest for practical actions that can improve a worried world. In our daily lives we are guided by the collective mind of our community: what do others normally do in the situation I find myself in? Cognitive gadgets are specific, hard-won answers to complex problems that the community once discovered and remembers because they worked. Since context is king, the gadgets useful in that first stage of reversing the downward spiral may differ from those that accelerate renewal once it is under way.

The gadget that arrests the spiral down always comes from within the society. It is unexpected sacrifice by those who are successful: a recognition of the obligations implied by shared citizenship. In a left-behind country, it is sacrifice by the selectariat who hold power. In left-behind regions of middle-income and high-income countries, the sacrifice must come from the successful regions. Being incompatible with the jaundiced hostility of the left behind towards the successful, the left behind notice it, and their surprise is the foundation on which they can build a less despairing view of their own future. Surprising sacrifice was the transformation that Helmut Kohl taught West Germans in 1992: a hugely costly moral duty accepted across the political spectrum which transformed the lives of East Germans. In contrast, cheap gestures of assistance too small to be effective are shameful. By raising false hopes soon dashed, their deception raises the bar: to shift expectations, a subsequent sacrifice will need to be larger.

The gadget that accelerates renewal once it is under way is rapid learning. Swallow pride and learn from others: although Whitehall is too arrogant to do so, it is exceptional. Experiment and learn from evaluating the outcomes: even when there is a loss of prestige from admitting the need to learn, it forestalls the greater embarrassment of confident promises that fail. Deng Xiaoping breached many of the tenets of twenty-first-century Western democracy, but by embracing rapid learning he transformed more lives for the better than anyone else in human history.

---

although a small minority, they are disproportionately active in the media and portray any centrists who oppose them as indistinguishable from their enemy.

The gadget that coordinates actions into a coherent whole is the dashboard that tracks three timeframes. 'Action this Day' and 'The buck stops here' pithily injected a sense of urgency to counter 'God make me good but not yet', the ubiquitous human reaction to an uncomfortable truth. To change outcomes, we need to make a start at changing our actions. Just as there are sham gestures of sacrifice, there are sham gestures of action: British commitments to net zero by 2050 and French commitments to global aid for the Sahel, neither of which have any means of enforcement. Alongside them, the third timeframe tracks whether missing capacities are being built. Is there a team learning how to collect taxes? In a left-behind country like Zambia, is there a team learning how to tax the mining companies without driving them away? In the poor regions of over-centralized Colombia and Britain, it is a switch from national to local taxation matched by fiscal redistributions that leaves poor regions with local control of revenues and better off. Is there a team learning how to maintain security? In the English regions menaced by 'county lines' and American cities where the police force has lost the trust of left-behind communities, is the police force improving? In Islamic State-infiltrated Mozambique, is the army increasingly trusted?

We know that we don't know everything

Sometimes, the woes of the left behind have multiplied and entwined beyond our capacity to understand what is causing what: too much is intertwined. Fortunately, remedies need not be related to causes: we can find them even though the causes remain uncertain. The approach in this book has been to find a middle way between the two methods that have been vying for supremacy in economics. Microeconomists are trying to identify each individual cause in the labyrinth of poverty. Macroeconomists are trying to find the one big cause. The middle way is to focus on a few processes by which the left behind can catch up, such as leadership and social movements; urbanization and resource management; taxation and security. Each has been informed by recent research across the human sciences, not just economics. I have aimed both to focus poverty research on the world's neglected and despairing places and to open up its study to a much wider range of scholarship. I opened the book with an agenda, and I draw it to a close not with definitive answers but with that new agenda. It will be for teams of younger scholars collaborating from different fields to take this work forward. Many will be from the left behind and, increasingly, they will be based there. There is enough work for a new generation who will leave mine in the dust.

Images that distil complexity

The processes that affect the left behind are complex. Our brains have evolved to grasp complexity most readily through images: scholars have used them to crystallize their ideas and to express them to others. Milton Friedman used the image of the plucked harp to capture how he believed market forces would enable a place disrupted by a shock to recover. In countering it, I used the image of dinghies sailing in gusty wind and then stacked up the evidence supporting that opposing account. The crucial process of renewal was distilled into the image of mounting a spiral staircase. In mounting it, a familiar scene is revealed from a new perspective in which features once thought to be disadvantages can be reassessed as opportunities. Such reassessments happened in post-invasion Ukraine, in post-Independence Singapore and in post-genocide Rwanda. Again, I delved into the sequence of actions and narratives by which these and other transformations were undertaken.

Such renewals are feasible, but around the world millions are still trapped in the syndrome of fragility – spiralling down. My own home region has become one of them: some of my relatives live in communities of distress that are now in their third generation of doomed life chances. Like my friend Fiona Hill, who grew up in the doomed town of Bishop Auckland and became the White House expert on Russia, I left when I was young. We both became successful exiles, and that status – Fiona calls us 'flukes' – gives rise to complex emotions, compounds of disbelief, guilt, anger and despair. Images again distil those emotions, the experts now being poets. For me, the most profound image of despair is that of Paul Celan, a survivor of the Holocaust. Writing in 1945 about witnessing the destruction of European Jewry, he used the image of ashes. In my bleakest moments, I fear that the dreams of millions of young lives among the world's left behind will be dashed to ashes by the ignorance and selfishness of those with power. But ashes are akin to embers, the image Coleridge used in 'Frost at Midnight' to celebrate his baby's joyful future. While ashes speak of death, embers can be reignited by oxygen. That is the hopeful closing image for this book, oxygen being the actions and ideas that transform.

In 2021 I was appointed to serve on a government committee that advises on 'levelling up'. By 2023, as the official attempts to disguise inaction as action became egregious, my mounting despair escalated into anger. I spoke out publicly, perhaps breaching some rule of confidentiality. Nothing happened, and then, when all seemed lost, fortune began to smile. In South Yorkshire, the mayor's new team bestirred itself. The inert British Business Bank got a new leader with energy. The government decided to use South Yorkshire as a pilot for devolving greater powers and some money. Five penitent former prime ministers and chancellors jointly called for devolution to the regions.*

Will it be another false dawn? You, reading this in what is for me the unknowable future, will be able to tell. But it reminds us that despair is unwarranted. Human energies can transform the future of every left-behind place. We have the privilege of living in the 2020s, the decade when the stasis of complacency cracked. We can use the rest of the decade to contribute to that goal. We all have agency, and now is the time for each of us to use it.

* 'Britain's growing regional divides: reviewing the regional economics, politics and policy making of the UK since 1979'. Three were Conservative, two Labour. Issued to the media on 23 October 2023.

Acknowledgements

The ideas and evidence underpinning *Left Behind* have evolved over a decade, driven by mounting evidence that, in many parts of the world, economic policy was failing many millions of people. I had to face the discomfiting recognition that ideas I had regarded as established truths of economics, and indeed taught, needed radical revision. In the quest for evidence, I have been helped considerably by the statistical analyses of Jim Cust and Alexis Rivera-Ballesteros at the World Bank and Sonya Krutukova and her team at the Institute for Fiscal Studies. Other specific assistance, such as from the Cities that Work programme by the team at the International Growth Centre, is acknowledged in the notes to the book.

Like most re-educations, it is impossible to disentangle all the personal influences on my thinking. I have been fortunate and privileged to work and talk with scholars far cleverer than myself; to teach students who questioned what they read and heard; to see the painful realities of mounting distress in many diverse communities; and to be confronted by the frustrations of those setting policies who witnessed outcomes that they did not fully comprehend.

Among the scholars, I will start with the immensely insightful interactions with my co-authors and co-directors on research programmes. Such collaborations forge a process of mutual understanding and learning. During the five years of writing *Left Behind*, I have worked with Tim Besley, Alex Betts, Robin Burgess, Stefan Dercon, Ed Glaeser, David Good, John Kay, Colin Mayer, Philip McCann, Dennis Snower, David Tuckett and Tony Venables. Complementing these people, I have been fortunate to be included in several scholarly discussion groups from whose members I have learned much. Among them, the most notable influences have been

Andrew Briggs, Ruth Chang, Nicholas Christakis, Joe Henrich, Celia Heyes, Mervyn King, Denis Noble, Michael Sandel and David Sloan Wilson. Quite evidently, none of these people bears any responsibility for the text or proposals of *Left Behind*, nor should this acknowledgement be taken as implying their endorsement. Other scholars may detect the influence of their work on what I have written and I will not dispute any such claims. I read widely and have tried to absorb many ideas.

Among the many students I have taught while writing the book it would be invidious to single out particular contributions, although many have found their way into improving the book. Necessarily, I make one exception since Anna Volynets was directly responsible for the remarkable Russian case studies in Chapter 5. The unrivalled resource of those ageing professors who have encouraged former students to stay in touch with them is a network providing insights that sometimes outclass those of official intelligence services. The discussion of the taxation of natural resources in Chapter 9 has benefited immensely from Ali Readhead, now a world authority on the subject. A further instance is the analysis in Chapter 11 of pressure from American NGOs on gay rights in Ghana. One of my many former Ghanaian graduate students, now a social media researcher, provided the information convincingly supported by evidence. For understandable reasons he wishes to remain anonymous.

Left Behind took far longer to finish than I had anticipated. Turning a repeatedly delayed and rewritten manuscript into a readable book has depended upon the patience, encouragement and skill of my editors, Laura Stickney at Allen Lane and Clive Priddle at PublicAffairs. Fortuitously, though Laura is responsible for tuning the book to a British audience, she is originally American, whereas Clive, responsible for my American audience, is originally British. This made collaboration seamless since they each had valuable insights on both. A final round of careful editing was contracted to Sarah Day, who had a keen and patient eye for my dyslexic howlers.

Acknowledgements

But from its opening page to its final words, *Left Behind* is written predominantly for a global audience. That it is simultaneously appearing in many different languages so soon after completion is due to Andrew Wylie and James Pullen of the Wylie Agency: true professionals.

Paul Collier, Oxford, December 2023

Notes

Chapter 1

1 Moral worthiness depended only on the intended consequences of individual actions. Its flaws were exemplified by the crypto-disaster of 2022 in which a million desperate people in left-behind places faced ruin, having been lured by Sam Bankman-Fried's promise of easy money. Instead of feeling shame and guilt, sheltered by his explicitly Utilitarian philosophy, he merely felt embarrassed over the mass misery due to his Ponzi scheme. As I finished *Left Behind*, he was convicted of massive fraud by an American jury.

Chapter 2

1 Tim Besley and I jointly developed the concept within a research programme which we co-led within the International Growth Centre, funded by the British Academy. The work was first presented at the 2018 Annual Meetings of the IMF in Washington DC and fed into a much larger programme with the Research Department of the IMF, culminating in *Macroeconomic Policies in Fragile States*, R. Chami, R. Espinoza and P. Montiel (eds), (2021), to which both Tim and I contributed chapters.

2 P. G. Rice and A. J. Venables (2021), 'The persistent consequences of adverse shocks: how the 1970s shaped UK regional inequality', in *Oxford Review of Economic Policy* 37(1).

3 The three giants who have revolutionized the field of social psychology are Nicholas Christakis (Yale), Cecilia Heyes (Oxford), who

introduced the concept of cognitive gadgets, and Joe Henrich (Harvard), whose books on the collective mind have been immensely influential. See N. A Christakis, *Blueprint: The Evolutionary Origins of a Good Society* (2019); J. Henrich, *The Secret of Our Success: How Culture is Driving Human Evolution, Domesticating Our Species, and Making us Smarter* (2016) and *The Weirdest People in the World: How the West became Psychologically Peculiar and Particularly Prosperous* (2020); C. Heyes, *Cognitive Gadgets: The Cultural Evolution of Thinking* (2018). I am fortunate to know these pioneering scholars. Social psychology and the closely related field of evolutionary biology are more important to economics than the more familiar field of individual psychology. N. MacGregor, *Living with the Gods: On Beliefs and Peoples* (2018) is a highly readable swing through many related ideas.

4 For a moving account of the industry, combined with a fascinating family story, see C. Bailey, *Black Diamonds: The Rise and Fall of an English Dynasty* (2008). The analogous coal story to the common purpose of steel workers and owners in founding Sheffield University was the dramatic threat of the Yorkshire coal miners to strike if the Labour government persisted with its plan of wrecking Wentworth, the magnificent country house of the local coal-owning family, by open-cast mining.

5 P. Collier and D. Tuckett, 'Narratives as a coordinating device for reversing regional decline', *Oxford Review of Economic Policy* 37(1), 2021.

6 A. R. Hochschild, *Strangers in Their Own Land: Anger and Mourning on the American Right* (2016).

7 E. Kaufmann, *Whiteshift: Populism, Immigration and the Future of White Majorities* (2018).

8 R. D. Putnam with S. R. Garrett, *The Upswing: How America Came Together a Century Ago and How We Can Do It Again* (p. 279) (2020).

9 See J. A. Kay and M. A. King, *Radical Uncertainty: Decision-Making for an Unknowable Future* (2020). On the neuroscience and psychology underpinning the concept, see S. G. B. Johnson, A. Bilovich and D. Tuckett, (2023), 'Conviction narrative theory: a theory of choice under radical uncertainty', in *Behavior and Brain Sciences*, 46, 1–26.

10 The sense of crisis is well captured by Martin Wolf in *The Crisis of Democratic Capitalism* (2023). The stand-out instance of overconfidence

is the Truss–Kwarteng faith in the Panglossian omniscience of financial markets as a means of reviving economic growth. The financial markets themselves had considerably less faith than they did, swiftly sinking their government with a rout of the currency. The theme is picked up more fully in Chapter 3.

11 See D. Yergin and J. Stanislaw (eds) *The Commanding Heights: The Battle for the World Economy* (1998).

12 'London's economic growth outpaces all other regions', *Financial Times*, 17 May 2023. The data are from the Office for National Statistics.

13 T. Besley and T. Persson, 'Democratic values and institutions', *American Economic Review: Insights* 1(1), 2019.

14 M. Seddon, 'Russia bans largest independent news website Meduza', *Financial Times*, 26 January 2023.

15 D. Rushkoff, *The Survival of the Richest: Escape Fantasies of the Tech Billionaires* (2022).

16 A. Davis, *Bankruptcy, Bubbles and Bailouts: The inside history of the Treasury since 1976* (2022) and S. Friedman (2023), 'Climbing the velvet drainpipe: class background and career progression within the UK civil service', *Journal of Public Administration Research and Theory* 33, 563–77.

Chapter 3

1 A hypothesis that a proposed in 2007, which I termed the *conflict trap*, was that many of the costs of war accrued long after the conflict was over. Due to problems of endogeneity, this has proved extremely difficult to test rigorously. Finally, as I was finalizing the proofs, two scholars have confirmed it, using the example of the unexploded ordinance accumulated during conflict in Laos. 'Collateral Damage', by F. Valencia-Caicado and J.F. Riano, is appearing in the first issue of *The Economic Journal* for 2024. I am grateful to the authors for alerting me. Sadly, precisely the same enormous future costs are accumulating during the on-going war in Ukraine, (see ACAPS, 'Ukraine: Humanitarian implications of mine contamination' also due to appear in early 2024.)

2 R. Chami , R. Espinoza and P. Montiel (eds), *Macroeconomic Policy in Fragile States* (2021).

3 T. Besley and T. Persson, *The Pillars of Prosperity* (2011).

4 'Eskom chief's explosive interview exposes ANC's rotten core', *Financial Times*, 27 February 2023.

5 F. Hill, *There's Nothing for You Here* (2022).

Chapter 4

1 S. Durlauf, A. Kourtellos and C. M. Tang (2022), 'The Great Gatsby curve', Working Paper 2022-29, the Becker–Friedman Institute, University of Chicago.

2 J. Knight and L. Song, *Towards a Labour Market in China* (2006).

3 R. Putnam, *Making Democracy Work: Civic Traditions in Modern Italy* (1993).

4 R. Putnam, *Our Kids: The American Dream in Crisis* (2015).

5 R. Layard, S. McNally and G. Ventura, *Applying the Robbins Principle to Further Education and Apprenticeship*, The Resolution Foundation (2023).

6 C. Crawford, L. Macmillan and A. Vignoles (2017), 'When and why do initially high-achieving poor children fall behind', *Oxford Review of Education*, 43(1).

7 Data on education are for 2021/22 on net current expenditure per pupil. See statistica.com/statistics/381745/education-exenditure-per-pupil-england-region-uk/. Data on health are from the Health Foundation – see 'The Crisis facing NHS GPs', *Financial Times*, 27 October 2023.

8 'Growing up North', *Children's Commissioner Report*, 2018.

9 L. Sibieta, 'School spending in England: trends over time and future outlook', IFS (2021).

10 Among them P. Johnson, 'Inequalities: what's been happening and what should we do?' IFS (2022) and P. McCann, 'Levelling Up Economics', IFS (2023).

11 D. Acemoglu and S. Johnson, *Power and Progress* (2023).

Chapter 5

1 See J. Tepperman, *The Fix: How Nations Survive and Thrive* (2016).

2 See K. Thomas et al., (2014), 'The psychology of coordination and common knowledge', *Journal of Personality and Social Psychology* 107, 657–76.

3 I would like to thank Sheila Khama for these insights. She is no relation to Sir Seretse Khama, but was for many years the CEO of Debswana, the joint venture between the government and De Beers. I came to know Presidents Masire and Mogae. As people, they were modest, humorous, and very shrewd.

4 Measured at 2021 Current International Purchasing Power Parity prices, on World Bank data. Mauritius, which is in the Indian Ocean but a member of the African Union, has done even better. The BRICS designation for Brazil, Russia, India, China and South Africa was coined by Jim O'Neill when chief economist at Goldman Sachs in his advice to its clients.

5 D. H. Yanagizawa-Drott (2014) 'Propaganda and conflict: evidence from the Rwandan genocide', *Quarterly Journal of Economics* 129(4) and A. Blouin and S. Mukand (2019), 'Erasing identity? Propaganda, nation-building and identity in Rwanda', *Journal of Political Economy* 127(3).

6 S. A. Haslam, S. D. Reicher and M. J. Platow, *The New Psychology of Leadership: Identity, Influence and Power* (2011). The quotes are from pp. 163–4.

7 S. Gachter and E. Renner (2018), 'Leaders as role models and "belief managers" in social dilemmas', *Journal of Economic Behavior and Organization* 154(C).

8 E. Fehr and I. Schurtenberger (2018), 'Normative foundations of human cooperation', *Nature Human Behavior* 2.

9 J. J. Van Bavel et al. (2020), 'Using social and behavioural science to support COVID-19 pandemic response', *Nature Human Behaviour* 4.

10 See J. Hjort (2014), 'Ethnic divisions and production in firms', *Quarterly Journal of Economics* 129(4), 1899–1946.

Chapter 6

1 R. D. Putnam, R. Leonardi and R. Y. Yanetti, *Making Democracy Work: Civic Traditions in Modern Italy* (1994).

2 R. D. Putnam and S. R. Garrett, *The Upswing: How America Came Together a Century Ago and How We Can Do It Again* (2020).

3 W. Jack and T. Suri (2014), 'Risk-sharing and transaction costs: evidence from Kenya's mobile money revolution', *American Economic Review* 104(1).

4 T. Bold, with M. Kimenyi, G. Mwabu, A. N'Gang'a and J. Sandefur (2008), 'Experimental evidence on health care reforms in Kenya', *Journal of Public Economics* 168, 1–20.

5 D. Tuckett, 'Explanatory models and conviction narratives', in *Thinking about Behaviour Change*, S. Michie, S. Christmas and R. West (eds) (2015).

6 J. Henrich, *The Weirdest People in the World* (2021), especially Chapter 13.

Chapter 7

1 D. Acemoglu and S. Johnson, *Power and Progress* (2023).

2 Sarah Richmond, 'A philosopher's philosopher', *Times Literary Supplement*, 6266, 2023, and the powerful critique of 'small world' reductionism by Nancy Cartwright, *A Philosopher Looks at Science* (2023).

3 'How to fix Britain's water industry', *Financial Times*, 15 May 2023. A further disastrous example is the privatization of bus services. As a result of the lack of coordination of competing services, bus usage has halved. Exceptionally, bus services in London were left under the ownership of Transport for London, controlled by an elected mayor. Over the period that usage of privatized bus services in the rest of the country halved, usage of London's bus services doubled. Belatedly, in 2023 the mayors of some regional authorities mutinied against the Treasury and adopted the TLF model.

4 S. Kaplan (2008), 'The remarkable story of Somaliland', *Journal of Democracy* 19(3), 143–57.

Chapter 8

1 This paragraph and much of this chapter draws on the work of the International Growth Centre's Cities that Work Programme, which distils current research on urbanization into practical advice for the mayors of low-income cities, all of which is available on its website. The programme is co-directed by Ed Glaeser of Harvard, who chairs it, myself and Tony Venables. The story of the Kampala airport road comes direct from the then president of the World Bank, who was infuriated by NGO naïvety but impotent to resist its pressures.

2 World Development Report 2015, *Mind, Society, and Behavior*, p. 53.

3 See J. Knight and L. Song, *Towards a Labour Market in China* (1995).

4 D. Gollin, R. Jedwab and D. Volrath (2016), 'Urbanisation with and without industrialisation', *Journal of Economic Growth* 21.

5 P. Collier and A. S. Venables (2018), 'Who gets the urban surplus?', *Journal of Economic Geography* 18(3).

Chapter 9

1 P. Collier and A. Venables (2014), 'Closing coal: economic and moral imperatives', *Oxford Review of Economic Policy* 30(3).

2 B. Klaas, *Corruptible: Who Gets Power and How It Changes Us* (2021).

3 P. Collier and A. Hoeffler (2009), 'Testing the neo-con Agenda', *European Economic Review* 53(3).

4 P. Collier and B. Goderis (2012), 'Commodity prices and growth: an empirical investigation', *European Economic Review*, 56(6).

5 J. F. Cust and D. Mihalyi (2017), 'The presource curse', *Finance and Development* 54(4), 37–40, and J. F. Cust and D. Mihalyi (2017), 'Evidence for a presource curse? Oil discoveries, elevated expectations, and growth disappointments (10 July 2017), World Bank Policy Research Working Paper (8140).

6 P. Vicente (2010), 'Does oil corrupt? Evidence from a natural experiment in West Africa', *Journal of Development Economics* 4(1).

7 N. Berman et al. (2017), 'This mine is mine', *American Economic Review* 107(6).

8 J. Gutierrez (2018), 'Oil and state capture: the subnational links between oil revenues and armed conflict in Colombia', D.Phil. Oxon.

9 B. Javorcik, A. L. Turco and D. Maggioni (2018), 'New and improved: does FDI boost production complexity in host countries?', *Economic Journal* 128.

10 S. Bhattacharyya and P. Collier (2014), 'Public capital in resource-rich countries: is there a curse?', *Oxford Economic Papers* 66(1).

11 P. Collier, 'Resource revenue management: three policy clocks', in R. Caputo and R. Chung (eds), *Commodity Prices and Macroeconomic Policy* (2015).

Chapter 10

1 See L. Heldring (2021) 'The origins of violence in Rwanda', *Review of Economic Studies* 88(2).

2 A. Bergeron et al., 'Optimal assignment of bureaucrats: evidence from randomly assigned tax collectors in the DRC'. CEPR Discussion Paper 16771 (2021).

3 P. Balan et al. (2022), 'Local elites as state capacity', *American Economic Review* 112(3), 1–36.

4 A .Q. Khan, A. I. Khwaja, and B. A. Olken (2015), 'Tax farming redux', *Quarterly Journal of Economics* 131, 219–71.

5 J. Naritomi (2019), 'Consumers as tax auditors', *American Economic Review* 109, 3031–72.

6 J. L. Weigel (2020), 'The participation dividend of taxation', *Quarterly Journal of Economics* 135(4).

7 A. Jensen (2022), 'Employment structure and the modern tax system', in *American Economic Review* 112(1).

8 A. Dixit, *Lawlessness in Economics: Alternative Modes of Governance* (2011).

9 A. Schipani, 'Rwanda flexes muscles in fight against terror in Mozambique', *Financial Times*, 3 October 2021.

10 C. Blattman, *Why We Fight: The Roots of War and the Paths to Peace* (2022).

11 S. Michailof, *Afghanistan: Autopsie d'un Désastre, 2001–2021* (2022).

12 A. Schindler, 'Warfare under scrutiny: British public perspectives of soldiers, and tactical behaviours in operation HERRICK', *Defence and Security Analysis*, September 2023.

13 S. Michailof, *Africanistan: Development or Jihad* (2018).

Chapter 11

1 See M. Sandel, *What Money Can't Buy* (2012) and *The Tyranny of Merit* (2020).

2 J. Henrich, *The Secret of Our Success* (2018).

3 R. F. Baumeister and R. E. Leary (1995), 'The need to belong: desire for interpersonal attachments as a fundamental human motivation', *Psychological Bulletin* 117(3), 497–529. On the dramatic consequences for longevity, see G. E. Valliant, *Triumphs of Experience: The Men of the Harvard Grant Study* (2012).

4 *25 Years of University Access*, The Sutton Trust, October 2023.

5 R. Chetty, D. J. Dening and J. N. Friedman, 'Diversifying society's leaders: the determinants and causal effects of admission to highly selective private colleges', NBER Working Paper 31492 (2023); and on the Supreme Court decision, 'Harvard faces federal probe over legacy admissions', *Financial Times*, 26 July 2023.

6 M. Daams et al., 'Capital shocks and UK regional divergence', Productivity Institute, WP034 (2023).

7 There is rightly far more attention now being paid to neurodiversity, which is not a mental condition to be treated but a valuable aspect of diversity in a community. All characteristics which have survived the winnowing of evolution are valuable to human communities when deployed in the right contexts. There is much that is not yet understood, but we have learnt that the neurodiverse are not exceptions to empathy. Neurodiversity can impair the ability to grasp how others will react to my behaviour, and so the neurodiverse may *appear* not to care about the suffering of others, but this is completely different from their capacity to *feel* empathy, which is often unimpaired.

8 P. Collier (2020), 'Diverging identities: a model of class formation', *Oxford Economic Papers* 72(3), 567–84.

9 M. Wolf, 'The G7 must accept that it cannot run the world', *Financial Times*, 23 May 2023.

Chapter 12

1 'More than half young Arabs in Levant and north Africa pin hopes on emigrating', *Financial Times*, 12 August 2023.

Index